Rainbow Girl

A Memoir of Autism and Anorexia
Livia Sara

LIV LABEL FREE

DOWNLOAD MY FREE GUIDE!

To say thanks for buying my book, I would like to give you my exclusive guide 100% FREE!

In this guide, you'll learn how 5 common autistic traits can manifest as eating disorder behaviors and how to use each trait to your advantage in recovery.
www.livlabelfree.com/rainbowgirlguide

PRAISE FOR RAINBOW GIRL

"Rainbow girl is an incredibly gripping read that exceptionally captures the autistic experience of eating disorders, which is so rarely discussed. While reading, it felt like I was simultaneously walking with Livia through her darkest and most vulnerable times but also that through her experiences, she was guiding me, sharing the light, perseverance, hope and joy. So much of Rainbow girl resonates with my own story and experiences as a neurodivergent individual. Livia's book highlights an empowering and authentic message that I will forever carry with me."

— **Lou Chandler @neurodivergent_lou**

"The co-occurrence of eating disorders and autism is prevalent, yet there is an alarming lack of awareness and resources addressing this overlap. The eating disorder treatment approach that works for neurotypicals often does not work for autistics, making stories of lived experience a vital part of understanding the connection. In this regard, Rainbow Girl stands out as a remarkable work that vividly illustrates the link between autism and eating disorders. I am very grateful Livia wrote this book!"

— **Bianca Toeps, author of *But You Don't Look Autistic at All***

"Rainbow Girl is more than a book. It is a moving experience thanks to Livia's embrace of vulnerability and relatable approach to storytelling. She shares her journey in a profound manner that captivates the audience while vividly illustrating the deepest valleys of an eating disorder and the highest summits of recovery. I appreciate Livia's direct approach to topics that are often marginalized in society and within the mental health community. She never shies away from sharing her true, authentic self, leaving the reader cheering for her throughout. Rainbow Girl is a life-changing resource for many and a narrative-changing piece of art for us all."

— Jason Wood, speaker and author of *Starving for Survival*

"Rainbow Girl is honest and inspiring. Livia Sara does a beautiful job of capturing the pain and struggle she experienced during her battle with an eating disorder, while also writing with hope and optimism. Her story is sure to be encouraging to many readers. Livia offers insights into her diagnosis of autism and provides important reflections into how being autistic played a role in her eating disorder journey. Teaching us the value of breaking away from certain labels and living a life free to pursue meaningful opportunities, Livia provides a great deal of hope and healing within these pages."

— Kelly Mahler, occupational therapist and author of *The Interoception Curriculum*

"What a gifted experience to read Rainbow Girl. I can feel deeply that Livia has written her book with vulnerability and insights. I am so grateful to Livia for writing Rainbow Girl as there are too few resources and references regarding the overlap of autism and eating disorder recovery. Through coaching, Livia has also taught me to do hard things and never give up. Livia's journey to recovery and discovering she is autistic illustrates to readers that nothing is impossible as long as we are willing to change our perceptions."

— **Tammy, course student and coaching client**

"I could not put this book down! This is such an important story that everyone should read. It shows the truth of how autistic people can be treated poorly within the medical system when trying to access help in eating disorder recovery. While reading Rainbow Girl, I laughed, I cried, and I got angry as it was so relatable to some of my own experiences. Livia's story is truly inspiring, so much so that I couldn't stop thinking about her book for days! I highly recommend everyone read Rainbow Girl by Livia Sara."

— **Lex, course student and coaching client**

"Livia is such a beautiful light to the neurodivergent community. She also writes in a way that touched my soul profoundly. It was through reading Rainbow Girl that I discovered that I am autistic. While reading her book, I saw myself clearly for the first time. I realized that I wasn't a problem to be fixed and the numerous psychiatric diagnoses I had were wrong. I just had a unique brain. Livia is a courageous coach and a survivor. I'll always carry her light with me."

— **Brianna, coaching client**

"I'm so grateful to have read this beautiful memoir by this lovely angel. Rainbow Girl not only sheds light on the anguish of battling an eating disorder, but also showcases Livia's triumphant journey of conquering the ED demon to emerge with wisdom and strength. As I had the privilege of being guided by Livia as my coach, I came to understand that my eating disorder stemmed from trying to fit into a neurotypical world as an autistic person. So, getting to read Livia's personal story moved me to tears time and time again! Rainbow Girl provides an enormous amount of hope for those struggling with an eating disorder as an autistic person, proving that no matter what obstacles life throws at you, you will always come out stronger!"

— **Abby, coaching client**

"This book should be recommended reading for anyone with anorexia and their loved ones. Livia has been through it ALL and shares even the darkest moments with her characteristic bright voice. This book instills hope that anyone, whether they be neurodivergent or have an eating disorder, can find health and happiness. Here's to living label free!"

— **Michelle Cen, counselor**

"Rainbow Girl is an autobiography by Livia Sara documenting her journey through an eating disorder, recovery, and eventual autism diagnosis. Livia's writing is so raw and genuine I couldn't help but see myself in her story. Once I started reading I couldn't put it down; I finished it in less than 24 hours. Livia's story reveals the most vulnerable moments of a person engulfed in an eating disorder and then shines through with a powerful message of hope. A message that anyone can recover from an eating disorder- no matter what they have been through or have been told by health professionals. Livia's book is the first place I have truly felt seen and understood. I cannot recommend it more."

— **Colleen @wildflower.autie**

ISBN 979-8-9875398-9-7
eISBN 979-8-9875398-0-4

Book cover by my sister, Mae van Aarsen

For more information, visit www.livlabelfree.com

To my family: for believing in me until I had the strength to believe in myself, for sticking with me through thick and thin, and for holding my hand so I could one day hold others'.

To my clients: for trusting me as your guide and inspiring me to keep improving as a coach. I am never not learning from you, and I am forever amazed by your resilience and commitment to do the hard work. Recovery from an eating disorder is no easy feat! Yet every session, every message, and every testimonial acts as a testimony to how worth doing the hard work really is.

CONTENTS

PART 1: COLORING INSIDE THE LINES

1

THE START

I never planned for my life to become such a mess. Quite the opposite, in fact. If I stuck to the rituals and routines that allowed me to feel safe, what could possibly go wrong? So I drew symmetrical rainbows and castles. I lined up the guests' shoes when we hosted a dinner party. I set up the yellow Playmobil mansion to match the picture on the box, then simply left it for display – not play – as soon as I had finished.

One of my most vivid childhood memories was the day we moved into a big yellow house of our own in Brookline, Massachusetts. The year was 2005, at which time my family consisted of four: Mom, Dad, me, and my younger sister, Mae. This was already my fourth time moving, but it's the first move I have a clear recollection of.

My first *actual* move was in 2000, when I was just a six-month-old baby. In the late spring of that year, my mom, dad, and I set out on a journey overseas. My mom had received a job offer from Harvard, which no one in their right mind would turn down. We packed our bags (well, my parents packed mine, even though I'm sure I would have wanted to pack them myself), left our little cottage in the heart of The Hague, and got on the plane to Boston that would eventually land us in Cambridge, Massachusetts.

The Maria Montessori School across the street from our house in Cambridge is where I drew my first rainbow. Whether my special interest in rainbows was nature, nurture, or a combination of the two, the school certainly influenced it. The classrooms in the building were organized by color, the interior of each room matching its corresponding streak in the rainbow. My own behavior followed a similar structure. I had all the stuffed animals of the *Teletubbies*, watched the show on repeat, and begged my parents to play the theme songs whenever we listened to music. Every single day until the age of ten, I ate the same breakfast, lunch, and dinner. If I liked a specific book, I needed every one in the series. Uncoincidentally, my all-time favorite series was Rainbow Magic, about two tween girls and their adventures with magical fairies.

Along with drawing perfect rainbows, I was artistically gifted in two other ways: drawing symmetrical castles and tracing coloring pages. I would often offer my most recent creation to one of my parents in the morning before school, then spend the whole day looking forward to a black-and-white coloring page in exchange. As soon as I saw that little stack of freshly printed pages slip out of my mom's or my dad's work bag, I would jump up and down in excitement, then race towards the window to carefully tape a blank sheet onto the edges of it so I could trace a new image.

As a purebred Dutch girl, I knew how to bike practically as soon as I could walk. I have no memory of learning how to ride my bicycle, but if you ask my dad, he will talk your ear off for hours about how he would run after me on my little purple bike. Apparently, I would take off and pedal as fast as I could, fearing that slowing down or stopping would result in an unpredictable yet inevitable fall. I'm sure we still have video recordings of me riding that purple bicycle across the tennis courts of the Montessori school.

Much more accessible are the old photo albums lining the shelves of the antique bookcase we inherited from my grandmother. From time to time, I adore flipping through them and looking at the photos of me bicycle-kicking my legs as I lie on the scale of Bronovo Hospital, clocking in at just barely over 2 kg (not quite 4.5 pounds).

When I tell people how small a baby I was, they're often surprised I was *not* born prematurely. I was rebellious from the very start, making my mom wait an additional two weeks after my due date to give birth to me on November 19, 1999 (at 11:09, mind you!). I kinda have a thing for the numbers 1 and 9, and maybe I was already planning this from inside the womb. I guess no one will ever know.

Something else no one will ever know is the impact of my birth experience on my future. It was a sunny November morning, with clear blue skies and not a cloud to be seen. This kind of weather is rare in the Netherlands, where the typical daily forecast is cloudy with an almost certain chance of rain. But not on the day little Livia came into the world.

Perhaps the beautiful weather compensated for the fear and stress my parents endured during my birth. Every time my mom pushed, the baby heart rate monitor would flatline. What was this all about? First, I decided to be late, and now I didn't even want to come out? It wasn't that I didn't *want* to come out; I simply *couldn't* come out. The umbilical cord was wrapped around my neck twice, cutting off my blood supply every time my mom pushed. The only way I was going to come out was via an emergency C-section. Obviously, I made it; otherwise, I wouldn't be here writing this book today. Or am I writing this book today *because* I made it? One of the therapists I eventually saw accused this "traumatic experience" of being the root cause of what developed into an eating disorder, but I'm going to save that story for later.

2

THE GOLDEN RULE

Although my life may sound picturesque thus far, how I truly felt was far from ideal. Sure, I attended birthday parties, participated in school activities, and was a star athlete on my soccer and gymnastics teams, but I never felt like I fit in. My interests were so different from those of other girls. I never enjoyed imitating doll voices or having imaginary tea parties, let alone engaging in the never-ending gossip on the sidelines of the soccer field. I wanted to run, score, and win, not chitchat about who had the nicest shoes or the softest scrunchie. During lunch break at school, I was the only girl to play soccer outside with the boys. Yet still, I wanted to be "a normal girl." I pretended I liked all the things the other girls did, just so I wouldn't end up alone at their birthday parties. I remember faking reactions to their gossip so they would keep including me in their conversations. I remember commenting on how incredible their Barbie collections were, just so they would keep inviting me over.

When you're a kid, you're practically forced to call everyone your friend. It's one of the first things you learn in school, along with the Golden Rule of treating others how you want to be treated. Was the girl whose party I got invited to and bought a new Barbie for *really* my friend, or did I just go to the party with a silly doll because a sparkly pink invitation arrived in the mailbox? When I wrote cards for every classmate on February 14, was it *really* because I wanted everyone to be my Valentine, or simply because it would be unfair if the popular kids got more heart-shaped cards? Either way, the Golden Rule will forever be one of my favorite concepts. I always tried my best (and still do!) to act from a place of what *I* would want when I communicate with others, even if this isn't always socially acceptable. The first and best example that comes to mind is regarding my birthday parties.

"Mama, can we please plan my birthday party?" I asked this question almost every night before bed. Even when my birthday was months away, I loved nothing more than planning every detail of the upcoming party. What would the theme be? Which cake flavor would match that theme? Should we have the party on my actual birthday or the nearest weekend? And, perhaps most importantly, what gifts did I want to receive?

I took my gifts very seriously, and when it came to this aspect of my birthday, I naturally applied the Golden Rule. If people were going to buy me presents, I had to ensure I didn't waste their time. I had to provide clear instructions so they wouldn't be overwhelmed figuring out the "perfect" gift to give me. I believed this solution was one of the kindest things I could have ever done for my guests. How could it not be? If I were going to *their* party, I'd want to know exactly what to do to make the birthday person happy!

So when I was turning eight, I came up with the genius idea of an Allowed Birthday Presents List. The concept was simple: I wrote down exactly what I wanted to receive and assigned each desired present to an invitee. All they would have to do is buy their assigned item, and voilà! I would be happy, and they would be spared the overthinking that often comes with gift-giving.

Apparently, some of the invitees' parents didn't agree. A few days after I handed out my first Allowed Birthday Presents List, my mom got a call from my "friend" Izzy's mom. Izzy's mom explained that it was absolutely ridiculous of me to expect such "behavior" to be tolerated, indirectly accusing my mom of allowing me to put out the list in the first place.

I have always been very independent, and most of what I know is self-taught. When Izzy's mom called my mom, my Allowed Birthday Presents List was news to her. Thankfully, my mom wasn't mad. In fact, I'm pretty sure she found the idea to be as genius as I did. My parents know me like no one else, including my need for predictability and order. If my Allowed Birthday Presents List would ensure both of those needs were met, what was the problem? In the end, I did receive the sleeping bag I had assigned Izzy, even if her mom thought the whole approach to ensure I would get it was ridiculous. Izzy was going to buy something for me anyway, so I guess her family figured buying a gift they knew I wanted was the most efficient solution after all!

3

JUSTICE

Another distinct birthday memory I have is my sixth birthday party. We hosted the party at our yellow house in Brookline, which we had moved into earlier that year. We spent the morning of the party setting up the interior of our home to celebrate my birthday. In the living room, about a dozen chairs were arranged in a circle for playing musical chairs. The halls of the house were lined with garlands galore, and the birthday girl's chair was enrobed with my favorite garland of them all. I had placed a large wooden laundry basket near the door for gifts and moved all of my family's shoes to make room for those of the guests.

As usual, the kitchen was a complete wreck: the sink was overflowing with dirty dishes, and it was hard not to notice the greasy spots on the stove. But none of that mattered today. The setup on the kitchen table made up for it. A brightly colored tablecloth disguised the punctured wood and fork marks (Mae loved to stab the table with her cutlery, a habit my dad couldn't stand), and polka-dot plates edged the table in perfect alignment with the surrounding chairs. In the middle stood one of my mom's famous home-baked birthday cakes (okay, maybe not famous in the traditional sense of the word, but her birthday cakes were simply the best!).

The cake was in the shape of a six, for which she followed the instructions of a Dutch number cake cookbook. That morning, we had spent hours slicing and assembling pieces of cake, then spreading thick layers of vanilla buttercream frosting on every surface and in every crevice. Because musical chairs was the main event of the party, my mom had used edible ink to draw chairs and music notes across the entire cake, resulting in an event-coordinated masterpiece. Everything was planned and prepared, resulting, without a doubt, in the best birthday party ever! My sense of confident excitement lasted until the third round of musical chairs.

Tiny and fast as I was, musical chairs was one of my favorite games. I always won, which was why I participated so confidently. The same applied to soccer, gymnastics, and any other activities I didn't shy away from. If I believed I could win, I would jump right in. So when the music stopped during the third round of the game and Gina pushed me right out of my seat, I was furious. Well, to be fair, I wasn't initially angry. Gina had simply cheated by pushing me out of my seat, and a quick explanation would keep me in the game and send Gina out. But no.

"Livia, you're out!" exclaimed my mom, serving as the game referee.

"No, I'm not! I was in the chair first! Gina pushed me out!" I responded hastily.

"I'm sorry, Livia, but Gina is clearly sitting in the chair right now while you're standing up. You're out of the game."

A tear trickled down my reddening cheek. "Mommy, I'm not out! She pushed me out! I promise! This isn't fair!"

My birthday party quickly devolved into a horrible meltdown, one that could easily have been avoided had my mom trusted me. Disqualifying me for no reason was one thing, but allowing Gina to stay in the game despite her cheating? It simply wasn't *right*. The injustice was unbearable. To this day, I still get a pit in my stomach when I think back to my sixth birthday party.

4

SISTERS

When I think back to my youngest years of sisterhood, I feel eternal joy. For as long as I can remember, I took pride in being the oldest sister. I wanted to be a role model, the person my sisters could turn to whenever they felt lost or needed an answer. I wanted to be their unconditional guidepost, the one person they knew would always be there for them. To my surprise, my sisters played a mutual role just as big in my life. In fact, I cannot even remember being an only child.

Mae was born in May of 2002, making our age difference a mere two and a half years. But our closeness defied any age difference at all, as Mae and I did everything together. When we were little, we wore matching outfits and pretended to be twins. We baked together and shared boxes of mac and cheese after school. We sat side by side in the big chair in front of the TV and watched shows punctuated with fake laughter until our eyes glazed over. After our parents kissed us goodnight, Mae would often crawl out of bed, carefully climb up the bunk-bed ladder, and join me on the top bunk. We would giggle and say "shhh!" to make sure our parents didn't catch us. We were as close as sisters could be, and when Amélie was born, there were three!

That was in March of 2006. It seems like just yesterday that I held Amélie in my arms, full of pride that I was now the oldest of not two but three girls. When my parents initially suggested the name Amélie, I was the first to exclaim, "That's it!" I couldn't have been more excited that her name contained her two older sisters' names, with "mé" reflecting "Mae" and "lie" reflecting "Livia." The amalgamation of both my and Mae's names symbolized a unity now bound by letters. Nowadays, we often call Amélie "Amie," which translates to "friend" in French. I'm a sucker for finding the deeper meaning in semantics, Amélie's birth being one of the earliest illustrations of that passion. My mom is incredibly indecisive, so I'm positive she appreciated my quick confirmation. I was, after all, her oldest daughter, so my opinion mattered!

Most of my time growing up was spent with my sisters. I loved taking care of them, but more importantly, I could be myself around them. I didn't have to pretend to be someone I wasn't. I was simply their older sister. When I was with people my own age, I always wore a mask. Pretending to be someone else is exhausting, so I didn't spend much time with others outside my family. Of course, it's impossible to keep – let alone make – friends when you aren't willing to invest time and energy in those relationships. This difficulty with friendships wasn't evident until much later, however.

5

FRIENDS

"**M**ommy! I have a new best friend!" I exclaimed after completing my first day of kindergarten at Lawrence School. The highly reputable public schools were one of the main reasons my parents had decided to move to Brookline in the first place. My transition from being an outsider in my own world to suddenly running home and begging for a playdate must have been the best confirmation of my parents' decision. Lexi and I instantly clicked that first day because she was the only other girl who actually wanted to do something *purposeful*. She was the only other girl who didn't want to talk about their dolls; instead, she came up to me and asked if I wanted to play checkers.

At first I was nervous. All my prior friends had been boys, probably because I loved running and playing sports as much as they did. Thankfully, a game of checkers didn't involve much talking, which gave me the chance to determine whether I could potentially warm up to Lexi's presence. This didn't take long. After just a few diagonal moves across the checkerboard, Lexi and I realized that the time we would spend together would go far beyond a simple game. I learned she was a gymnast like me, and that same year, we would both score spots on the same soccer team.

From that first game of checkers, Lexi and I were inseparable. We did backflips on her trampoline and played double Dutch. We had lemonade stands and baked endless batches of chocolate chip cookies and fudge brownies. Lexi became part of the family. We introduced her to Dutch holidays such as Sinterklaas (Saint Nicholas) and played Dutch board games such as Ganzenbord (Game of the Goose) and Mens erger je niet! (the American version of which is called Sorry!). When she slept over, we would wake up to the buttery, sweet smell of my mom making *poffertjes*, mini Dutch pancakes that were the only exception to my usual bowl of Froot Loops or Cinnamon Toast Crunch that I allowed. For the first time in my life, I could be myself around a girl I was not related to by blood.

Over time, Lexi and I grew apart. As we progressed through elementary school and classes began to mix, Lexi started making new friends. But I didn't, nor did I want to. Lexi was *my* friend, and I didn't want to share. Unfortunately, Lexi's friendships were out of my control. I was without a best friend until fifth grade, when I met Mila, who had recently transferred from another Brookline public school to Lawrence.

Even though Mila wasn't an athlete like I was, her honest personality and unique sense of humor brought us together. I convinced her to play soccer outside with me while the rest of the girls in our grade stayed inside to gossip, and I taught her how to ride a bike without training wheels. She loved good food as much as I did, and we taught ourselves to cook and bake by tasting and criticizing each other's creations, like in the reality TV show *Chopped*.

Now that I think about it, my friendship with Mila was almost inevitable. Like mine, Mila's family wasn't from the US. Because she had recently moved, she was just as much in need of a new friend as I was. So it was that, at the end of the first day of fifth grade, I ran home, yet again exclaiming, "Mom! I have a new best friend!"

6

NUTRITION CLASS

In fifth grade, we started learning about nutrition. That was the first year our health was to be evaluated by the school nurse, including height, weight, and various forms of fitness. As soon as my teacher, Ms. Raven, informed the class of what we could expect in the upcoming months, I grew as stiff as a board. Competitions of any kind stressed me out, but competitions that involved measuring athletic performance brought this stress to a whole new level.

For instance, before the PACER test, which involves running back and forth at a pace that gets progressively faster after each beep, my gym teacher said, "Remember, everyone: this isn't a competition." But it *was* a competition, both the PACER and the rest of the fitness metrics we would be measured by. My identity was tied to athleticism, and this competition was going to prove that I was the best. To optimize my chance of winning, I needed to optimize my health. What better way to do that than to apply everything I was learning in health class to my life?

During class, I diligently took notes on weight, diet, and exercise. I wrote that a healthy weight is one that falls within a certain BMI range. I wrote that you should always choose an apple instead of a cookie. I wrote that you should exercise for at least sixty minutes each day. Every statement I learned related to health translated into a rule in my black-and-white composition notebook. These new rules meant that a lot was about to change. I could no longer eat my favorite cereals for breakfast. I had to swap white bagels for whole wheat bread. Instead of baking, Mila and I would have to find a more beneficial way to spend our afternoons. Namely, training for the FitnessGram.

"We're going on a diet!" I told Mila as I handed her the health program I had created for us. After hearing about the FitnessGram from my gym teacher, I used my parents' big iMac computer to research what this fitness evaluation program entailed. Along with the PACER test, we had to perform push-ups, pull-ups, sit-ups, and flexibility moves. The training program I had created for Mila and me dictated that we would spend sixty minutes being active after school every day. I already had soccer and gymnastics practices scheduled throughout the week, so I didn't necessarily *need* to exercise for another full hour each day. But I did it anyways because the rule in my notebook stated *at least* sixty minutes of daily physical activity. Besides, the more, the better, right?

I ran around the block as Mila bicycled after me. I joined the cross-country and track teams and showed up to school an hour earlier to practice. I started running around the Muddy River with my mom and dad, often leaps and bounds ahead of them as they panted after me.

"Wow, she's so fast! You must be such a proud parent!" nearby dog walkers exclaimed. I would grin discreetly, then quicken my pace. I was on the road to winning the PACER and getting a perfect score on all the other elements up for evaluation.

7

FINANCES

E ven while I was obsessed with my physical fitness and nutrition, it was during my training for the FitnessGram that
I stopped feeling hungry. By this time, I had been packing not
only my own lunch for school but also lunch for my two sisters.
My dad had been laid off from his graphic design job a few years
earlier and had seized the opportunity to take care of us while
my mom continued to work full-time as a cancer researcher
in Cambridge. Even though my dad had chosen his role as a
stay-at-home dad, he was always complaining. He groaned about
how all three of us kids had different taste preferences, making
the assembly of our lunchboxes more difficult than that of a
1,000-piece puzzle. He called himself a "taxi driver" when he
drove us to and from sports or extracurricular activities and a
"cleaning lady" when he stood above the sink, soaking bowls
whose interiors were encrusted with the remains of mac and
cheese or sticky milk and cereal.

The constant quarrels between my mom and dad always gave me
a stomachache, so I did my best to relieve my father of his irri-
tants. I obviously couldn't take over driving or other grown-up
responsibilities, but I *could* take over the lunchboxes and keep
the sink empty. Making our lunches was a win-win for everyone;
I could pack according to the rules of my new health plan, and
my dad could sleep an extra hour.

For myself, I packed sprouted multigrain bread with a thin layer
of peanut butter made from 100% peanuts and sugar-free jam.

Even though I didn't mind the crusts, I trimmed them off to cut back on calories. Because I didn't want to hurt the crusts' feelings by throwing them away, I'd eat them for breakfast instead of my usual bowl of sugary cereal. This was definitely a huge adjustment, but at least I could still taste hints of the peanut butter and jam. While I savored every bite of the bread trimmings, I was already dreaming about lunchtime; then I'd get to eat my *real* PB&J. The crusts were just my appetizer.

For my sisters, I packed the same thing, but different. Instead of multigrain bread, I gave them dense white bread. Instead of the thin layer of all-natural no-sugar-added peanut butter, I gave them a thick smear of creamy Skippy. Instead of the aspartame-laden jam, I specifically selected the jam with the highest calories at the grocery store. This one happened to contain high-fructose corn syrup, a food that was written in the OFF-LIMITS section of my composition notebook. Ms. Raven had said that high-fructose corn syrup could contribute to obesity, and obesity was the *last* thing I needed if I was going to win the PACER.

Now, don't get me wrong. I didn't want to make my sisters obese either. I just had to be certain they were eating more than me. I became so furious when their lunches came home half-eaten that I would stomp my feet and burst into tears.

"They don't appreciate my efforts!" I yelled when my parents asked why I was so upset about something as insignificant as them leaving two bites of a peanut butter and jelly sandwich.

"What can we do to help you calm down?" My parents would lay a hand on my shoulder.

"Mae and Amélie need to finish their lunches. Look, I did!" I replied. I held out my arms to show them the empty contents of my lunchbox.

"Okay," my mom or dad would utter tiredly, calling in my sisters to finish whatever was left of their lunch.

"I don't want the rest of my food," they would say. "I'm full!"

I'm sure they were full, as the half-full lunchbox scenario often happened when the whole family was home, after my sisters had grabbed snacks with their friends or eaten the copious amounts of desserts I baked. But then I would stomp my feet and burst into tears again, not stopping until my sisters gave in. They would grudgingly pop the now stale pieces of bread into their little mouths, allowing me to breathe again.

8

WORRIED

Even the temporary relief of my sisters finishing their lunches was lost when my mom got laid off in January 2011. I was about halfway through fifth grade, submerged in the pressures of harder tests, training for the FitnessGram, and the increasing seriousness of my sports. *This couldn't be!* I thought as I lay wide awake at night, fearing we would be evicted from our house. If that happened, we would end up in a shelter, and I would no longer be able to make my own food. All our income was thanks to my mom's job, which was now gone. What was I going to do?

Not one to leave anything up to chance, I tried to take control. I ran lemonade stands outside our house, which to this day my dad calls the start of my entrepreneurial journey. At one point, I even started selling my drawings to people walking down our street! I baked even more so I could hold bake sales in the school playground. I added more butter and sugar to whatever I was making, so that everyone who indulged in my treats would moan even more deeply with pleasure and delight. At the same time, I ate less to save on groceries, insisting that I didn't want to burden my parents more than I already was.

I did whatever I could to support the family, but I could tell my mom was still stressed. My efforts would never be good enough. So I turned even more fiercely to what I knew I *could* be good at. I stopped hanging out with Mila after school to make more time for homework. I got straight As and infinite praise from Ms.

Raven. I completed my daily miles even faster, leaving me more time to clean the house.

In May 2011, the day I had trained for had finally come: it was time to run the PACER. I didn't sleep the whole night prior as I trembled with nerves, but I was full of energy that morning. I had spent months preparing for this; now all I had to do was execute. Not surprisingly, I won! I had proven myself and my athletic capabilities, which meant I no longer had to keep training. But somehow, breaking my grade level's record on the PACER test – as a girl at that – didn't make a difference. Instead of being relieved that this challenge was over, I felt even more pressure to keep going.

When I came home from school that day, I told my mom I wanted to run a marathon. "I want to raise money for cancer!" I exclaimed, secretly hoping we could also save some of that money to support our family.

"What a lovely idea for the future," my mom replied gently, half gazing at her computer screen, where a LinkedIn page was displayed. The future? What did she mean, *the future*? I wanted to run a marathon *now*! I needed something new to train for.

"You're a bit young, honey," she reassured me. "Eleven-year-olds shouldn't be running marathons. Besides, you're running so much already!" I could hear the worry in her voice. For the first time since she had lost her job, it was worry about something other than her work. She was worried about *me*. But why?

9

NATALIE'S OFFICE

I t all unfolded in June of 2011, the moment we stepped foot in the small office of Natalie, my favorite pediatrician at Harvard Pediatrics.

"So, tell me – what's been going on, Livia?" Natalie's voice was the cheerful one I associated with her. I shrugged as I stared at the blue-speckled tiles that lined the floor. Before I could even ponder a word, a phrase, anything, my mom interrupted: "She hasn't been eating enough. She's always running. She doesn't spend time with anyone anymore, and every conversation nowadays seems to be about food!"

"Is that so?" Natalie turned slightly, shifting her gaze from my mom to me. Though I was still staring at the floor, I could feel Natalie's eyes like lasers beaming onto the crown of my head. I was cornered, a wild animal realizing its visibility on a trail where hunters are actively seeking prey. The metallic base of a tall body scale was apparent from the corner of my eye, but I kept my head locked into position, fearing that even a glimpse at the scale would somehow trigger Natalie to make me step on it. I knew why we were here long before Natalie had asked me her initial question.

"I know I lost some weight," I murmured, almost inaudibly.

"How about we take a look?" Natalie responded, still cheerful as ever.

Dammit.

I got on the scale reluctantly, already aware of what the number would read before my bare feet met the cold metal. I had weighed myself that morning, just like I had every morning for the past three weeks.

"What does it say?" my mom asked insistently, balancing on the edge of her seat, unable to read the number from a distance.

Natalie answered my mom and finished with, "Let's get a height, too."

The forty-five-minute conversation that followed was like a pinball machine that bounced between dozens of phrases containing the words *BMI, growth curve,* and *zero percentile.* I had lost just a couple of pounds since my eleven-year well-child visit a few months prior, but it was enough to put me below the growth curve for my age and height. Natalie told me about the importance of healthy eating and highlighted the benefits of carbs and fats. She explained the growth curve to me, drawing her finger along the bottom and eventually pointing to my position on the chart.

Did she think I was ignorant or something? I knew what healthy eating meant! It's what I had been doing ever since we started learning about it in class. If anything, Natalie had to brush up on *her* knowledge of nutrition. She said whole milk was *good* for me. Clearly, she was not familiar with the part in our textbook that read, "Aim for three 8-oz. servings of low-fat or skim milk products each day." Every time she mentioned a food I *should* be eating, I hit back with a piece of knowledge from my research. But somehow, my words seemed to go in one ear and straight out the other. When I realized this, I just started nodding, ambivalently agreeing to eat more from now on.

And I did. A few days after that visit with Natalie, my mom got a call from Dana-Farber Cancer Institute. She had just landed a position as a senior scientist. Woohoo! We were safe! When my mom announced the terrific news at the dinner table that night, I ate my entire plate. I didn't skip dessert either.

A month later, we were back in Natalie's office for a follow-up visit. I was praised for my weight gain and told to continue my healthy eating patterns, which I would do without a doubt. Life was so much simpler when it was predictable, and I no longer had to worry about the responsibilities that come with friendship and spontaneity.

Every day was the same. Upon waking, I would do my exercises, make my bed, and brush my teeth. I would go downstairs to make the lunchboxes, saving my crusts for an effortless breakfast. At the same time, I would hound my sisters to finish their cereal, not taking my eyes off them until they also drank the sweet-flavored milk that remained in the bowl.

From 8:20 a.m. to 2:20 p.m., my sole focus was school. The only time I spoke was to answer one of Ms. Raven's questions after she'd called on me. Mila no longer came outside to play soccer with me. Instead, she joined the other girls in their gossip about who-knows-what. Whereas I used to care, I didn't have the energy to occupy my mind with anything other than food, exercise, and keeping the house clean. I no longer had the energy for sports, either. On the days I had soccer or gymnastics practice, I woke up already counting down the hours until the sport was over. I felt exhausted and lifeless, with eating being the only thing I looked forward to.

In July 2011, we were back in Natalie's office for the third time that year. This time, however, my mom didn't go on about my food choices or rigid exercise routine. My obsession with order and routine seemed to have become a routine in and of itself, so much so that my family had gotten used to it. I couldn't imagine what there was to worry about now.

"She seems so depressed," my mom said. Based on her tone of voice, I was certain *she* was the one who was truly depressed.

"Can you tell me a little more about your mood, Livia?" Natalie tried to saw away at the tightrope of tension suspended between my mom and me.

I shrugged. Since the last visit, the only difference between that shrug and my earlier one was that my shoulders were now bonier. "I just feel sad," I responded, aiming my answer at the tiled floor.

"Do you always feel sad?"

"Not all the time. It makes me happy when people like the things I bake." I felt a flutter of excitement. "I actually baked a lemon poppyseed loaf yesterday! I used whole wheat flour and honey and applesauce to make it healthier, and still, everyone loved it!"

They thought I didn't notice, but my mom and Natalie glanced at each other. We spoke again about the importance of allowing all foods, but this time it was *my* ears Natalie's words went in and out of. Considering all our conversations up until this point, I was certain no one knew what healthy meant as well as I did. After all, *I* was the one constantly researching and applying it to my life!

The last visit to Natalie that year was my well-child visit in September. The topics of conversation didn't seem to change; it was all healthy food this, hang out with friends that, blah blah blah. I knew what I was doing, and I didn't need anyone to tell me otherwise.

At the start of sixth grade, my parents forced me to see a therapist, but I refused to continue going after a couple of sessions. I knew *something* wasn't right, but I couldn't figure out *what*.

It became clear that the therapist didn't know either, which is why I no longer wanted to waste money on something that was obviously a waste of time.

My parents were at a complete loss as to how to help me. They were trying their best. They encouraged me at mealtimes and reassured me that I was allowed to rest when I was too tired to run, but I couldn't stop what I was doing. It had become my routine, my schedule, my life. It was what I knew, and I thought doing what I knew would keep me safe.

It wasn't until the first month of seventh grade that we were back in Natalie's office again, but this time, the conversation was different than it had been precisely a year before. Instead of Natalie's usual encouragement to eat more, talk to friends, and continue trying to find joy in my sports, her tone was cold and serious.

Within five minutes of that appointment, I was diagnosed with anorexia nervosa and depression.

Author's note: As I read through countless medical records while writing this book, I came across an email my mom had sent prior to this appointment. I believe my mother's raw, unfiltered words enrich this story, which is why, with her permission, I have chosen to share it here:

Hi Natalie,

I hope we can talk before today's appointment this afternoon. We feel we are drifting into an increasingly taxing and awful situation, Livia is getting more and more hard to deal with and it may be teenage independence combined, but Jan and I are at wit's end with approaching the food. Yesterday we went to endocrinologist, Livia is now X lbs, and there seems to be no other (endocrine) issue than the weight loss which will have to turn around to have her grow, so...she needs to eat way more...

She says she will but is so resistant and finicky about everything, disrespectful, defiant and resentful to us about offered help or suggestions. One example: bought Ensure to give her a daily boost (suggested by endocrinologist, but negated by Livia because she thinks she might not like it) and Livia called me all kinds of things for doing that and [said] she would eat instead, freaked out over the ingredients on the label which she insisted was high fructose corn syrup which she learnt is BAD so etc etc big unproductive discussions...

Her sisters are getting to be afraid of her, she is bossy, unkind, pushy, always irritated and obsessed with food and homework. Nothing else. It breaks my heart...

You have been such an important voice in this process and I hope today's visit will at least help to get her paired up with a nutritionist ASAP; we need INTENSE monitoring and some support in our parenting as well. Livia is seeing a therapist at Brookline Mental Health, and is telling stories there that may not necessarily reflect the situation as is...Jan and I will be going too, and we feel very motivated to work through this, but admittedly are a bit desperate at this point.

Hope you don't mind my venting. Whew. Talk soon,

Louise

PART 2: SINKING INTO LABELS

10

ENSURE

I plugged my nose and sank into the bathtub, sliding down until I was fully immersed in the hot water. Sometimes I wondered what it felt like to drown. As I lay there, covered in what felt like the accumulation of the tears I had shed in the last two hours, a vivid memory of a movie started playing in my head. I don't remember which movie it was, but the opening scene showed a couple skating on a frozen pond. They were smiling and moving with a playful grace, but the music that accompanied the scene gave the viewer a feeling of tension and unease.

CRACK!

There it was: the moment that had been just a shadow in the background since the start of the story yet had only become certain once the ice had broken.

You have anorexia. The words echoed between my ears again, like they had mere hours before, but this time, the sound was intensified by the pressure of the water that encased my entire body. The moment Natalie said it, I started to fight. I begged her to take it back, explaining that someone who *really* had anorexia would think they're fat. I pleaded that I just wanted to be healthy, admitting that I had perhaps taken things too far. No matter how hard I tried to defend myself – seeking desperately for an opening in the wall of ice I had just fallen through – there was no going back. I guess this was what it felt like to drown.

During the appointment (with a record-breaking duration of time spent in that little Harvard Pediatrics office), I was told to eat six small meals and drink one Ensure nutrition shake per day. At least, that was the plan until my next doctor's appointment with what Natalie called a "specialist" at Children's Hospital Boston. She had already scheduled the intake for the following Monday, September 24, as that was the first availability considering this was a Friday. Because I had learned that nothing I said seemed to matter anymore, I agreed to go to the appointment on Monday and to drink the Ensure shakes over the weekend.

As I nodded, using all my willpower to contain the mass of tears building behind my eyes, I already knew I was *not* going to drink those shakes. They contained high-fructose corn syrup, listed as the second ingredient at that! When I said I wanted to try to gain weight at home, I meant it. When I said I would eat more, I had every intention of doing so. When I said I knew I was too thin, I wasn't lying. But there was *no way* I was going to drink an Ensure shake.

11

Dinner

We had family dinners as often as possible. The makeup of our typical meal was straightforward: protein, carbs, fats, and vegetables. Because my parents were both born and raised in the Netherlands, they had been brought up on this type of meal, called Aardappels, Vlees, Groente (AVG'tje), translating to "potatoes, meat, greens." For me, up until the age of ten, this looked like macaroni and cheese, chicken nuggets, and steamed broccoli. My parents often encouraged me to try a bite of their baked potatoes, steak tips, or sautéed asparagus, but as with everything, I stood my ground: it was either mac and cheese or nothing at all.

When I first embarked on my journey to becoming "healthier," I finally ventured out. Change had always been difficult for me, but if there was a strong enough *reason* to change, I'd at least try. I learned to love sweet potatoes, chicken, and some other vegetables. Even though I didn't like fish, I would eat fish sticks dipped in applesauce as my mom and dad ate salmon with dill sauce.

I knew that after I got out of the bathtub, it was time for dinner. When I came downstairs that night, wearing loose pajamas in a pointless effort to hide the fact that I was now officially "anorexic," my plate was waiting for me: sweet potatoes, spinach, and fish sticks with applesauce. I felt okay about it and was ready to sit down, until I saw the empty glass with an unopened bottle of Ensure next to it. I started to tremble, hoping my parents would notice my unease. All I wanted was for them to comfort me, to tell me everything was going to be okay. Instead, I was met with anger and impatience.

"What took you so long?" my dad said as he finished portioning everyone else's plates. I looked over at my mom in desperation.

"Livia was diagnosed with anorexia today," she announced.

"Shhh! I do *not* have anorexia!" I yelled.

"Ano-what?" Amélie asked, her five-year-old voice curiously sweet and innocent.

"Anorexia," I answered. "But I don't have it. Natalie has no idea what she's talking about!" I was ashamed of the label while at the same time angry because it was just plain *wrong*.

As part of nutrition class in school, we learned that there are three types of eating disorders: anorexia, bulimia, and binge-eating disorder. The biology textbook gave each disorder one small paragraph, anorexia being extra privileged in that it got a picture to go along with its description. My way of thinking – in images rather than words – was why the illustration of anorexia remained so clear in my mind, even several months after having seen it. I was intrigued by the visual, utterly floored by the possibility that anyone so thin could see a fat version of themselves in the mirror. I guess that's why the authors had included that graphic in the first place: it seemed impossible.

I knew I couldn't have anorexia because I never saw myself as fat, nor did I want to lose weight. All I wanted was to be healthy! Somehow, my attempting to be healthy had resulted in losing a few pounds.

"Can we please eat?" Mae insisted, energetically bobbing up and down at the opposite end of the table.

"I can't eat," I said softly. "My stomach hurts now." It was true; my tummy felt like it had been put in the washing machine and set on *super cycle*, twirling and whirling every which way.

"You have to eat, Livia." My dad handed me my fork, attempting to comfort me with a smile.

I was torn. I wanted my dad to keep his smile; I wanted to be a good daughter and to eat and pretend that what happened in Natalie's office today never happened. But it *had*, and for whatever reason, the very thought of consuming anything numbed me.

"Please, Livia," my mom begged. "Please eat." The look in her eyes was almost as desperate as mine when I had glimpsed that bottle of Ensure.

"Well, I'm not going to let my food get cold," my dad said, scooping a piece of sweet potato into his mouth. "Mae and Amélie, let's eat."

Oh, how I wanted to do the same. "I'm so sorry, but I can't. Not with that Ensure staring right at me!" I was trying to buy myself time, hoping it would somehow lessen the anxiety building up inside.

"Livia, remember what we agreed on in Natalie's office. You promised to drink the Ensure." My mom's announcement dually chastised me and acquainted my dad with this new protocol.

"The only reason I agreed to drink it was so that we could leave! I'm not going to drink that!" I wanted to grab the bottle and throw it at the wall.

My mom's face scrunched up. "Why aren't you going to drink it?"

"Because it has high-fructose corn syrup. And not only that, just look at the rest of the ingredients!" I grabbed the bottle, flipped it over, and read the tiny print aloud. "I mean, what even *is* that?"

I asked mockingly as I attempted to pronounce the ingredient *DL-Alpha-Tocopheryl Acetate.*

My dad put his head in his hands. Seconds later, my mom did the same.

I darted for the stairs, needing to escape from this prison that the label "anorexia" had locked me in. But even in the familiarity of my own room, I felt trapped. I thought about jumping out the window but knew I would never actually do it. I thought about the relief that would come if I could just disappear into thin air, slightly comforted by the thought of how much my family would miss me if I did. I started pacing between my bed and bookcase while I waited for someone to follow me.

When ten minutes had passed and no one had come, I started doing push-ups. After my arms shook so much that I collapsed onto the fluffy rug that matched my bedspread, I flipped over and started doing sit-ups. An untamable fireball of energy raged inside me, and seeing as I couldn't run outside without having to pass the kitchen table first, exercises in my room would have to suffice.

After each set of precisely counted reps, I scurried over to the door to check if anyone was coming. Part of me wanted them to stay away and leave me to my exercises, but a greater part wanted someone to come. I wanted a reason to stop making my arms tremble and my legs quake, a reason to rest.

Finally, I heard the faint sound of footsteps, followed by intensifying creaking noises on the floorboards outside my bedroom. Then came a knock, followed by a forceful push on my bedroom door.

12

MEADOWBROOK

O ur house on Meadowbrook Road was an old house, which was why the floors creaked, the doors got stuck, and my dad had to remove all the bathroom locks after my sister got locked in one the first week after our move. But to me, the house still felt new. We had moved in the fall of 2011, when I was a couple of months into sixth grade at Lawrence School. I always loved looking inside open houses, creating fantasies of which room would be mine and how I'd decorate it. But that's all they ever were: fantasies.

We already lived in a beautiful yellow house on Brook Street, with an open playroom filled to the brim with every set of Playmobil toys. My sisters and I would create cities and towns inspired by the pictures on the boxes, and instead of playing with the figures ourselves, how we engaged with our creations was even better: we let our hamsters run the action! When the hamsters' short lives came to an end, we got kittens. Kiki and Sammy were beautiful blue point Siamese twins (as in Siamese cats that were twins; they were not physically attached) who spent their first years of life sniffing and making our home on Brook Street theirs, too.

It was on Brook Street that I operated my lemonade stands, ran to and from Lexi's house just a couple of blocks away, and could walk to Lawrence School in less than ten minutes. Brook Street was my home – but it could no longer be once our landlord informed my parents he was increasing the rent.

We had been renting on Brook Street for over five years by the time our landlord broke the news. Considering the house's sublime location just a few miles from Boston, those five years had cost my parents a pretty penny. They had initially put off purchasing a home, uncertain how long we would live in Brookline, but when our rent increased, they decided it was time.

I visually furnished "my room" at every open house we went to, and I pictured myself in the kitchen, baking brownies or cooking up a feast for the rest of the family. I was anxious about where we would move, yet at the same time, I was enthralled by the novelty that was to come. My family searched long and hard for a house that would fit our now family of five (actually seven, because Kiki and Sammy were 100% part of the family). However, each house we visited was either way above our budget (with my mom still the sole breadwinner of the family) or too small to accommodate us all.

Then, our family friend and realtor, who also lived on Brook Street, sent us the link to a house on Meadowbrook Road. It was located in Chestnut Hill, a part of the Greater Boston Area that was almost a suburb compared to the location of our home in the center of Brookline. Although living on Meadowbrook Road would mean driving to school and sports rather than walking or bicycling as we had done for years, this house was not only affordable but a beautiful Victorian built in 1924.

During the open house, my mom jokingly told my sisters and me to make loud, overdramatic remarks about everything that was "wrong" with it. "Oh, look how annoying! The doors get stuck!" I would blabber, winking at my sisters, who would follow with, "And the floors creak!" Even though it probably made no difference, my mom wanted to scare off any potential buyers who might want to place a bid on the home. This house was a steal, and it was going to be ours.

13

Do You Love Me?

When my dad entered my room, he was holding my dinner plate in one hand and a glass filled with thick, cream-colored liquid in the other.

"I already told you, I'm not hungry!" I yelled, trying to disguise my shortness of breath and my cheeks that were red as a tomato. I thought my dad would ask what I had been doing, but we both knew it was obvious. "I'm not hungry!" I repeated, set on edge by the uncertainty that accompanied the silence.

"Mama tells me you agreed to drink this." His voice was calm as he held up the glass. I hated when my parents did this: one asked the other to take over a task when the initial attempt had been unsuccessful.

"I know Mama sent you," I mumbled angrily. "Why doesn't she come up herself if she truly loves me?" My dad sighed. It wasn't the first time I had used this tactic to get my parents to express their love for me. Deep down, I knew they loved me – but a part of me always needed to hear it again.

"You know we both love you very much, Livia. That's *why* we want you to drink this."

"See, I knew it!" I took a step back and pointed at him. The truth was exposed by his choice of words. "*You* just want me to drink it. If you truly loved me, you would let me do what *I* want!"

"Doing what *you* want will land you in the emergency room!" My dad was clearly losing his patience. When I started trembling, his expression softened.

"Emergency room?" I whimpered like a scared dog.

My mom seemed to come out of nowhere. "You got that right! If you don't eat your dinner right now, we're taking you straight to the hospital!"

If I had felt imprisoned before, now it was as if I had been brought to one of those prisons where you know the other inmates are going to destroy you with their own hands. Even though I was always cold, my palms became sweaty. The very thought of eating food transformed that fireball of energy previously inside of me into a giant ring of fire...and my parents were asking me to leap right through it with no opportunity to practice jumping through regular hoops first.

I looked up at my mom, then at my dad. "Do you love me?" I asked.

"Honey, of course we love you!" My mom squeezed me tight, and the pressure intensified as my dad joined in on the hug.

"I'll eat my dinner, but please don't make me drink the Ensure." All three of us knew this compromise was a steal, so my parents took it.

14

ADOLESCENT MEDICINE

During French class the following Monday, I couldn't keep my eyes off the clock. The gentle ticking was like a time bomb that would explode when the school office rang the French teacher to tell her my dad was here to pick me up. The appointment with the "specialist" was at 2:00 p.m. It was only a ten-minute drive to Children's Hospital Boston, but we would need to be on our way well before 1:50 to allow time for traffic and parking. I became increasingly nervous when the phone still hadn't rung by 1:40 p.m. Not because I wanted to be on time for the appointment (I would have done anything to miss it) but because events that didn't happen as scheduled were events that held uncertainty.

"I know I'm late. There was traffic on the way here," my dad said at 1:47 p.m. when I finally met him in the Lawrence School lobby. My dad was almost always late, so any excuse would have been equally meaningless. One day it was traffic. Another day it was losing track of time. Another, it was someone else's fault for calling him at an inconvenient time. Whatever the reason, my dad could never admit to *just being late*.

He hurried towards the car while I took my sweet time. "Livia, hurry up! We're already running late!"

He was late for this appointment *I* didn't even want to go to, so why should *I* hurry? I didn't want to stress him out more than he already was though, so I picked up my pace.

The drive to the hospital parking garage seemed to pass in a flash. I didn't even notice we had arrived until the car stopped, my mind occupied by the unpredictability of what the appointment would entail. Who even was this "specialist"? What were they going to ask me? Why did *both* my parents need to be there?

"Finally!" my mom hollered as soon as she saw us approach the building across from the main hospital. "Come on, we don't want to miss this appointment!" We rushed inside and waited for the elevator to take us to the fifth floor. If I were by myself, I would have taken the stairs. Scratch that: if I were by myself, *I wouldn't even be here*. But if I were by myself here, I would have most definitely taken the stairs. And not because I have a fear of elevators like my mom has, but because that's another thing I learned in my research: when you have the option, take the stairs.

When the elevator finally came, I was grateful to find it empty. Those moments of awkwardness with strangers always made the hairs on the back of my neck stand up. And recently, that image had become more than just an idiom. My mom first pointed out the lanugo when she was braiding my hair (on my head, not my neck!) a few weeks before, and it certainly contributed to her increased worries since then. On the contrary, when I learned that lanugo is one of the body's adaptive mechanisms to keep itself warm due to lack of body fat, I wasn't the least bit worried. In fact, I was astounded by my body's incredible ability to adapt to new circumstances. Not enough body fat? No problem! That's what extra hair is for, right? I still couldn't understand why everyone was making such a big fuss about a mere five pounds of weight loss.

After checking in at the front desk of the Adolescent Medicine Department, a nurse told me to pee in a cup and then wait in a small hallway until I got called for my weight and vitals. These measurements were taken in a much more advanced way than in Natalie's office. Instead of the manual, pump-type blood pressure meter, my arm received a cuff that tightened with the single press of a button. Suddenly, a machine that resembled a robot on wheels emitted beeps and flashes. Instead of the scale in Natalie's office, made up of a small base and a single rod with a small gray screen at the top, the hospital scale consisted of a platform with handrails on each side.

The nurse handed me a speckled blue gown. "Take everything off except for your underwear, then let me know when you're ready," she said, drawing a curtain with an orange and blue block pattern. So far, the curtain was the only colorful thing I'd seen in this place.

"I'm ready," I said moments later, turning to face the scale.

She opened the curtain. "Step on backward for me, please."

Backward? Why? I'd always been allowed to know my weight! But now was not the time to ask questions. I turned around and followed her orders, tormented by the knowledge that I couldn't see the number.

I got dressed, returned to the hallway, and sat in the chair between my mom and dad. When twenty minutes had gone by, I became annoyed. "I shouldn't have left school early for this." I groaned. "I could have finished French class instead of just pointlessly sitting here."

My mom sighed, and my dad tapped his feet. "Welcome to the hospital," he said in Dutch. "You always gotta wait here." It was true; wait times in medical settings were unpredictable. Still, this knowledge didn't make it any less annoying. Being in this new location was hard enough, never mind not knowing when the appointment would even start. I blinked a few times to make sure I wasn't having a nightmare.

"Livia?" A plump lady with short blond hair and a face full of pimples looked up from her clipboard. I raised my hand, an almost automatic response that I had school to thank for. "I'm Dr. Jones. It's nice to meet you," she said as she greeted us with a half-smile. The three of us rose. My mom and dad shook her hand, but I just stood there, waiting for her to guide us to the next colorless room.

"I actually want to speak to you alone first!" She looked into my eyes, and my gaze immediately shifted to her light brown cowboy boots. Eye contact had always caused me discomfort, but with today's circumstances, forcing myself to make eye contact would have been downright painful.

Dr. Jones asked me all kinds of questions about food and exercise. Did I fear weight gain? What were my thoughts about eating sugar? How often did I exercise? I gave her answers I thought she would not expect. I made a game out of this stupid appointment I never should have gone to in the first place. If the hospital was going to play games with me by hiding my weight, making me wait, and putting me in depressing rooms with doctors who clearly didn't take care of their own health, the least I deserved was a bit of fun, too.

Even though she seemed surprised by my not-typical-for-an-anorexic answers, everything I said was true: I told her I didn't fear weight gain, leaving out the part about not *wanting* to gain weight. I told her I ate sugar every day, leaving out the part about how it had to be *all-natural* sugar. I told her I exercised the recommended sixty minutes each day, leaving out the part about how it was *at least* sixty minutes each day. By playing my cards in a way that would catch her off guard, I believed I could win this game and would be free to go. That was until she threw in a joker.

Dr. Jones called my parents into the room and told us all how concerning my situation was: I was severely underweight, and my heart rate was less than 40 beats per minute (bpm). My parents looked at each other in shock, and my dad shared how his heart rate had been 35 bpm when he was in a coma after suffering a brain aneurysm in 2003. I remember that day very well. Even though I was only four years old, it seemed like yesterday that I was giggling at my dad's half-bald head from the hospital bed after the surgery that saved his life.

Today, no one giggled. I didn't know why Dr. Jones needed to ask me all those questions beforehand, because the news she bore seemed to be what she had known all along: "With this low of a heart rate, Livia should immediately be admitted to the hospital." My heart sank. I looked over at my parents, my eyes flashing back and forth between them. But they didn't look back at me. Instead, they held their heads in their hands and cried.

15

CHILDREN'S HOSPITAL BOSTON

We crossed the street to enter the main hospital, which was surrounded by taxis and kids in wheelchairs. Most of them were obviously being treated for cancer, as they wore caps on their heads and were attached to machines holding bags of liquid. I wondered what their parents thought. Did they cry, too, like my parents had in Dr. Jones's office? How long had they been sick? I wanted to ask them what it was like being in the hospital. Were the beds comfortable? Was the food any good? How did they get their schoolwork done? My brain flooded with so many questions, it paralyzed me. And just like a person physically paralyzed, I was lying in a hospital bed before I knew it.

My room was on the eighth floor, diagonal from a large, round desk occupied by what seemed to be nurses clicking away at large computers. I couldn't tell who was in the room to the left because the curtains were closed, but the room to the right gave me the slightest glimmer of hope that this wasn't *the* most depressing place on Earth. Fluffy stuffed animals lined the foot of the bed, and the wall at the head of the bed was decorated with dozens of colorful cards. There were so many balloons that the room could have easily been mistaken for a birthday party if not for the ginormous white bed in the middle. The only thing missing was the birthday cake, but judging by the gaunt face of the girl who occupied the bed, I didn't think she was missing the cake one bit.

A nurse who introduced herself as PJ helped me settle into bed, rattling off a whole list of what to expect during my stay. She was going so fast that I was afraid I was going to forget something super important, but her friendly smile and peaceful demeanor put me at ease – at least, as close as I was going to get to feeling "at ease" in these circumstances. She explained what the machines did and showed me how to adjust my bed with a remote. Up down, up down. Cool! My bed at home didn't do this!

"And this button" – she pointed to a big red button at the top of the remote – "you press this button when you need help."

I didn't think I would ever press that button, but PJ pressed it for me, proving *how fast* another nurse would come. When the out-of-breath nurse exclaimed "PJ!" before sighing in relief, PJ winked at me. As PJ continued explaining all the particulars of my hospital stay, I was surprised to hear that I wasn't allowed to get up to use the bathroom.

"But it's the *bathroom*," I protested in the kindest possible way. "I'm for sure going to need to go!"

"I know, hon." PJ grabbed a metal contraption with a bucket from under the bed. "Due to your low heart rate, you're not allowed to get up at all. When you need to go, just press that red button, and a nurse will help you."

I couldn't believe this. Did they think I was some kind of invalid who couldn't walk? I had walked (and run, for that matter) every day for the past three months without anything happening, so why shouldn't I be allowed to take a mere three steps to the bathroom?

"Okay, well, how about showering? Surely you don't have a portable shower contraption!" I hoped this clever remark would change the rules.

"Sorry, hon. No showers until your heart rate is up." PJ seemed to really mean her "sorry," as her words echoed with empathy. I knew she didn't make the rules, and I wanted her to keep liking me, so I nodded in understanding.

That afternoon, I met with all kinds of doctors who asked me all kinds of questions. The psychologist and psychiatrist asked me about my feelings and mood, which I really didn't like to talk about. I knew I was scared of being in the hospital, but beyond that, I truly didn't know how I felt. They asked me if I knew why I was here. I answered, "Yes, because my heart rate is too low." But when they asked me what deep, dark hole in my life had triggered me to use food and exercise to "cope with my emotions," I shrugged. *If I knew, I wouldn't be here, you dumbo!*

When the nutritionist came in, I felt a tingle of excitement: we were going to talk about food! I knew I had to eat – especially now that I was in the hospital – so I couldn't wait to have all my questions answered. Who prepared the food? Could I choose my meals? How often were mealtimes? Not only did the nutritionist answer my questions, but she gave me something that would become my lifeboat for the next seven years: a meal plan.

I quickly learned the ins and outs of my meal plan as the nutritionist and I worked our way through the pile of papers on her clipboard. She explained the exchange system, which was basically just a way of structuring my intake based on food groups. There were six categories of exchanges: starches, fats, proteins, calcium/dairy, fruits, and veggies. She had assigned me a specific number of exchanges for each category, and all I would have to do was mix and match foods by selecting them from the exchange list. The list was closer to a novel than an actual "list," as it went on for at least ten pages. It was neatly organized in a table, with the food, serving size, and specific exchanges from left to right.

1 slice of bread equals 1 starch

1 tablespoon of peanut butter equals 1 protein and 1 fat

1 cup of milk equals 1 dairy

1/2 banana equals 1 fruit

When the nutritionist left, I spent a good hour reading through the exchange list. The time passed so quickly, the list might as well have been a good book! I filled in my food choices for that night's dinner and snack, as well as my entire meal card for the next day. For the first time since being in the hospital, I felt a sense of relief. I was finally *allowed* to eat all the foods I had been dreaming of, and better yet, it was all according to a simple structure.

That night, I enjoyed every bite of the chicken parmesan (2 starches, 2 proteins, 2 fats, 1 veggie) I had selected for dinner. Even though it was made with regular white pasta and topped with full-fat cheese, I didn't care; it followed the exchanges, which was all that mattered. I ate my dinner as PJ lounged in a chair near the foot of my bed, telling me about her kids and what she liked to do when she wasn't being a nurse. My parents and sisters had visited to help me decorate my room between the several meetings with doctors that afternoon and were now having their own dinner in the hospital cafeteria. It felt odd not knowing what they were eating, but just as with the meal plan, it brought relief. I no longer had to compare my intake to anyone else's.

I had to eat all my meals in the presence of a nurse. When I asked why, the nutritionist said it was to make sure I ate everything.

Of course, I was going to eat everything! What did she think, that I didn't enjoy structure? Thanks to the meal plan, my current life's mission was to follow it perfectly! I ate every morsel of food served to me and grinned in satisfaction as the nurses and nutritionists applauded me for my 100% completion. When they asked if I found it difficult – eating all the food, that is – I truthfully answered that I didn't. That was until the night of the baked potato.

16

BAKED POTATO

On the third day of my stay, I ordered a baked potato (2 starches), grilled chicken (3 proteins), green beans (1 veggie), and a side of butter and sour cream (2 fats) for dinner. It was also my first dinner with a glass of milk (1 dairy). The nutritionist had been increasing my meal plan bit by bit, and I was still quite full from earlier meals when 6:00 p.m. rolled around.

"Can I please eat my dinner a little later?" I asked the supervising nurse as she wheeled the meal cart into my room. My mom was visiting, and I wanted to finish playing our card game.

"No can do – dinnertime's at 6:00 p.m.," she replied. "Hospital rules."

I looked over at my mom, hoping she could save me from this desperate situation, as she'd always done when I needed an out.

"Honey, I guess it's time to eat your dinner now. We can finish afterward, okay?" I knew she felt conflicted. On the one hand, she wanted to make me happy; on the other, she wanted to make me *healthy*. She had put her trust in the hospital's rules for the latter.

I grunted but cleared my tray of the cards to make room for dinner. When I lifted the lid off the plate, I instantly regretted my choices. The baked potato was *huge*. How was I going to finish it, let alone the rest of the meal?

"Mommy," I whispered. "I don't think I can finish this. I'm still so full!"

I could tell my mom wanted an out at this point, too. She clearly wanted to sprint for the exit and leave me with the nurse, but she was just as stuck as I was. "Livia, you haven't even started yet. Just take one bite at a time, and you'll finish, just like you've finished all your other meals so well." I stared at her, silently pleading for one last sign of encouragement. She gave me a nod that held the words *you've got this*.

I picked up the fork, followed by the knife, and cut into the chicken. *One bite at a time.* I spread the sour cream across the baked potato and inserted my fork into the starchy flesh. *One bite at a time.* I melted the butter atop the green beans and scooped the vegetables into my mouth. *One bite at a time.* I took a sip of milk and wiped my mouth with the napkin. *You've got this.* Slowly but surely, I made my way through the meal, looking over at my mom for approval every time I completed another milestone. She smiled at me. Suddenly, I hit a point where no number of smiles was going to get me through. I was absolutely stuffed, and I couldn't bear the thought of consuming even a single green bean more.

"Can I please take a break?" I signaled the nurse to look up from her book. "I really want to finish, but I'm too full. My stomach is going to explode if I eat another bite right now."

She glanced at her watch. "You have thirty minutes to complete the meal, and twenty have already gone by. You can take a break if you want to, but if you ain't finished before 6:37, you're going to have to supplement."

No no no no no! I couldn't drink the supplement. I *had* to finish this food!

"Deep breaths, honey," my mom reminded me as she rubbed my back.

"Mommy, I'm *so* full! I can't do this!" But we both knew she couldn't save me. As the clock on the wall struck 6:30, I became increasingly anxious. I forced down the last piece of chicken and finished my milk, but there was no room for anything more. "I feel like I'm going to throw up," I moaned, collapsing back onto the bed.

I could see the nurse already calculating what percentage of my meal I had eaten. "Well, the good news is that you completed over 50%, so that's just one Ensure."

Just one? Did this lady not know how to do math? All that was left on my plate was a quarter of the potato and half of the green beans. "But I'm practically finished!" I motioned towards the plate. "No way an Ensure is equal to this," I protested.

With no sympathy whatsoever, the nurse responded yet again, "You know the rules." That was true; I *did* know the rules, but it hadn't occurred to me how preposterous they were until now. I still had that slip of paper from the nutritionist somewhere, though I hadn't given it much thought because I'd decided it wouldn't apply to me. Suddenly, the phrase about meal completion came to me as a carbon copy of the paper flashed in my mind.

Patient is to complete 100% of all meals according to selected choices from exchange list. In the case of non-completion, supplementation will be given as follows:

0-49% completion: 2 Ensures

50%-99% completion: 1 Ensure

Given those percentages, I calculated my completion to come up with a compromise. I was willing to drink Ensure but would only drink as much as was equal to what I had left on my plate. After all, supplementation came down to meeting my exchanges, right? When I finally proposed my idea to the nurse, she declined it without a pause.

"So, even if I had just left a *single* green bean, I would still have to drink an *entire* Ensure?" I asked, testing her logic.

"That is correct."

"But that doesn't make any *sense!*" I pleaded, shifting my desperate gaze towards my mom once again.

It was clear my mom felt sorry for me. She said, "Livia's practically finished. Can't she just supplement what's left on the plate?" For a moment, I was hopeful.

"If we have to calculate the exact percentage of completion for every patient that doesn't finish, things would be incredibly complicated around here," the nurse explained. "That's what the rules are for." I wanted to scream. The nurse went on. "You can decline the Ensure, but–" She didn't need to finish. If I didn't finish my food and didn't drink the supplement, I would get a tube down my throat. And I was going to do anything to ensure *that* didn't happen.

Given the choice, I agreed to drink the Ensure. I received an additional twenty minutes to finish it, which helped. Still, I could not believe I was consuming more than my exchanges. I had been on a meal plan for less than a week and had already failed to follow it perfectly.

17

WALDEN

I was finally allowed to shower on the morning I was discharged from the hospital. I had been lying in bed for a week, so my legs felt like Jell-O when I got up for the first time. After breakfast (oatmeal with nuts, raisins, and a glass of milk every single day), there was a meeting with my parents and someone I had never seen before. She introduced herself as Nancy and represented Walden Behavioral Care.

"It is critical that Livia continues receiving support as she transitions home," Nancy said. She explained what the Partial Hospitalization Program (PHP) at Walden entailed. I would be sleeping at home but spending most of each day at a clinic in Waltham. Here, I would learn to make my own meals according to the exchange system and engage in therapy with other individuals who had eating disorders. "It will be great for Livia to talk about her issues in a group setting." My parents nodded hopefully, but I was ambivalent. A part of me wanted to connect with others and express my frustrations with people who understood, while another part couldn't shake my unease at the thought of a "group setting."

Growing up, I always preferred to do everything alone. I hated group projects at school so much that I often announced I'd do the whole project by myself. In exchange for letting me take the lead, I'd give the rest of the group members the gift of taking an equal amount of the credit. Even though I enjoyed playing with Lexi and Mila when we were friends, when we grew apart, I was relieved to no longer bear the responsibility of making sure they liked me. Nowadays, when I talk about hating parties, my mom reminds me that nothing has changed: "As soon as we arrived, the first thing you'd ask is when we could leave!"

After a week of being sedentary in the hospital, I was ready to leave this party as well. I didn't like what Nancy told us about Walden, but I stayed silent. I was not going to screw up my chance to go home.

We drove directly from the hospital to the clinic. Thirty minutes had passed when the GPS announced, "You have arrived." My dad pulled into a large parking complex surrounded by tall brick buildings. It was clearly a medical area, as I noticed words such as pathology, fertility, pharmaceuticals, data, and dermatology all around.

If Adolescent Medicine on the fifth floor across from Children's Hospital Boston had been colorless and depressing, Walden's waiting room was exponentially so. Black chairs lined the windowless space, and the only semi-interesting object in sight was the cabinet on which a water dispenser stood. Just like at my first "specialist" appointment, I was told to pee in a cup and had a nurse take my weight and vitals. Again, I had to step on backward.

When we finally got called into an office (thank goodness this one had windows, albeit with a view just of other buildings), I was asked the same flood of questions as during my first appointment with Dr. Jones. Did I struggle with body image? What was my mood like? Was eating difficult for me? How often did I exercise?

I was tired of hearing the same questions over and over again. Didn't these people have ways of communicating with each other? Not a very efficient system for people who call themselves "specialists," I thought. At this point, I stopped trying to play games or do anything besides nodding my head in agreement.

My parents wanted to save me, and if I had any chance of being a perfect daughter, I had to let them.

The moment we stepped into the group room, all three of us knew Walden was most definitely *not* going to save me. There were girls of all shapes and sizes. Some were lounging around on the couch watching TV, while others sat crouched in the corner, hidden behind a sudoku book. Two girls were playing a game of cards, but judging by the tempo at which one of them shuffled the deck, this was their last resort to kill time. My mom, dad, and I received a tour of the kitchen, where every food-containing jar or container was labeled with exchanges and measurements.

Even though I wasn't going to be sleeping at Walden, the staff member gave us a peek at one of the bedrooms. Apparently, their residential (inpatient), PHP (Partial Hospitalization Program), and IOP (Intensive Outpatient Program) were all mixed together, with certain meal and therapy times overlapping. The only distinguishing factor for each level of care was the daily duration an individual would have to spend in a higher level of living hell. Even though I could tell that my parents' feelings about this place were as distasteful as mine, they mutually agreed to have me start the program. It was the specialist's recommendation, and the specialists knew best, right?

I went to Walden for two days before my parents and I decided I would not continue, against my treatment team's recommendation. My parents wanted to give me a chance to gain weight and become healthy again at home, which I had promised to do if they took me out of this horrible place.

"Being here is just making everything worse!" I exclaimed when my dad picked me up on the first day of PHP. What Nancy had said about getting to make my own meals wasn't true, as the staff prepared everything for the patients. "They're forcing me to eat foods I don't even like, and we don't do anything besides sit around all day." Aware that I had always known *exactly* what I wanted and stubbornly resisted what I didn't, my parents trusted their instinct, which told them to give me a chance.

18

IBS

When I returned to school after the hospital and a mere two days at Walden, I pretended nothing had happened. I told everyone I had the flu, and I was ready to catch up on all the homework and assignments I'd missed. The girls from my soccer team knew that wasn't true, since they had come to visit me in the hospital the week before. I was furious when they showed up. Not with them – I thought it was sweet that they cared about me (or at least pretended to) – but with my mom.

"Why do you always tell everyone *everything*?" I yelled after my teammates had finally left.

"Honey, I want to inform parents of our lives. If my daughter is in the hospital, *of course* I'm going to tell people!"

The *of course* emphasis was completely beyond me, as I was the total opposite when it came to sharing others' private information. I didn't gossip or talk behind people's backs because I didn't want people gossiping or talking about me behind *my* back. Had my mom never learned the Golden Rule? No matter what I said though, my mom stood her ground as stubbornly as I always did. Perhaps I got that trait from her.

"I'm your mom and I can share what I want" – that was how the heated discussion finally ended. After that, I tried even harder to hide, protecting myself from the looks of the parents (who had inevitably told their children), which would never be the same again. The only thing I had control over was schoolwork, food, and exercise. I continued to get straight As and maintained my weight. Not that I had much choice in the weight department, as visits with the doctors at the fifth-floor Adolescent Medicine had become part of my weekly routine. But the fact that I now had a meal plan to follow – along with the terms that I could continue to play sports if I followed it – gave me just enough autonomy to keep my balance.

My stomach didn't seem to agree. About halfway into the stressful year that was seventh grade, I started experiencing horrible digestive issues: bloating, gas, diarrhea, vomiting – you name it. I hadn't changed what I was eating (every day was practically the same), so I didn't understand why I was experiencing so much discomfort. Only during my work as a recovery coach years later did I discover the power of the gut-brain connection and the impact stress can have on our entire body. Embarrassed, I shared my symptoms with Dr. Coleman at Adolescent Medicine (Dr. Jones had moved back to Texas – don't mess with the cowboy boots!), who referred me to a gastroenterologist at the hospital.

Even though my aversion to hospitals had grown since being diagnosed with the "A" word, I was excited for my GI appointment. I wanted to figure out what was wrong so I would know how to fix it. Before meeting the doctor, I was instructed to drink a thick pink liquid. I hesitated. How would this fit into my meal plan?

"Is there something wrong?" the nurse asked as I stared blankly at the cup's contents. I tried to act as normal as possible, not wanting her to think I had lost my way and should have been in the psych ward rather than the gastroenterology department.

"What is this?" I asked in a shy voice.

"It's a barium drink." As soon as she noticed my widened eyes, the nurse laughed and said, "Don't worry. I don't expect you to know what that is! Barium is an element that coats the inside of your upper GI tract. It absorbs X-rays, meaning we can use it to observe what might be going on in your tummy."

I sloshed it around in the cup.

"You like strawberry?" she asked, putting her hands on her hips.

"It's my favorite fruit!"

"Well, it's strawberry-flavored, so I'm sure you might even like it." She winked.

"May I know the ingredients?" I hoped this information could give me a clue as to what this drink's exchanges might be.

The nurse looked slightly puzzled. "Honestly, I'm not sure, but I can definitely go and ask the doctor if you'd like?"

I felt so bad for this poor woman. "It's okay, thank you." I brought the cup to my lips.

"You're so brave!" she exclaimed, putting her hand on my shoulder. "I know hospitals can be scary." *Hell yeah, they can be.* To me, the fact that I didn't know the exchanges of this drink was scarier. The liquid was sweet and tasted a bit like a strawberry milkshake, so I decided to play it safe and label this foreign substance as 1 dairy and 2 fats.

After the procedure (it was fascinating seeing that barium drink travel through my body on the X-ray scans), it was back to the waiting room. I really hoped the doctor would find an explanation for what was wrong.

"Well, I have good news and bad news. Which do you want first?" The doctor was a friendly man in his early thirties with an upbeat voice.

"Good news!" I chirped, attempting to match my tone to his.

He held up some images of the scans. "Alright. The good news is that we didn't find any abnormalities in your scans."

"What's the bad news?" I asked impatiently, wondering what could be worse than no physical explanation for all the digestive issues I was experiencing.

"Well, since you're experiencing these issues: gas, cramping, on-and-off diarrhea, and constipation," he stated, tapping his outstretched fingers as he listed the symptoms, "and there are no physical abnormalities, I'm diagnosing you with irritable bowel syndrome, or IBS." He handed me a paper with the words *Foods suitable on the low-FODMAP diet* at the top. "I recommend you start following a low-FODMAP diet. It should reduce your symptoms."

I quickly scanned the chart, and the foods listed under the heading *Eliminate foods containing FODMAPs* immediately caught my eye: high-fructose corn syrup, cow's milk, ice cream, wheat, and other forms of gluten. There were also specific fruits and vegetables listed, along with certain legumes. I was disappointed to no longer be allowed to eat beans and chickpeas, but I was willing to accept the limitation. A valid excuse to eliminate certain sugars, dairy, and gluten from my diet was well worth the trade-off! I left the appointment with a new sense of purpose. As soon as I got home, I would research and plan all the ways in which I would master my meal plan, low-FODMAP style.

Going on the low-FODMAP diet felt like an adventure to me. I never missed a trip to the grocery store with my parents. Checking the labels of every gluten-free bread or dairy-free yogurt and finding the best-tasting "healthy" ice cream gave me a sense of euphoria. I also decided to become a vegetarian. Ironically, the limitations of the meal plan and this new diet made it monumentally easier for me to eat and maintain my weight. Even though my parents practically had a heart attack every time they saw the price of the specialty products at the checkout counter, I was eating – and that was priceless.

It wasn't until the summer of 2014 – over a year later – that I started running into problems with my perfectly constructed food routine.

19

HOCKEY CAMP

For as long as I can remember, we took a family trip to the Netherlands during summer vacation. It was our home away from home, where we would spend three weeks hanging out with my parents' old friends, watching late sunsets on Scheveningen beach, and eating more Dutch *poffertjes* (mini pancake puffs), *pannenkoeken* (pancakes), and *boterhammen met hagelslag* (sandwiches with butter and sprinkles) than our tummies could handle. The school summer breaks in the USA are long – about three months – so our trip in July was always a great switch-up from the camps that were supposed to keep us occupied.

The trip to our home country in 2014, however, was different. Instead of playing it by ear, my parents had signed up my sisters and me for hockey camp. Field hockey is a massive part of Dutch culture, with the national women's and men's teams winning the world championship more often than not. My parents had both grown up playing field hockey, and they often said "what a shame" it is that field hockey isn't as popular in the US. According to them, putting us in a hockey camp for one week of our annual Dutch trip would be "a great way to immerse us in the culture." Not only would we be playing the sport and engaging with "true Dutch kids," but my parents could get a full week to themselves. Their relationship had been unstable for a few years, and they were hopeful this opportunity would give them space to "find love again."

When my mom and dad announced these vacation plans to us, I was furious. "There's no way I can be away from home for that long!" Besides the fact that I wouldn't know anyone and my field hockey skills would be a joke compared to the Dutch kids who lived and breathed the sport, this camp was a *sleepaway* camp. Having to go there felt like being hit in the head with a field hockey stick. There were too many unknowns; I had no idea how I would survive this.

"It'll be a great way to make new friends," my parents said. But nothing anyone could say or do was going to shift my perspective.

"What am I going to eat?" I asked shakily, worried about how on Earth I would follow my meal plan in this unpredictable place.

"You'll eat your meal plan just like you've been doing," my dad answered, "only among new people and in a different country."

Among new people and in a different country. That was the very problem! I had been doing such a great job following my meal plan *because* everything was predictable. At hockey camp, nothing would be.

"I bet they don't have gluten-free bread! Or soy milk!" I cried. "And oh, how am I going to be able to measure anything?"

My mom reassured me that she'd speak with the camp managers, trying her best to ease my worries as much as possible. But I knew this wasn't going to work.

I was right. My first appointment back at Adolescent Medicine at Children's Hospital Boston revealed that I had lost over five pounds.

"I told you guys. I should have never gone to that hockey camp!" I exclaimed in Dr. Coleman's office. The hockey camp barely had any foods suitable for my low-FODMAP and vegetarian diet, and with all the physical activity I was doing, the whole situation had been the ultimate recipe for weight loss.

"It's not just the hockey camp," my mom announced, evidently struggling to keep her voice stable. Dr. Coleman turned to face her as my dad drew closer. I *hated* when my parents did this: suddenly exposing me during an appointment without any kind of warning. They would join forces with the doctor or therapist and corner me with ultimatums, resulting in a meltdown afterward. My heartbeat quickened.

"She's not gaining weight," my mom said. "We believe she needs more support than we can give her at home."

Before my mom could add anything, I interrupted: "But I've been following my meal plan perfectly! The only reason I couldn't was because *you* decided to put me in hockey camp!"

As soon as Dr. Coleman saw an open spot in the conversation, she leapt in. "That's the very problem, Livia. The fact that such changes *are* so incredibly difficult for you shows us you're not in a good place."

I looked down at the gray tiled floor. A whirlwind of words zoomed through my mind, but I was unable to piece them together to create even a single sentence. No one would ever understand, and I was incapable of making them. The lengthy appointment ended with me in tears as the group of joined forces decided I would return to treatment.

20

CEDC

I started the Partial Hospitalization Program (PHP) at Cambridge Eating Disorder Center (CEDC) a week later. At least it was still the summer, which meant I didn't have to make anything up about why I was missing school. All I had to do was make sure I was out of treatment by September so I could start school without anyone knowing where I had been.

The ambiance of CEDC was a lot better than that of Walden. The downstairs lobby was lined with large and lively plants, and the main group area on the second floor was filled with motivational posters. Unlike Walden, we were allowed to make our own food, with measuring cups and all! The food itself wasn't half bad, either. It was the therapy sessions and groups I dreaded. I was assigned a therapist named Scarlett, a thirty-something-year-old woman with blue eyes, long ginger hair, and a soft smile. Scarlett was kind, but like all my previous therapists, she didn't understand me.

I don't remember much now from the years of therapy I endured as a minor. I was so absent during the sessions, exhausted by the constant searching for a supposed void in my life that I was trying to "fill with an eating disorder," according to the therapists. Group therapy was even worse. People in their fifties who had struggled with alcoholism and drugs after their partners had left them told stories of how their addictions had phased into disordered eating. When it came to people somewhat closer to my age, they often spoke about body image issues or wanting to look a certain way. Even though these people's stories were supposed to resonate with me, my detachment from their experiences couldn't have been greater.

The days passed so slowly that they felt like centuries. I would gaze at the clock, only to be reminded of how many more hours remained until my parents would pick me up. At night I would struggle to fall asleep with the anticipation of needing to do it all over again the following day. I was 100% meal compliant from the start, hoping that would result in an exit ticket a few weeks later.

During our therapy sessions, I gave Scarlett the answers she wanted to hear. When it came to groups, I figured out how to strategically place a captivating novel within a large therapy book, so I could be in my own world without anyone else knowing it. After a few weeks of abiding by the laws of CEDC, I asked Scarlett when I could be discharged.

"I am so proud of you for being so committed to your recovery." That was how she replied to my question. I had learned about Scarlett that she always started off with an encouraging remark when she was going to say something bad. "However, the team and I don't believe you're ready to step down."

"Why not?" I already knew the answer, but I wanted to hear it from her to avoid suggesting something she might not even have considered.

"Sometimes the body can take longer to catch up. Even though you're doing such an excellent job with the meal plan, your weight hasn't been trending in the direction we'd like it to." She spoke in her typical tone, gentle and comforting. But I was not comforted.

"So, when *can* I leave?" I asked.

"I've already spoken with Irene, and she will increase your meal plan at your next nutrition appointment. We really need to start seeing shifts in your weight, and only then can we start looking at the possibility of a step-down."

I was so sick of this. Not only was I putting up with the food and therapy, but I had also stopped exercising, a recommendation that would support a quicker restoration of my pre-hockey-camp weight. Because movement had always been one of my main pastimes, I needed to find a new hobby. That's why I started my own vegetable garden. It was rewarding to tend and care for something that was mine yet had nothing to do with my physical body. The understanding that produce could only grow when given nourishment and love acted as a constant reminder that I needed to treat my body the same way. When I shared my newfound love for gardening with Scarlett, however, it was like I was hit in the head with a hockey stick again.

"I think it's so great you've found a new passion." Scarlett started up in her usual way, foreshadowing my disappointment. *But...* I thought to myself. "But with your weight stagnation, the team and I think it's best you step away from gardening for now." I chuckled at my precise prediction of how she'd end her sentence, but that chuckle quickly turned into a deep sigh.

"But it's gardening! It's barely movement!"

Scarlett explained that it was best to minimize movement as much as possible, even if it was just gardening.

"Gardening is truly the only thing that's keeping me motivated right now." I went on, telling her how it dually acted as a metaphor for my recovery as well as a way to keep my cool without actual exercise. I threw my hands up in the air. "This place has already taken so much away from me. Please don't take this away too."

"Trust me, Livia, I think it's great you're being so flexible. And that's why I have no doubt you can find another hobby that requires less movement!" She smiled, but her words betrayed any possibility of solace. Scarlett had emailed my parents to take over my garden for the time being, so going on with it wasn't even an option.

I was trying my best and they were punishing me for it. I was no longer going to tolerate this. I was done following the rules for nothing. It was time to start doing things my way.

To get out of CEDC as quickly as possible, I concocted a plan to ensure my weight would go up. At least, I was going to make it *seem* like my weight was going up. Now that gardening had been taken away from me, I had no choice but to start exercising in secret. Every chance I got, I would pack in as many reps as possible of high-intensity movement. During group therapy, I would excuse myself to do jumping squats and push-ups in the bathroom. Then I would splash cold water on my face to revert my flushed cheeks to their natural color. Of course, I couldn't allow this increased exercise to reflect itself at my weekly weigh-in. My solution? Water.

I started by drinking one large 16-ounce glass before treatment (16 ounces of water is equal to 1 pound, or 454 grams). Because water is not relatively dense, I quickly realized I would need to expand my resources if my upward trend on the weight chart were to continue. I emptied my piggy bank and weighed the coins on my food scale: 5.3 pounds (2.4 kg). "This should keep me stocked for a while!" I whispered with a grin.

For five weeks, I made my point on the weight chart go up in an almost flawless curve. After eight weeks, I was discharged from CEDC – just in time to start my first year of high school in September! But the upward trend couldn't stop there. The weight I had "gained" at CEDC was merely debt I had paid back after my hockey camp weight loss.

PART 3: MANIPULATION

21

BHS

My first weeks at Brookline High School hit me hard. Not only was BHS exponentially larger than Lawrence – accepting ninth graders from Brookline's total of eight public schools – but it was scholastically demanding in a way I had never experienced before. The stress piled on quickly, but that wasn't even the worst part; the isolation was. I had made the varsity soccer team along with several of my other teammates, an aspect of high school I was beyond excited about. When Dr. Coleman said I was not allowed to play in the fall, however, my heart sank. After being discharged from CEDC, I had to prove that I could continue gaining weight at home. Only then would the possibility of movement come back into the conversation. But as with all the other limitations put on me, this no-exercise protocol had an adverse effect.

Every day after school, I would run up to my room, shut the door, and lay out my red yoga mat. I followed dozens of high-intensity workouts on YouTube and secretly ordered dumbbells off eBay to add an element of challenge. During study halls and in between classes, I would run the four flights of stairs at school until my legs quaked. I often sought out the bathrooms no one else was occupying so I could do jumping squats until I heard the door swing open. A true moment of excitement was when I discovered after-school pickup soccer in BHS's gym. I had always loved indoor soccer more than outdoor, so I was curious how this new dynamic was going to play out. I was equally nervous to be playing with people I'd never met before, but if I had any chance of playing soccer, this was it.

"You can pick me up later today," I told my dad one morning before school. I had stuffed my athletic clothes in the bottom of my bag and couldn't wait to change into an outfit that had been sitting on my shelf for far too long. "I want to stay and study."

"What about your afternoon snack?" he asked. The kitchen was always the first stop before I could retreat to my room for daily exercises.

"I'll bring it with me and eat while studying. Being busy with schoolwork helps distract me anyways," I lied. Because I was committed to following my meal plan, I *was* planning on eating my snack – just not while studying.

Even though my dad thought this was a fair solution, he expressed frustration about the later pickup time. "I must say, Livia, it is quite inconvenient to pick you up later. It means I'll have to get in the car to pick up Mae and Amélie from Lawrence, drop them off at home, then get in the car *again* to pick you up. Can't you just study at home?"

Our move to Chestnut Hill was why my sisters and I relied on being driven everywhere. At our home on Brook Street, everything was within walking distance, meaning my dad "only" had to drive us to sports or other extracurricular activities. But now, living on the outskirts of Brookline, every destination required a driver's license. "I've become a taxi-chauffeur!" my dad often complained when my sisters begged for a playdate.

You chose to be a stay-at-home dad, I thought. *Welcome to parenting!* But he didn't seem to realize that was his choice, the most frequent topic of argument between my parents.

"I'm the only parent around here!" I would hear my dad yell from the kitchen as I scrambled to complete homework past midnight. "You're never home!"

Offended, my mom would rebut, "I'm working full-time! How else are we supposed to pay the bills?"

I tried my best to drown out the conversations, and I knew my sisters did the same – but even someone without a nose could have smelled the tension from miles away. After a while, my sisters stopped asking for playdates. In the rare times they did, Mae and Amélie made sure to arrange the dates so that the other parents would drive. Just as my feelings of responsibility around making the lunchboxes should have never belonged to an eleven-year-old, feelings of guilt around wanting to play with friends should never have existed in the hearts of my two little sisters.

Despite my guilt for lying, I insisted on the later pickup time so I could fulfill my desire to play soccer again. "Please, Dad. I always go straight home and never get a chance to spend time with people from school." We both knew this was true, as my already scarce social life had dialed down to zero since I started my healthy eating regime. My lie felt slightly more excusable considering that playing soccer was an opportunity to spend time with other students, even if I didn't know them yet.

"Fine," he agreed. Before I knew it, I was running, shooting, and scoring in the Brookline High School gym.

"How was studying?" he asked when he picked me up in front of school. The question might as well have been rhetorical. I didn't even need to use words to respond; my tomato-red face spoke for me. "You know, you can tell me if you're playing soccer, Livia," he said. "I totally get it. I would probably do the same." This was one thing I loved about my dad: he understood me in ways no one else could and trusted me in ways no one else would.

It was only years after I chose recovery that my dad explained why he had been so lenient in letting me go against the advice of the professionals. "I know what it's like to not be allowed to do the things you want to do," he said. This wasn't the first time he had told somber stories from his childhood. "I played hockey with two different patched-up hockey shoes," was how he started one of them. "My parents believed it was ridiculous to buy new shoes if you could find used ones, even if they didn't match." He also shared what would happen if he or one of his brothers tried to sneak a potato before dinner had been plated: "If our dad saw our little hands go into the potato pot, he'd take a fork and hit our fingers with it."

I never knew why my grandparents on my dad's side were the way they were. I dreaded visiting them when we traveled to the Netherlands in the summer. Their home in the middle of the woods was gloomy and depressing. My grandpa was always smoking a pipe and sitting in his big leather chair, while my grandma stood in the kitchen and got angry with anyone who wanted to make as much as a cup of tea. *She* was the keeper of the kitchen, and anyone who entered her domain was a possible destructor of her dynamic. Given what I now know about autism, I have no doubt about which side of the family I inherited those genes from.

Being a twin was one of the most challenging aspects of my dad's childhood. He and his brother Geert were inseparable growing up, but my dad often expressed feelings of inadequacy regarding their capabilities. "I was always the second choice." My dad's tone was dismal. "Geert got good grades and praise, while I was artistic and would work *so* hard to barely score a passing grade on my assignments. Even my art skills weren't good enough. If I showed my father one of my creations, he'd tell me he'd 'give it a six.'"

I couldn't help but feel my dad's pain when he shared these things with me. I believe autistic people have a sixth sense for emotions, especially when it comes to the emotions of other autistic people. I never knew what it was, but I can instinctively tell when someone is "just like me." Years later I discovered that being "just like me" meant being autistic. Furthermore, it was only after my own autism discovery that I recognized that my dad is on the spectrum too.

I continued playing indoor soccer after school, and it served me well. I still received straight As in all of my honors classes and was the epitome of a high performer. At least, on the outside. My external achievements were a mask for the loneliness and inadequacy I felt inside, acting as a mechanism for both external and internal validation. Faking my weight at the doctor's served the same purpose.

22

LUCKY PENNIES

Ever since being discharged from CEDC, my point on the weight chart had moved upwards. Just like I had done in treatment, I meticulously calculated every additional ounce of water I would need to drink before my next weigh-in. To prepare myself for what was to come, I used my body as a guinea pig to test its water limit. When dizzy spells came upon me one afternoon, I realized that three 24-ounce bottles was my max. One more sip, and surely I would have fainted. Luckily, I had my coins.

When I first started using coins as my secondary source for weight manipulation, I hadn't used all the contents of my piggy bank. I had only used three of the five pounds, supplementing any additional weight with water. I knew I would have to train my water-drinking capabilities if my plan had any chance of being sustainable, which was why I continuously relied on water to some degree. If I didn't *have* to feel dizzy or nauseated, I wouldn't.

To transform my 5.3-pound pile of coins into a format that would fulfill its new purpose, I distributed the contents evenly over two mini purses, stuffing them to weigh 2.5 pounds each. I saved the remaining 0.3 pounds for later, as I needed to remain perfectly clear on where each ounce was coming from. When the nurse closed the curtain at the doctor's office so I could change into a gown, I quietly removed the purses from my backpack, carefully placed them in my underwear, and yelled, "I'm ready!"

as I had done so many times before. By the start of November, I "weighed" 9.5 pounds more than I truly did.

On November 17, however, those 9.5 pounds would no longer be enough. I began dreading the appointment the moment it had been made two weeks before, knowing that I was going to have to do something I really didn't want to. For the scale to reflect an increase in weight, three bottles of water and two purses of coins wouldn't cut it. I needed to attach another two pounds to my body, which meant I needed to possess more coins. I scoured the house for whatever I could find, opening drawers and looking under couches. I found a few lucky pennies, but they were far from enough to achieve my current mission. That's when I stole from my sister's piggy bank.

As I sat on Mae's shaggy green bedroom rug, my fingers gently smoothing over the silver and copper discs, I gloried in the relief that I would have enough coins for my weigh-in. Nevertheless, I could not shake a deep sense of guilt. What I was doing was wrong, and I knew it. Hell, what I had been doing for the past several months was wrong, and I knew it! But I also knew that I wasn't going to let anyone tell me what to do. If my parents and everyone else in their coalition were going to steal my life, stealing some coins from my sister's piggy bank wasn't even worth batting an eye over.

23

WISH NOT GRANTED

On the day of the appointment, I couldn't stop thinking about the upcoming weigh-in. As I headed to last period, I stopped by the water fountain and filled my blue water bottle to the 24-ounce mark. During the last fifteen minutes of math class, I sipped my water while I attempted to solve for x and y – but an attempt was about as far as I was going to get to nearing a solution. By the end of class, I already needed to pee. *Just for today*, I thought.

When the clock struck 3:00 p.m., I rushed back to the water fountain with my empty water bottle, filling it to the 24-ounce mark one last time. I briskly walked towards my locker and sipped until the bottle was empty. Three two-pound purses of coins, a history textbook, a physics textbook, *The Odyssey* by Homer, and five half-inch binders weighed down my backpack. After gathering my things, I walked to the bathroom and took the big stall. Having the toilet right there was tempting, but I had to hold it in. *Just for today.* I dug the coins from the depths of my backpack and traded their place with my lunchbox. I would need quick and easy access when I was at Adolescent Medicine.

When my phone vibrated, I didn't even have to check to know who it was. "Where are you?" my dad's message read. Not wanting to seem suspicious, I quickly typed, "I'll be right there." I ran through the halls and out of the school as fast as my little legs could carry me. My back hurt. My legs hurt. My whole body hurt. I could hear the water sloshing around in my stomach and the coins jingling in my backpack. The weight was unbearable, but I reminded myself, *Just for today*. I had to keep going, just a little further, just a little faster.

Before I finally exited through the back of the school – a detour to the car – I skidded to a stop. I walked off Welland Road, took a left on Tappan, then another left on Greenough. I spotted our silver Subaru in the distance. I walked briskly towards the car, indicating my hassle to be on time, even though I knew I was ten minutes late. My dad's face expressed his rage, and my sisters gazed out the window impatiently.

When I got in the car, no one said a word. My dad cruised through the crowds of teenagers, then slammed on the gas pedal as soon as a clear street appeared. Mae and Amélie darted inside the house as soon as we pulled into the driveway on Meadowbrook Road. I wanted to follow them, to use the bathroom, to lay on my bed – but the imaginary thoughts of relief disappeared in a flash. I had to conquer this doctor's appointment. Wiggling in my seat, I reminded myself to hold it in just a little longer.

Neither my dad nor I said a word during the fifteen-minute drive to Adolescent Medicine. After checking in, I was again asked to pee in a cup. I rushed to the bathroom, the temptation to let it all go at an all-time high. But I didn't come this far to only go this far. I filled the cup halfway, using every last bit of my physical strength to hold in the rest. I flushed the toilet, screwed the white cap on the cup, and placed it in the little metal door in the wall before exiting the bathroom as quickly as possible.

As I waited for the nurse to call me in, I dreamt about peeing. It resembled a frequent type of dream I used to have as a kid, in which I would dream I was using the toilet only to wake up to wet sheets the following day. When I snapped out of my short daze, I checked my seat's cushion to ensure it was still dry. Thank goodness! *That* would have been embarrassing.

After ten minutes, a nurse finally called my name. I jumped up, a bit lightheaded as a result. I walked into the room, trying my best to avoid conversation. Not only would silence spare me the misery of small talk, but it would hasten my ability to use the bathroom.

"Just let me know when you're ready." The nurse closed the curtain and exited the room. I stripped off all my clothes except for my underwear and bra. I quietly unzipped my backpack and slipped one of the purses into my underwear. I divided the remaining two among the cups of my bra and covered it all up with a hospital gown.

"I'm ready!" I pulled aside the curtain and turned my back to the scale before she even entered the room. I was doing everything I could to speed up this process. Every second mattered.

"Step on," she said. As soon as I lifted my foot, I felt a warm trickle run down my leg. In a matter of seconds, I had peed all over the floor. The nurse must have paged Dr. Coleman immediately; suddenly, Dr. Coleman stood in the doorway with her hands on her hips.

"Go use the bathroom again, Livia," she demanded. "Get changed, and leave your backpack in my office." I lugged myself towards the bathroom and emptied myself of it all – the water, the coins, and any hope of relief. I repeated the same process I had failed to do correctly five minutes prior and stepped back onto the large metal platform. I knew what it read but had no idea what was about to come.

"We are deeply concerned about you, Livia," Dr. Coleman said as soon as I entered her office. Instead of waiting to call my dad in, she already had him seated beside her. "In all my years as a doctor, I have never seen anyone manipulate their weight to such extremes."

I reverted my gaze to where it always went when I couldn't find the words, hoping the gray tiles would somehow turn into a wishing well. Instead, they reflected the dullness I felt. Dr. Coleman called my mom and put her on speakerphone, and the coalition took the reins again. I had lost this battle and I was going to pay for it – a payment that came in the form of Walden Residential.

24

ROUND TWO

Returning to Walden after all these years felt like I had climbed a mountain only to have slipped and slid all the way back down to the bottom. To make matters worse, the intake took place on my sixteenth birthday. It was the most not-so-sweet sixteen I could have ever imagined. When my mom broke the news the day before, my lack of fury surprised her. Whether the intake was on my birthday or any other day, I didn't care. What was the point in celebrating if I couldn't enjoy it? What was the point in challenging myself to eat cake if it was just a matter of days before I would be surrounded again by sugary and fatty foods?

The most celebratory part of my birthday was the fact that the water dispenser in the windowless waiting room had moved to a new spot. Even though I knew the staff – not to mention my parents – were now hyper-aware of my water consumption, I was tempted to get up and grab a cup. Water loading before weigh-ins had become such a habit – a feeling so natural – that it drew me in like a magnet. I got up and walked towards the water dispenser.

"Now, don't go drinking water, Livia," my mom said.

"Oh, it's just one cup," I replied, aiming to piss off my parents for bringing me back to this horrible place.

"Fine, but no more after this," my dad said. I guess I wasn't the only nervous one.

"Livia?" a lady called out as she emerged from an office. I quickly gulped down the last of my water and stood up. "Come with me, please."

The routine was the same in every medically related place: pee in a cup, vitals, weight, talk with me, ask my parents into the room, talk with everyone.

"So, tell me why you're here today." The woman attempted to look into my eyes.

I averted my gaze to the ground. "My parents forced me here."

"And why do you think that is?"

I revealed what had gone down in the past several months, sharing the most condensed version of the story I could come up with. She already knew why I was here. Why else would she be tilting her clipboard to hide a stack of email printouts? When my parents were away from the computer, I often tried to log into their email to read the messages between the joined forces. I was successful a few times, finding emails from my nutritionist, Dr. Coleman, and anyone else who claimed to "want the best for me." But how on Earth could they even know what was best? The fact that I was back at Walden proved quite the contrary!

Despite my efforts to explain why residential was not going to help me, my parents sided with the "professionals," resulting in my losing another case of *Coalition v. Livia*. I would be given the evening to pack my things and was to return to Walden the following morning.

25

MISUNDERSTOOD

I barely slept that night and decided to skip breakfast altogether. I felt incapable of following my meal plan, knowing that my routine would be disrupted in a matter of hours anyway. To my surprise, my parents didn't say anything. They didn't need to; I could practically see the future them, sighing with relief the moment I was taken off their hands. Before I knew it, I was sitting across from my new nutritionist.

"Are you familiar with exchanges?" Diana asked in a cheery voice. *HA!* I wanted to exclaim. Am *I* familiar with exchanges? In an effort to come across as polite, I pretended this was not the most ridiculous question I had ever heard.

"Yes, I have been following a meal plan for the past couple of years."

"Wonderful, so you already know how all this works!"

Apparently, I didn't know how *all* of it worked, because she went on to explain that the staff prepared all of the patients' meals and snacks.

I nodded, but my hands began to tremble. "What if I don't like what they give me?" I asked.

"That's a great question! We're going to come up with a couple of lists that the staff will use for reference. Let's start with foods you really like."

All of my favorite foods flooded my mind, and I said the first things I could think of. "Oatmeal, yogurt, strawberries, and peanut butter."

She scribbled on her clipboard. "And what are some foods you dislike?"

"Blue cheese, seafood, candy bars, chips" – I started to list, immediately fearful that I would be served something I had forgotten to put on my dislikes list.

Diana frowned. "Hmm, are candy bars and chips *really* dislikes? They sound like fear foods."

"I really don't like them. Candy bars get stuck in my teeth, and chips always cut the top of my mouth," I replied. When she continued looking at me in disbelief, I told her about trick-or-treating when I was younger. "Ever since my first Halloween, I never ate the candy. I'd walk past the houses, put candy in my bag, then dump it all into the candy bin in front of our house. I figured, if I'm going to spend all that time collecting candy, I might as well make other kids happy with it."

She seemed more convinced after I told this little backstory, but I could still sense her wariness. "Alright. We can write those foods down for now, but the more honest you are in treatment, the better we can help you."

My trembling hands clenched into fists. I *was* being honest! Why did disliking an unhealthy food automatically make it a fear food? Besides, she couldn't look into my brain, so she had no right to accuse me. Obviously, I didn't say any of that out loud.

After meeting with the nutritionist, it was time for group therapy. Just like in CEDC, I mastered the art of hiding novels or puzzles behind clipboards or therapy books. My favorite time of day was the two hours of "school time." Daphne, the "teacher," was responsible for communicating with Brookline High School and ensuring I received the work I was missing. During free time at Walden, I was the only one who sat behind the computer to study. I had always loved learning, and it seemed a much better use of my time than lounging around on the couch or playing cards with girls I didn't connect with.

Another activity I became particularly skillful at during this time was secret exercise. Unlike CEDC's partial program, Walden's staff monitoring protocols were similar to that of a totalitarian government. If I needed to use the bathroom, I wasn't allowed to flush the toilet until a staff member had checked the contents. When I was informed about this rule, my face reddened. *But what about when I poop?* I was too embarrassed to vocalize my thoughts.

"Don't worry, the staff is used to it," one of the staff members reassured me.

"I've never thrown up though!" I protested, knowing this was the reason for the rule. "Besides, I would never do that!"

"I hear you," the staff member replied, "but sometimes patients develop new behaviors when other behaviors such as restriction and exercise are reduced."

They didn't trust me. And for precisely that reason, I did whatever I could to continue exercising. While showering in the morning, I would balance my body across the bathtub, placing each of my hands and feet in a corner. I did push-ups until failure, the shower stream masking the noise of my breathing. When I emerged with my typical post-exercise reddened face, I said, "I take really hot showers!" Every day, I looked for new ways to incorporate secret exercise. One of my favorites was doing planks while "resting" on my bed.

In mid-December, insurance cut my stay at residential. Whether I liked it or not, I had steadily been gaining weight, given my 100% meal plan compliance since day one. My BMI was now "within normal range," which, according to the insurance, meant I could step down to Walden's partial program. Luckily, I was never offered one of my dislikes-that-I-feared-I-would-forget while in residential. I was, however, often frustrated with the food combinations the staff members came up with. To eat without anxiety, I needed certain textures and flavors to complement each other, and the items needed to be arranged in a certain way on my plate. Out of fear they would say these preferences were "my eating disorder talking," I never said a word. I needed to be the perfect patient – or at least, to appear like it.

When I heard that I was stepping down to PHP, I was excited to finally make my own food again. I missed eating the same things every day, as that was another aspect of residential that kept my skin crawling from nerves: the constant change. One day, the staff would give me a bagel with cream cheese as my starches and fats, and the next it would be cereal and peanut butter. None of the patients knew what they would be served until the moment we were sitting at the table, an unpredictability that left me with perpetual anxiety.

While we were waiting for lunch one afternoon, I tapped a fellow patient's shoulder. "How does it make you feel that we can't know what we're having in advance?"

She turned to me with a big smile on her face. Helen was one of those girls who always followed the rules, even those that were stupid and made no sense. "Honestly, I love it! I don't have to worry about the meal beforehand, which allows me to be more present during groups and therapy."

I looked at her, dazed. "Hmm" was all I could muster. Helen's reasoning couldn't have been more perpendicular to mine, as it was precisely the not knowing that *did* make me worry and *didn't* allow me to be present during groups and therapy. With yet another piece of evidence that I wasn't like anyone else here, I requested to speak to my nutritionist.

"I want to be honest with you," I said, knowing Diana would appreciate my implementation of her initial request. "I find it very difficult that I don't know what food will be served at my next meal or snack. Can I please know in advance?"

"I appreciate your honesty, Livia." She clasped her hands and rested them gently on the table. "But we can't do that. These rules are in place to help you recover."

I was utterly confused. "How will not knowing what I'm going to eat help me recover? It makes it so much harder to eat!"

"It sounds like I'm talking to the eating disorder right now," Diana replied. "What would the healthy Livia say in this situation?"

"She would say the same thing, I promise," I mumbled, afraid that Diana would accuse me of being dishonest again.

"Well, that's hard to believe, seeing as the real Livia isn't here right now, hmm?"

"I swear, I'm this way with everything! I've always been this way, always wanted to know things in advance!"

"In recovery, you're going to have to do things that make you uncomfortable, Livia. Accepting unpredictability around meal-times is a key part of that."

Whatever "key" Diana was referring to didn't fit into my lock. I needed to know things ahead of time – whether it was an appointment, a school project, or anything that had to do with food. But my wish, yet again, was not granted.

26

MAUDSLEY METHOD

On the day of my step-down to PHP, my nutritionist, my parents, and I joined my therapist, Noreen, in her office.

"To make your transition home as smooth as possible, your parents and the Walden staff will continue to prepare all your meals and snacks," Diana said, shifting her gaze from my parents to me, then back to my parents.

"WHAT?" I shrieked. "But I'm going home! I've been making my own food for years. I'm not some baby that needs to be spoon-fed."

"Livia and I have discussed the importance of getting uncomfortable in recovery," Diana explained to my parents. "Letting go of control is a big part of that."

I shifted in my seat as Noreen took over the conversation. "Here at Walden, we believe involving the entire family is crucial to an individual's recovery. That's why we use the Maudsley Method." My parents looked as if Noreen were speaking in a foreign language. "The Maudsley Method is an evidence-based therapy practice that is used to treat a wide range of eating disorders. It will involve having you take over the preparation of Livia's meals at home." She gestured towards my parents, cupping her hands out to them as if handing them control over my food. "And of course, the staff will continue preparing her meals and snacks when she's here. As Livia progresses in her recovery, she will slowly be handed back control over her food choices."

"We just want to make sure it's Livia making those choices, and not the eating disorder," Diana chimed in.

I seethed. "I am fully capable of making my own food choices! I've been eating everything the staff gives me, and still, you guys don't trust me!"

My mom rested her hand on my knee. "It's not that we don't trust *you*. It's that we don't trust the *eating disorder*," she said. Apparently, my therapist's office had magically turned my mom into a chameleon.

My dad's shoulders were hunched. "So, how exactly is this going to work?" Considering his preexisting feelings of parental over-whelm, I figured making and monitoring my every bite was the last thing he needed on his plate.

Noreen and Diana went back and forth explaining the ins and outs of the Maudsley Method, a therapy originally formulated by Christopher Dare and his colleagues at the Maudsley Hospital in London in 1985. Also known as family-based treatment (FBT), this approach directs parents to take an active and positive role in an effort to help restore their child's weight, then slowly phase into handing the control back to the child to encourage normal adolescent development.[1]

Every word they said about this approach made me want to cringe. I would have no say when it came to decisions about food. I was no longer allowed to come to the grocery store. I wasn't even allowed to be in the kitchen when my food was being prepared. Judging by the look on my parents' faces, they weren't enthusiastic about this either. Our family had never been the hierarchical type. We never had rules around food or eating,

---

1. LE GRANGE, D. (2005). The Maudsley family-based treatment for adolescent anorexia nervosa. World Psychiatry, 4(3), 142–146.

and I was always free to grab whatever I wanted whenever I pleased. Sure, I was encouraged to eat my vegetables and finish my plate, but it was never an ultimatum for my daily dessert. To my parents and me, the Maudsley Method sounded like a regression to the Middle Ages in which the King and Queen were superior to anyone below them. It didn't match our family dynamics. More importantly, it didn't match *me*.

But what did? My parents were at a complete loss. They were willing to try anything that could save me, especially if it was "evidence-based." According to a clinical trial conducted at Stanford University and the University of Chicago, 75 to 90% of adolescents treated with FBT were still doing well five years later, compared to 36% of the teens who received individual therapy.[2] Of course, statistics based on a study with a mere 121 participants begs the question of what dynamics were present in the participants' families. Not to mention, one of the criteria for participation was an absence of diagnosed comorbid mental health issues. Would autism, obsessive-compulsive disorder (OCD), anxiety, depression, and the several other underlying aspects of my eating disorder that would only come to the surface years later make me part of that 75 to 90%? Back then, we didn't know. So why *wouldn't* my parents agree to an approach that promised such a high success rate?

---

2. Lock, J., Le Grange, D., Agras, W. S., Moye, A., Bryson, S. W., & Jo, B. (2010). Randomized Clinical Trial Comparing Family-Based Treatment With Adolescent-Focused Individual Therapy for Adolescents With Anorexia Nervosa. Archives of General Psychiatry, 67(10), 1025.

27

INCONSISTENCIES

My first dinner back home was rice, a veggie burger, and broccoli. Beside it stood a glass of whole milk filled to the tippy top. As soon as the plate entered my field of vision, I started clenching and unclenching my sweaty fists.

"Come and sit. It's time for dinner," my dad said. While the rest of my family sat at the table, I stood behind my seat. I was numb and shaky, wanting to say *the words* but fearing what they would lead to.

"Livia, what's going on?" my mom asked.

Silence. She repeated herself.

"I can't eat," I mumbled.

"Why not?"

I was caught in a déjà vu of the night I was first faced with a bottle of Ensure. "That's too much rice."

I had finally said it. I closed my eyes tight, hoping it would somehow protect me from the situation that would follow.

"It's one cup," my dad replied. "I measured it." At his words, I felt even more pressure to comply, fully aware of how greatly he despised exchanges and measuring cups.

"That's definitely more than one cup," I mumbled. "I only need two starches at dinner."

"Like I said, Livia, I *measured* it." The impatience in his voice started to grow.

"But I can see it's more." I half hoped my words would remain unheard.

I almost lost my balance as my dad stood up, stomping towards the sink filled with dirty pots and pans. He loudly rinsed the white one-cup measuring cup, patted it dry with a paper towel, then proceeded to stuff the white basmati rice into it.

"I knew it was more!" I shrieked, pointing at the heaping cupful of rice.

"Are you blind?" my dad asked in astonishment. "It's exactly one cup!"

I backed away as he brought the measuring cup close to my face.

"It's one *heaping* cup," I said. "I only need one cup!" I was furious that my parents were already trying to sneak me more food. They didn't trust *me*, but it was also clear I couldn't trust *them*!

"Jesus, Livia," my dad said. "What difference are we talking about?" He used my fork to toss off the additional rice and finished by patting the fork firmly onto what remained in the cup.

"Now you're even pressing it down to make it seem like less!"

My parents looked at each other and rolled their eyes. Mae and Amélie avoided my gaze.

My dad flipped the measuring cup onto the plate, revealing a perfect dome of rice when he lifted it. "There," he said, "does this match your exchanges now?" By the way his voice softened, I could tell he really was trying. I knew he didn't want this responsibility either, but he took it because of what had gone down in my therapist's office several hours earlier.

I felt so bad for what I was about to say, but I said it anyway, quietly: "Can you please re-measure the milk too?" At Walden, all the plates, bowls, and cups were the same. I always knew that the contents matched my exchanges because a glass only held so many ounces.

At home, everything was different. We had porcelain, pottery, and plastic bowls in every size and color. We had big plates, kid plates, breakfast plates, and dessert plates. We had glasses and mugs of every size imaginable, with a few mugs belonging to my dad (he only drank his coffee out of mugs with thin rims). When I made my food, I always used the same crockery. When I weighed food on the kitchen scale, I used one specific bowl. I knew my red plastic bowl weighed exactly 76 grams, so as long as my scale read 76 grams upon initial use, I could trust that it was working properly.

But right now, with the milk filled to the very top of a glass I had never drunk from before, there was no way of knowing. If I was going to sit down and complete my dinner, I had to see it to believe it.

Probably using his last bit of patience to ease my worries, my dad fetched the liquid measuring cup from the drying rack. He transferred the milk into the measuring cup, pouring quickly to avoid spilling.

"Have a look." He waved towards the measuring cup on the kitchen table. I bent down to align my eyes with the sides of the measuring cup. The top line of the milk was, indeed, perfectly aligned with the red dash that marked one cup – 8 ounces. I guess my parents weren't *that* deceptive. Still, I was glad I checked.

28

IOP

I was in Walden's PHP for only two weeks before insurance cut benefits again, resulting in a step-down to their IOP. Walden's Intensive Outpatient Program was three evenings a week, meaning I would finally return to school in January 2015. Considering I had missed almost two months, I was worried about how behind I would be in all my classes. Also, how was I going to explain my extended absence?

Brookline High School was incredibly supportive of my transition. "Your health is the most important," the dean said on my first day back. Apparently, I wasn't the only one at BHS who had missed school for an extended period due to health issues. Upon my return, I was warmly welcomed into Bridge for Resilient Youth in Transition (BRYT), a program of the Brookline Center for Mental Health.

The BRYT room was on the school's third floor, just around the corner from my English class. As I eased back into a full-time school routine, I spent most of my days studying in the peace and quiet of that room. When the period bell would trill, I gladly didn't have to risk getting run over by the mobs of students who swarmed the halls in a hurry. BRYT gave me space to attend school on my own terms.

During my transition, however, food and exercise were not (yet) on my own terms. To abide by the Maudsley protocol Walden had prescribed, every meal and snack needed a chaperone. I was too uncomfortable eating in front of a BRYT staff member (eating in front of others has always been difficult for me), especially if I knew I was being watched. Walden's solution for this? To have my dad drive to school and watch me while I ate lunch in the car. My dad was as much against the idea as I was, but what could either of us do about it? He wanted to maximize my chances of recovery, and I didn't want to sit across from a BRYT staff member. Having him chaperone seemed to be the best solution.

Three days a week, I spent three hours at Walden's IOP. While parents received guidance in a separate room on how to best support their child, patients were required to engage in group therapy such as dialectical behavioral therapy (DBT) and cognitive behavioral therapy (CBT) as we sat around a large table eating our afternoon snacks. Occasionally, a fellow patient would be called out of group to attend a private family therapy session. Each day's program ended with the families gathering in the dining room to eat dinner in a "therapeutic setting." After we arrived home, it wasn't long before I needed to eat my evening snack. Because it seemed like I was constantly eating and wasn't allowed to exercise, I adopted a new habit: hiding food.

29

UNDERWEAR

The first time I hid food was in my dad's office. On the two days a week I didn't have IOP, I had to sit on the couch as he sat behind the large family iMac. My afternoon snack consisted of two Pop-Tarts, two cheese sticks, almonds, and a large glass of orange juice. My naturally fast metabolism and the amount of weight I was expected to gain led to an insanely high meal plan, so most of my snacks had similar exchanges to my meals. Dense foods were a win in my parents' book and, as I quickly learned, also in mine.

One afternoon, I pondered my new idea as the "snack" plate stared back at me. My dad was so absorbed in checking his emails that I wondered whether he was even paying attention to me. Almost certain that he wasn't, I decided to test the boundaries. First, I wondered how long it would take him to say something if I just sat there and didn't eat.

After about three minutes, he turned his head. "Are you going to eat your snack?"

"Yep! Just finishing this chapter!" I chirped. I pretended to immerse myself in a novel I had to read for English class.

So he *was* paying attention...but *how much*? I broke a Pop-Tart in half, took a bite of the slightly smaller half, and slid the other half into my underwear. I quickly started pulling apart one of my cheese sticks, trying to act as nonchalant as possible. This time, he didn't turn his head. So I took the second cheese stick, slid it into my underwear, then divided the original one into as many strings as possible. This setup would make it seem like I was eating both simultaneously. I took a small sip of my orange juice. He still hadn't turned to look at me. Full of adrenaline, I popped one almond into my mouth, crunching loudly to amplify the sounds of its consumption. While he opened and closed emails, I slid the almonds to land alongside the hidden Pop-Tart and cheese stick. I took another sip of orange juice – that would be harder to hide.

"May I go to the bathroom?" I asked.

My dad looked at my plate. "Sure," he said, "but don't be long. You need to finish your snack."

My parents had picked up on several of the ways in which I tested their patience, slow eating being one of them. As soon as my dad's eyes darted back to the iMac, I took a huge sip of orange juice and hurried into the bathroom.

There, I spit the juice into the toilet, then grabbed the chunks of smushed Pop-Tart from my underwear and tossed them into the orange water. I tore the cheese stick into more pieces before adding it to the bowl of mush, followed by the almonds. I couldn't wait to change into new underwear, as the greasy, sticky concoction of snacks had caused my skin to itch. I hung over the toilet, trying to shake off any excess Pop-Tart crumbs. I flushed, guilty as I saw the uneaten food circulate down into God-knows-where, thinking about some starving child that would have beamed at the thought of eating a strawberry Pop-Tart and real cheese. I wished I could flush those feelings away, too.

When I returned to my spot on the couch, I finished what remained of my snack with a sense of euphoria. "I finished! Are you proud of me?"

"Good job, Livia." My dad glanced away from his computer for only a moment.

I was certainly proud of me. My meal plan had increased so much since I had stepped down from residential, which my nutritionist attributed to "a natural increase in movement as you participate in the activities that come with daily life." It wasn't that I didn't *want* to follow my meal plan; I just didn't *trust* the nutritionist. She was the same person who stood behind this whole Maudsley Method, which clearly wasn't working. Not only that, but hiding my food was yet another way I could defy anyone who tried to control me.

After my initial victory in the family office, I hid increasingly more food. I stuffed muffins and granola bars in my underwear and wore baggy sweatshirts with pockets to hide additional items. I discovered that I could even hide cooked oatmeal if I wrapped it in a paper towel enough times, so I ensured my backpack always contained a spare roll.

Physically, my relief increased as a result of my decreased food intake. I no longer felt full the whole day, which allowed me to concentrate on my schoolwork better. Mentally, however, mealtimes became increasingly more challenging. If I hid a certain amount of food one day, I had to hide at least the same amount the next. I started to worry more and more about what would happen if I got caught, traumatized by the very event that had landed me in Walden – and family-based treatment – in the first place. Meanwhile, my treatment team was worried about something completely different: why wasn't my weight going up?

30

PUNISHMENT

"**A**re you participating in secret exercise?" asked Richard, our family therapist, during one of our sessions. I was doing push-ups, sit-ups, and jump squats in my room every morning, but it was nothing more than I had already been doing in residential.

"No," I lied, justifying myself with the words of my nutritionist. "I'm just naturally moving more now that I'm going to school and everything."

Richard let out a sigh. "Your weight isn't going up. Why do you think that is?"

I shrugged, but I immediately knew what I had to do. "I don't know. Can we please just give it some more time?" I would start water loading again.

"More time?" my mom cried. "Livia, we've been at this for seven weeks, and you've barely gained weight since starting IOP!"

"Well, maybe this whole Maudsley Method doesn't work!" I practically yelled, emphasizing "Maudsley Method" with air quotes.

"Your weight has nothing to do with the Maudsley Method, Livia," Richard said defensively. "You're simply not consuming enough calories to compensate for whatever activities you're engaging in." He lifted his hands to imitate my use of air quotes: "Even if you're just naturally moving more, now that you're going to school and everything."

How dare he mock me? I looked down at the dark gray carpet to hide my anger.

"What are the next steps?" my dad asked, wanting to get to the point of the conversation, like I often did.

As if Richard had not inflicted enough pain already, he started talking about a higher level of care. "Since she's not gaining weight, not to mention her resistance to the treatment, I am recommending she be admitted to Alcott."

I shuddered, disbelieving. Although my parents looked puzzled, all the patients knew about Alcott. It was Walden's hospital unit, a locked ward for the sickest of the sick. One of my fellow patients in residential – Bella – had gone to Alcott, only to return two weeks later with horror stories.

"While you're sleeping, they come to check on you every thirty minutes," Bella told the group, in the same way kids tell scary stories at summer camp. "You have to get blood drawn twice a week. And the worst part is, all the food is delivered in packages like the frozen meals at the supermarket!"

Richard's mere mention of Alcott practically transported me into Bella's horror story. I had promised myself never to allow things to get *so* bad that I'd have to go to the hospital again. Yet here I was, on the edge of admission.

"I don't understand! Why don't I just go back to PHP? My weight is higher than it was in residential!"

My parents turned their heads in unison, from me to Richard, equally curious about his answer.

"Like I said, Livia isn't making any progress here in IOP. She is not following the recommendations of the Walden staff, so we need a more rigorous approach. Much more rigorous than PHP or residential can offer," Richard said slyly.

"You just want to punish me!" I shrieked. "Is this your version of revenge?" It was a rhetorical question. I knew Richard was trying to teach me a lesson.

I looked over at my mom, whose face filled with compassion.

"Isn't it a bit extreme?" she asked. "I know Livia's struggling, but isn't that to be expected with this illness?"

I was grateful for my mom's words, although I still denied calling whatever this was an "illness."

"We need to be extreme," Richard said. "Family-based therapy only works when it's all hands on deck. Livia may not agree to these decisions, but remember, you, as parents, have the final say in Livia's treatment. To maximize her chances of recovery from this illness, I strongly urge you to follow through with my recommendation."

Suddenly, I wasn't the only one who felt cornered. My parents quickly exchanged glances, then nodded at Richard. Their unease radiated like soundwaves, but no amount of doubt could trump their feelings of responsibility as my parents. If I didn't recover, they would blame themselves for not following through. So follow through they did.

31

ALCOTT

The admission routine I had become so accustomed to – pee in a cup, weigh-in, take vitals, and hours of questioning – was different at Alcott. Instead of me changing into a gown only to change back into my clothes the moment I stepped off the scale, my clothes were searched. Not only that, but *I* was also searched. An Alcott staff member swiftly brushed their arms along every crease of my gowned body like a security officer at the airport. Careful not to uncover my private parts, she inspected every inch of my skin. Although I had never self-harmed, her meticulous inspection almost made me suspect she *would* find something – just like a movie in which the innocent victim pleads guilty after being brainwashed into thinking they committed the crime.

"You're all good," she said, picking up the belt from my jeans, "but you can't keep this."

"Why not?" I reckoned all the possible ways a belt could be used beyond keeping your pants up.

"Policy" was the only word that came out of her mouth.

She moved on to the suitcase I had packed the night before, splitting its contents over two heaps. On the right, she placed T-shirts, pajama pants, underwear, socks, and, after flipping through the pages, my books. She unzipped my bag of toiletries, carelessly dumping all of the items into a white bin. "You can ask for your bin during hygiene hours," she said without looking up.

On the left, she placed my belts, necklaces, and sweaters with drawstrings. If it weren't for this investigation, I would have never considered a sweatshirt a potential murder weapon.

When the inspection was over, I was led to a large room with two single beds. The staff member, who I came to know as Ruth, placed my suitcase on one of the beds.

"May I please use the bathroom?" I asked shyly, intimidated by the strict policies, which would only get stricter.

"Sure." Ruth grabbed a bundle of keys out of her baggy jeans and unlocked the bathroom door. "Remember not to flush." *Here we go again*, I thought.

Bella's stories were not far from the reality of Alcott. I was constantly watched like a hawk, I had to endure my fear of needles twice a week, and the food was, indeed, similar to the frozen meals from the supermarket. But Alcott wasn't all that bad. The same sense of relief I had at Boston Children's Hospital washed over me, as if I were being comforted by a weighted blanket. It was impossible to hide my food. It was impossible to exercise secretly. All the manipulation, lying, deceit – they were impossible. I was finally allowed to be real.

When I was discharged from Alcott ten days later, I went straight back to IOP at Walden. Although it had given me room to finally breathe again, my time in Alcott was far from the spiritual awakening Richard had hoped for. If anything, I now felt extra pressure to swindle the system. He thought he could teach me a lesson by sending me away? Clearly, he didn't know what I was capable of! I resumed every manipulative behavior I had engaged in before, from hiding food to secretly playing soccer. After the humiliating accident that had prompted my admission to Walden in the first place, I never wanted to put myself through the misery of water loading again. But if this whole Maudsley thing was ever going to end, I had no choice.

Up until my IOP discharge in late March, I ensured that my weight continued its artificial upward curve. I did my best to give Richard the answers he wanted to hear and focused on excelling in my honors classes at BHS. Unfortunately, I had to miss yet another opportunity to play varsity soccer in the spring, but this disappointment was far greater than I had previously felt. I wouldn't only be missing one more chance to play soccer; I'd be missing my *last chance to play soccer in the United States.*

PART 4: THE NETHERLANDS

32

ROCKING THE BOAT

M oving to the Netherlands had been only an idea at the start of 2015. My mom had been looking for job opportunities here and there, similar to how one might browse Zillow for dream houses they'd never buy. We loved Brookline and the wonderful community it offered, but the dynamics in our family were teetering. My dad consistently expressed feelings of overwhelm in his paternal role, accusing my mom of being an absent parent – all while she worked full-time.

On the nights she engaged in her hobby as a jazz singer, my dad uttered phrases at the dinner table such as "Your mom chooses her hobby over her family." I felt guilty for having him act as my chaperone per Maudsley Method policy and responsible for making him feel better. That's when my mom and I first talked about moving back to our home country.

"What do you think?" she asked me one night as she scrambled to finish a work deadline around 2:00 a.m. I had gone downstairs because I couldn't sleep, anxious about one of my own deadlines for school.

"Of moving?" I always knew what topic my mom was referring to before she even had the chance to mention it, a sense of mine that astounds her to this day. "I think it's an excellent idea!" In truth, it wasn't the act of moving across the ocean that I deemed a good idea but rather the chance to escape the life that trapped me.

"Do you really?" My mom sought confirmation for an answer she already felt in her gut. "Because there's this job—"

"Yes, mom," I interrupted. "I want a fresh start. I'm so sick of the doctors and the nutritionists and the therapists. Plus, me and Mae and Amélie will be able to bike everywhere. Finally, Dad won't feel like a taxi driver anymore." The very thought of such independence made my stomach flutter with excitement.

She sighed in relief. "Thank you, Livia!" Although my opinion wasn't the sole driver of the decision, I knew it mattered greatly to my mom.

In May, she and Mae traveled to the Netherlands to see how this idea would play out. They visited my mom's potential workplace and explored nearby schools, wanting to feel the ambiance before making any important decisions. When they returned, it was official: we would move "home" in July.

I was over the moon about the upcoming change of tides. I was finally going to be free from everything that was holding me back, and I couldn't wait for a chance to start over. I fantasized about all the Dutch foods I missed, finally permitting myself to eat them because no one was forcing me to. I imagined playing soccer again, going for bike rides, and walking on the beach to watch the summer sunset. There would be no more fighting, no more Maudsley, no more pain. Everything would be *perfect*.

In anticipation of our move, I stopped caring about the opinions of Dr. Coleman. I water-loaded and used coins to make my weight go up, even if it was just on paper. During these last few months, I even admitted to every manipulative thing I was doing. It didn't matter anyway, as I was leaving the country!

33

UITSMIJTER

The moment we arrived at Schiphol Airport in Amsterdam, I tugged at both of my parents with a huge grin. "Can we go sit in that café?" I pointed to a little restaurant displaying large images of bread and cheese on its menu. My parents looked at each other in surprise but couldn't have loved the idea more. I ordered an *Uitsmijter*, a classic Dutch sandwich made with bread, butter, eggs, and cheese. The word *uitsmijter* literally means "to forcefully throw out." Legend goes that this dish used to be served in cafés late at night, just before the bouncer kicked you out at closing time. An *Uitsmijter* is not a meal for dainty eaters; it's a monster of a sandwich meant to satisfy serious hunger. And seriously satisfy my hunger it did. My parents watched in amazement as I demolished three fried eggs with fresh Dutch bread and all the fixings. I hadn't willfully eaten a meal this big since the age of ten. This move was a good decision after all!

For the first few weeks following our arrival, we stayed in a furnished home of friends as we waited for our belongings to arrive at the Rotterdam seaport. I turned my dreams of food into reality as I consumed everything I had loved as a little girl. Though I was anxious to start a new school in August, the anxiety was covered in excitement as I tasted freedom after all these years. If I could turn my life around just like that, surely I could conquer any challenges that a new school brought with it! Little did I know my mom had scheduled an appointment at an eating disorder clinic on August 4.

The appointment had already been on the calendar for over a month when my mom finally told me. I later discovered in old medical documents that my entire treatment team in the States had been part of the scheme. Here's an excerpt from my final report at Adolescent Medicine, dated July 15, 2015:

> 15 y/o female with longstanding restriction, hyper-exercising, water loading. She is now about 5 years into her illness. She has had limited ongoing in-depth therapy as she had only intermittent care with a long-term therapist who was also working with parents. She has been engaged with a new therapist for the last few months but does not feel that she made any progress. She is scheduled to see Priscilla in Utrecht in 2 weeks who will provide ongoing specialized eating disorder care. I feel that this is a time to deepen her therapy rather than considering easing up, as I worry that this may become a lifelong issue limiting her development.

During our last appointment, Dr. Coleman stressed the importance of having a support system in place. I believed we would cross that bridge after settling into our new home, and I was under the impression that my parents believed the same. I couldn't have been more wrong.

"Livia, I'd like to tell you something." This was how my mom introduced the subject. I thought she might tell me how proud she was of my new eating behaviors, but judging by her tone of voice, I knew it was not positive news. Well, at least not for me. "We're attending an appointment next week."

"What kind of appointment?" I asked suspiciously.

"Well, you know me and your dad only want the best for you," she said, "and we want to support you in getting healthy."

"I *am* healthy!" I pleaded. "Don't you see how I've been eating since we got here? I told you I just needed a fresh start!"

"Yes, honey–"

"Don't tell me it's an appointment with someone who's going to talk to me about eating disorders," I interrupted. "That's the very reason I wanted to leave Boston!" My heartbeat quickened as the look on my mom's face confirmed my fear.

Just like that, all the hope I had for this new start was forcefully thrown out the window.

34

RINTVELD CLINIC

Rintveld was in the town of Zeist, on the outskirts of Utrecht, on a quiet terrain behind bushy trees. As we turned onto the gravel road that led to the clinic, my stomach reminded me of my unease. I was so focused on the rain pattering gently on my window that I barely noticed my dad shift into park. When he opened the back door of the car, I met a thick, humid smell that intensified my nausea. My dad, mom, and I sauntered towards the entrance, where the words "Altrecht eetstoornissen Rintveld" were printed in blue letters across the glass doors. Altrecht was a mental health establishment with locations across the Netherlands, Rintveld being one of them.

"Can I help you?" an old, white-haired woman asked from behind a large desk. Aligned in square formations on each side of the entrance were chairs, two of which were occupied by a man and a woman who appeared to be in their early fifties. They were reading magazines, although I wondered how they could focus with the girl pacing back and forth behind them. I guessed she was their daughter, and they were here for the same reason I was, except this girl clearly needed to be here more than I did. Her gangly figure had the ability to catch anyone's attention, with twigs for arms and knees that protruded from their sockets. Her lightweight summer clothes revealed pale skin and visible veins. When I glanced at her eyes to make sure she didn't just have albinism, my heart sank at the blue circles that dipped into her hollow cheeks.

"Yes, hi." My mom rushed over to the white-haired woman as she pulled her silver handbag closer to her side. I shifted my focus from the gaunt girl to the front desk, walking briskly to join my mom and dad. "We're here for an appointment with Priscilla Vilain," my mom said.

The woman clicked away at her computer for a few moments, then looked up at me. "Livia?"

"Yes," I replied shyly, avoiding the woman's eyes.

"Have a seat." She directed a hand towards the empty side of the waiting area. "Dr. Vilain will be with you in a moment."

Priscilla Vilain had an impressive track record: appointed professor of clinical psychopathology at Utrecht University, medical director of the Rintveld Clinic, and co-founder of the Utrecht Research Group for Eating Disorders. No wonder this woman was regarded as one of the top eating disorder specialists in the country. My mom had made an appointment with her specifically because, of course, she only wanted the very best for me.

When Dr. Vilain finally called us into her office, her appearance was not at all what I expected. Instead of a bright, smiling woman in colorful clothing, Priscilla had short gray hair and wore a suit of the same color. A neat row of diplomas and certificates hung on the wall behind her large desk. After giving each of us a firm handshake, she motioned for us to take a seat at the round table in front of her desk.

"So, you all just moved back to Holland, and Livia is here to get help for her eating disorder," Priscilla stated, getting straight to business in the typical Dutch direct manner. "I spoke to Dr. Coleman a few weeks ago, and she told me Livia is not doing so well." Her accent when she pronounced "Coleman" almost made me choke with laughter, but I forced myself to hold it in. She turned to face me. "I've heard you've been resistant to treatment and have manipulated the system on multiple occasions."

It's nice to meet you too.

When I didn't say anything, my mom jumped into the conversation. "We just want to do what's best for Livia." She looked over at my dad, who nodded in agreement. The conversation morphed into a complete history of my life since fifth grade, with my mom doing most of the talking. When the story had come full circle and landed in the present, Priscilla asked me what I thought would be the best course of action.

"I've been eating really well since we got here," I offered with a slight smile. "I needed a fresh start, and I really hope you guys can trust me for once." I looked at both my parents.

"Do you trust her?" Priscilla asked.

"We really want to," my mom said, "but it's hard when there's been so much manipulation. We know it's not Livia. We know it's the eating disorder–" She looked out the window as if the words would somehow transcribe themselves onto the rain-fogged glass. "We just want to make sure there's a support system if things go in the wrong direction."

"A plan B," Priscilla confirmed.

"Yes, exactly!" My mom's face brightened, grateful for the mutual understanding.

"Well, I think we have a plan then," Priscilla said in an emotionless tone, which I quickly learned was distinctive to her. "I recommend Livia start outpatient therapy and see a nutritionist here at Rintveld." She shifted her gaze from my parents to me. "And if you are unable to handle things on your own, we will discuss going inpatient."

This was not happening. Had I come all this way, endured all this change, just to be in the same helpless position as I was before the move? Despite my efforts, they still didn't trust me. If they did, they wouldn't *need* a plan B.

"Please, can you just give me a chance to do things without more therapists and doctors?" I begged. "They don't help!"

"Honey," my mom said in a loving voice, "we've been at this for years. We just want you to get better."

Even though Maudsley was finally over, there was officially a new coalition between my parents and Rintveld. As I remained unable to express myself in a way that would get through to them, my mom and Priscilla set up weekly appointments for the coming months. I would be attending Gerrit Rietveld College at the end of August, but with the ultimatum of concurrently attending outpatient nutrition and therapy appointments at Rintveld. When my parents and I emerged from the clinic, I felt a wet droplet stream down my cheek. Though it was raining harder than before, that droplet wasn't rain.

35

GERRIT RIETVELD COLLEGE

Three weeks after the appointment, I believed there was still a slight chance of a new start on my first day of 3 VWO (comparable to ninth-grade honors/advanced in the US) at Gerrit Rietveld College. Unlike in the US, the Dutch word "college" refers to high school in the Netherlands. When talking about the American version of college, the Dutch use the term "universiteit," which literally translates to "university" in English. Gerrit Rietveld College was conveniently located just around the corner from our new home, which we were slowly settling into as we unpacked dozens of boxes on the daily. On the first day of school, I felt like a character that had been dropped into a video game to which it didn't belong. I was a year older than my new classmates, and almost everyone already had a friend group.

Further, the teaching style was drastically different from what I had become accustomed to in the US. My years at Lawrence and BHS were filled with clarity, support, and guidance. When I was given an assignment, it was accompanied by a "criteria for success" sheet. As I learned how to write an essay, I was provided with templates to structure my work. I learned about different ways to hook your reader, the importance of supporting evidence, and the components of a strong conclusion.

When I was given my first assignment at Rietveld – a book report about my summer reading – that was about as far as the instructions went.

"What are the criteria for this assignment?" I asked my teacher after class. It took all my willpower to approach her, as asking questions had never been my strong suit. But if I was going to get a good grade, let alone make a good impression, I needed to know.

"You're going to write about the books you read this summer. Analyze them, share what you thought of them, and say whether or not you would recommend them," she answered.

It seemed simple enough, but dozens more questions buzzed in my mind. Analyze them *how*? Recommend them to *whom*? How *long* was this report even supposed to be? Because I didn't know which question to ask next, I didn't ask any of them. Everyone else had already left class, and I could tell my teacher wanted to do the same. At home that afternoon, I started on the book report with a heavy feeling. If I didn't know exactly what to write about, I'd write about it all – just to be safe. Similar to every assignment I completed during my school career, that book report exceeded my Dutch teacher's expectations.

On another occasion, during physics class, I had to compute a distance using a scaled example. To calculate an exact result, I needed more information than was given in the book. I spent practically the entire class ruminating on how to work around the lack of critical information, reading and re-reading the question a million times over. Surely, I was missing something! While my classmates left without homework, I still had most of the questions to answer. Unable to figure out what I'd missed, I decided to stay after class to ask my teacher for elaboration.

"Hi," I said. "I've been trying to answer this question for the past hour, but there's no way to calculate the distance without knowing the exact distance of the scaled model."

"Ah, yes." He took the open textbook from my hands and placed it on the table in front of him. "Do you have a ruler with you?"

I grabbed a triangular ruler from my fully stocked pencil case and laid it atop the book.

"In this case, since the question doesn't specify an exact answer, you just measure as best you can, then provide an estimate of the final distance."

Estimate? How on Earth was I supposed to answer anything if I couldn't be precise?

Within the first week of school, I was drowning in the workload. I was constantly studying or doing homework, yet I still felt behind. Why was I so *slow*? It turns out, I wasn't. I just took in every detail. Even when the bell rang, I was always the last one to have my bag packed. And not because I lacked the muscles to lift books into a bag or zip it shut, but because I ensured the books were placed as efficiently as possible and the zippers were fully closed. Every time my classmates forgot their books (or, on some occasions, even claimed to have *lost* them), I was reminded of why I couldn't afford to be anything *but* precise.

36

DIETITIAN

My first outpatient appointment back in the Netherlands was with Rintveld's dietitian, Johanna. When I told her how I had been eating for the past five years, she looked at me as if I was speaking a foreign language. To her, I was. In Europe, no one used measuring cups – we used the metric system. From nutrition facts to recipes, everything was measured in grams or milliliters. *Okay, so I can just replace the measurements on the exchange lists with the metric version*, I thought. But it wasn't going to be that simple. Johanna had never even *heard* of the exchange system.

After I tried to explain the exchange system, Johanna was still confused. "How are we supposed to work together without a meal plan?" I asked.

"Well, there *is* a meal plan." She pulled open a heavy file drawer. She grabbed a printout that read "Voedingsadvies" (literally translating to "feeding advice") at the top and handed it to me.

My eyes quickly scanned its contents. "That isn't a meal plan," I said. "That's just an example of one day of eating."

"Sure it is!" she replied defensively. "This is the way I work with all my clients."

Her version of a meal plan labeled the exact foods I had to eat, with minimal options to switch things up. Breakfast was two slices of bread, both buttered, one with cheese and one with something sweet, such as sprinkles or jam. Alongside it, a bowl of yogurt and granola. Lunch was three slices of bread, all buttered, one with cheese, one with deli meat, and one with something sweet. Dinner was an Aardappels, Vlees, Groente (AVG'tje) meal, in which similar amounts of pasta or rice could be subbed for the potatoes, chicken or tofu for the meat, etc. The snack options were typical Dutch treats, such as *stroopwafels* (waffle wafers filled with caramel) and *ontbijtkoek* (a rye sweet bread), or chips and cheese for those with savory preferences.

"This is too different from what I'm used to," I said helplessly. "I never eat bread for breakfast, always oatmeal. Also, I don't like those snacks. And besides, how can we ever make increases or decreases without using exchanges?" My voice shook.

"We can create some options," Johanna replied encouragingly. "Let's start with oatmeal. Instead of two slices of bread with butter and toppings, you can have 40 grams of oatmeal with nuts and fruit."

I sighed with relief. "What about snacks?"

Johanna pulled another document from her file drawer. She handed me the stapled stack of printouts. "Here's the list of snack options."

I quickly skimmed through it and immediately noticed that the snacks were categorized into three sections: big snacks, medium snacks, and small snacks. "How do I know when to have which size snack?"

"You have three snacks per day," she replied. "Your daily snack average should come down to three medium snacks. So, say you have a small morning snack, you would need to have a large snack for either your afternoon or night snack to balance it out."

My brain liked the logic behind this snack system, yet part of me was still ambivalent. I had been using the exchange system for years, and now I was expected to change everything and trust the plans of a woman I'd just met? The very fact that I was at Rintveld in the first place was because they didn't trust me. The least I could do was return the favor.

37

TRUST

What I lacked in trust – both at school and between the Rintveld/parents coalition – I made up for at home. Because I was no longer working with a nutritionist who understood measuring cups, I fully switched to using my food scale. If we needed to change my plan, I had to speak a language my new dietitian understood. I removed single oat flakes to ensure the weight was exactly 40 grams. I cut corners off slices of bread to ensure they matched the exact weight on the nutrition label. I left teaspoons of yogurt in practically empty tubs to ensure I was consuming only the serving size.

Whereas I started strong and hopeful upon arrival in the motherland, my health declined as the weeks progressed. I was so hyper-focused on food that I could barely concentrate on my schoolwork. The obscurity of the teaching style only amplified this. My obsession with exercise intensified by the day, as I constantly felt I had to add more. If I had done twenty push-ups one day, I had to do *at least* twenty the next. But when I reached a new minimum, I increased the reps and set the bar higher. I absolutely dreaded the way I was living, but I didn't know how to change. I needed something to hold onto – something I could trust – and this was the only way I knew to achieve it.

38

UNIT 1

In September 2015, my weight reached a critically low point, and I was admitted to Rintveld's Unit 1. Rintveld had three units in total. Unit 1 was for adolescents under eighteen, Unit 2 was for adults, and Unit 3 was the long-term eating disorder unit. In an interview I found online, Priscilla Vilain describes the purpose of Unit 3: "In Unit 3, full recovery is no longer the goal. Rather, it's about striving to improve the overall quality of life while living with an eating disorder."

Author's note: I simply cannot find the words to express my pain when writing about Unit 3. At the time of my admission to Unit 1, I was so young that I didn't realize how incredibly harmful such a philosophy is. Only after reaching full recovery and now guiding others to do the same can I look back with this insight. You will continue to read about my journey to full recovery as you progress through this book, but I already want to tell you now: don't EVER stop making full recovery the goal. An eating disorder is NOT an illness you "just have to learn to live with," no matter how long you've been struggling.

The admission took place on September 16, my mom's fiftieth birthday. Rather than joining the family for dinner that night, I unpacked my suitcase in a room with cold gray floors and an uncomfortable bed. My first roommate at Rintveld was Minnie, a ten-year-old girl who came across as very shy. I didn't blame Minnie for her isolative behavior, as her age made it incredibly difficult to connect with the rest of us in Unit 1, all teenagers. I quickly learned that Minnie hadn't eaten in over a year, which was why she received daily tube feeds. Sometimes, we overheard Minnie crying and screaming from the nurses' office as they held her down during tube feeding. I can't even imagine the pain that poor girl must have endured.

Perhaps this daily coercion was a significant part of the reason for Minnie's secretive exercise behavior. She may have been young and shy, but she was equally sly. Whenever I'd leave our bedroom for a moment, I'd hear banging and pounding as Minnie did jumping jacks and burpees. Maybe we weren't so different after all. However, when I tried to speak to her, sharing my own story and asking about hers, she refused to open up. Everything I knew about Minnie were details that other group members overheard from the nurses' meetings.

Clearly, the nurses weren't very good at overhearing secret exercise because that's how I spent my days at Rintveld. Unlike the inpatient and residential treatment centers I had endured in the US, Rintveld had no therapy groups. When my mom asked one of the nurses why, she answered, "Eating moments are therapy moments." Therefore, outside of mealtimes, I was free to do whatever I wanted. When Minnie occupied the bedroom, I would hide my laptop under my bathrobe and casually walk to one of the large disabled bathrooms to "take a shower." I spent hours watching YouTube workouts, and not once did a staff member knock on the door. This very carelessness made me hate Rintveld even more.

Despite their "mealtimes are therapeutic" claim, the staff didn't seem to care much during meals either. Rintveld had a phase system in place, through which patients progressed during their stay. In phase one – the "motivation phase" – staff plated all the patient's food and selected their bread toppings at breakfast and lunch. In phase two – the "try-out phase" – a patient was given more autonomy. They were allowed to choose their own bread toppings, pick their own fruit at snacks, and plate themselves at dinner. In the third and final phase – the "transition phase" – a patient mapped out a plan for follow-up treatment and would go to school on some days. I barely remember anyone being in phase three during my time there.

I vividly remember one Rintveld mealtime when the staff made fun of one of my fellow patients. Although she had already been at Rintveld for over half a year, Anela was still in phase one because she wasn't fully meal compliant. We were all sitting at the lunch table one afternoon, and Anela was having an especially tough day. When a staff member had assigned *hagelslag* (chocolate sprinkles) as one of her bread toppings, she spoke up.

"I'm having a really hard day," Anela said. "Can I please have an easier topping?"

"Even on the hard days, you have to do the hard work," responded Boris, one of the staff members.

"Please," Anela begged. "I do want to eat. I don't want to supplement. I am just incapable of eating hagelslag right now. I promise I'll eat it another day."

"Ohhh, I'm so scared of the hagelslag!" Tanja, another nurse, mocked her.

Boris laughed. "Here, how about Nutella? Or are you scared of that, too?"

"That's even scarier!" Tanja replied, and they both burst out laughing.

I looked at Anela, who was crying. I wished I could help her, but I didn't dare to put the nurses in their place. Who knows how they'd make fun of me if I did.

Rintveld's phase system created incredible tension between patients. Everyone seemed to be competing with one another, regardless of which phase we were in. In phase one, patients were given portioned butter cups at breakfast and lunch. The rule was half a butter cup per slice of bread. So two slices of bread meant an empty butter cup at the end of the meal. One of the privileges of phase two was that you could use butter from the big tub. Whereas this privilege assumed a newfound awareness of portion sizes and responsibility, one would have to be blind not to notice how thinly the phase two patients smeared the butter on their bread. Apparently, the staff *was* blind; they constantly encouraged the phase one'ers to "look up to" those above them.

Dinner was no different. The purpose of a phase two patient's privilege to plate their own food was to lead by example, but it was crystal clear to everyone in phase one that they were doing just the opposite. The phase two'ers would scoop their potatoes onto the plate, spreading and flattening them to make them appear like more. When it came to dessert – always a different flavor of *vla* (Dutch custard) – the phase two'ers would under-portion themselves again, spreading the thick pudding up the sides of the bowl to trick the staff into believing an optical illusion. The staff fell for it every time. I had hidden food in the past, but this could barely be called hiding; this was *hiding in plain sight*. The phase one'ers would compare their own fully loaded plates to the flattened, cut-up, and spread-out creations of the phase two'ers with envious eyes.

Even though the portion sizes varied, every patient always finished at the exact same time: after thirty minutes, on the dot. This was yet another way the patients competed with each other, and in this regard, those in both phases one and two had an even playing field. At Rintveld, just like at my past treatment facilities, food had to be completed within a certain amount of time: thirty minutes for meals, twenty for snacks. During my first dinner at the clinic, I had eaten my heaping pile of rice and chicken stir-fry in ten minutes flat, only to realize the rest of the group had practically their whole meal left. Since then, I had learned to pace myself, closely observing the others' tactics. Small pieces, putting my utensils down between every bite, chewing slowly...all the way up until the last two minutes, in which everyone would run a consumption sprint to ensure completion by minute thirty. This, the staff *did* seem to pick up on.

"If you didn't take such mouse bites, you wouldn't need to make such a sprint to finish in time," a staff member would often say, as all the patients shifted their focus from each other to cleaning their plates.

"Hmm hmm," we would mumble through our full mouths, knowing that their words wouldn't change a thing.

39

LEADING BY EXAMPLE

The staff often had something to say about crumbs, too. Another way patients at Rintveld hid food in plain sight was by crumbling anything that could be crumbled. The crevices of the couches were filled with bits and pieces of *Liga* and *Sultana* (two brands of Dutch fruit biscuits), chips, granola bars, *speculaas* cookies, and more. When one of the staff members noticed a trail of ants creeping along near one of the couch legs, she called for a community meeting.

"It has not escaped our notice that a negative behavior has infiltrated the group," Astrid said on behalf of the five present staff members. "Everyone seems to be crumbling their food, which is obviously not the purpose of snack time."

"To create a therapeutic environment, you must encourage each other to recover and lead by example," added Willeke, another staff member.

But what if we didn't *want* to recover? What if, to us, leading by example meant teaching the other group members how to manipulate the system? Every patient shared these thoughts seemingly through telepathic powers, and using these same powers, we knew not to say a word.

Because the phase one patients didn't have the luxury of hiding food in plain sight like the phase two patients, they found other tactics. One morning at breakfast, I tilted my chair backward as I waited the remaining few minutes for the meal to be over. I balanced on the two hind legs and placed my hands under the table to stay in position, wanting to irritate the staff by doing something they'd consider "dangerous." Only once my hands met a greasy, melty gob did I realize I really *was* in danger.

"Ewww!" I jumped up from my chair to look under the table. An entire square of smashed butter was right where my hands had been. But even if I had been sitting somewhere else, I would have been met with the same stroke of bad luck – the *entire* underside of the tabletop was covered in everything spreadable or sticky, reminiscent of dried gum under the table of a diner. Peanut butter, Nutella, jam; the combination of hidden splotches was enough to top an entire meal's worth of bread!

If *I* – a master at hiding food – had made this discovery only after a *whole month* in the clinic, it didn't surprise me that the staff was just as flabbergasted. The next community meeting was identical to the crumb talk, except this time, the staff used more intense phrasing, such as "toxic group environment" and "negative influence." If they actually thought any of us patients would be influenced by their words, though, they were seriously fooling themselves.

When I realized how easy it was to get away with certain be-haviors at Rintveld, I started testing the waters. Not only did I continue water loading and putting coins in my underwear as I had done years prior, but I learned a new behavior: purging.

Just like at the clinics in the US, the bathrooms at Rintveld were officially off-limits for an hour after meals and snacks. However, unlike my previous admissions, the Rintveld staff did nothing to enforce this rule. When a "therapeutic" eating period ended, the nurses retreated to their little office, babbling away until it was time for the next "therapy moment." Some patients would rush to their rooms to do sit-ups and jumping jacks, while others would scurry off to the bathroom to get rid of whatever they had just consumed. One day, too exhausted to squeeze in yet another exercise session, I decided to join my fellow patient Fien for her routine bathroom trip.

"How do you do it?" I had never considered vomiting before, as I associated it with the nausea and discomfort of having the flu.

"You take your finger and stick it down your throat, as deep as it will go," she explained as if it was common knowledge.

"But what if I choke myself to death?" I asked with wide eyes.

"You won't choke," she replied, almost choking on her laughter. "You'll gag at first, but you just keep going. Eventually, the food will come right up."

Fien was right, but I never threw up again after that. The pounding headache that came with the act made me feel as if my head was going to fall off, a sensation I'd rather not endure on a regular basis. So I stuck to my tried-and-true methods: exercising, hiding food, and water loading.

40

SYSTEMS THERAPY

B esides the "therapeutic eating moments," I was forced to engage in family therapy while at Rintveld. Once every two weeks, my parents and I (and, on occasion, my sisters) would meet with Hedwig, who called herself a "systems therapist." "The goal in systems therapy is to uncover problems within the family system," she explained during our first session. "An eating disorder is a coping mechanism for deeper emotional pains, and these often have their roots in dysfunctional family dynamics."

During our sessions, Hedwig would sketch elaborate figures on her whiteboard, pointing out problems in our family system. According to her, one core issue was that my parents were no longer in their position of hierarchy. "This is what your family is supposed to look like," she said as she scribbled a family tree with her squeaky marker. She started by drawing a circle and a square, connected with a horizontal line, to represent the relationship between my mom and dad. From there, she drew another series of lines and three circles to represent my sisters and me. "The problem in your family is that Livia is no longer next to her sisters," Hedwig said as she crossed out the circle on the bottom left of the family tree. She drew a new circle at the same level as my parents' symbols. "Livia has taken on the responsibilities of the parents, which has caused harm to her adolescent development. For your family to function normally again, the parents must unite, and Livia must return to the position in which she belongs." She drew an arrow from the top circle back down to the one she had previously crossed out.

When Hedwig mentioned my parents needing to "unite," tension filled the room. Their quarrels had gotten progressively worse, despite attending couples therapy. To everyone besides Hedwig, it was crystal clear they weren't going to "unite" anytime soon. My mom placed her hand on my dad's, and I noticed how it took all his willpower not to pull away. I knew that though they may no longer have been united by love, they'd always be united in supporting me. By the sullen looks on their faces, I could tell Hedwig's words about their lack of unity contributing to my illness stabbed them in the deepest points of their heart.

The truth is, however, neither my parents nor I was responsible for my lack of progress. Rintveld created a toxic environment. After nearly four months of inpatient treatment there, the only change had been the further decline of my mental and physical health. And I'm not an anomaly when it comes to this experience; at the time of this writing, only a fraction of my fellow patients there are still alive. I knew that if I stayed in this clinic, the outcome would not be favorable. But my self-created secrecy trapped me, and I feared that opening up about my true feelings would land me someplace even worse.

"You need to take me out of here," I begged my parents one weekend. Thankfully, going home on weekends was a privilege that all patients received after their first week in the clinic. Weekends were always tough, involving endless arguments about portion sizes and movement, but every night in my own bed made me realize how much I yearned for more. Although I still did my daily push-ups and hid any food I deemed "too much," I wasn't compelled to compare, eat slowly, or watch endless hours of exercise videos just to pass the time. When I was home, I felt safe. When I was at Rintveld, I felt poisoned.

"She keeps talking about wanting to come home," my dad said during the routine "weekend conference" held between each patient, their parents, and a Rintveld nurse. "We don't know what to do, as it seems she hasn't made any progress since her admission. Whenever she comes home, we're always arguing."

"She still has a long way to go." The nurse cunningly used her power position to keep me trapped.

"This place isn't helping me!" I pleaded. "The environment is so toxic, everyone is manipulating and comparing, and if anything, Rintveld is just making me *sicker*!" It occurred to me that this was the first time I'd ever admitted to being sick.

"You do realize, Livia, that you are part of the group," the nurse said. "You need to be a role model to your peers if you want to prove you are ready to leave."

"That is *not* my role," I responded angrily. "You people are supposed to support us, and all you do is make fun of people and chitchat in this little office." I threw my hands in the air. "I'm trying my best, but it's impossible to make any progress if I'm constantly surrounded by people who don't even want to eat or get back to real life."

The nurse took a moment to find her words. She turned to my parents. "If you take Livia out of treatment, you're making a deplorable decision." And with that, the decision was made. My parents trusted the specialists out of fear that they couldn't trust themselves. But *I* trusted myself and knew that deep down, my parents' instincts aligned with mine. There was a fire inside me, a burning desire that told me I *had* to leave. I was holding on by a thread, and that thread would snap if I didn't escape soon.

41

ESCAPE

On a rainy Wednesday night not too long after that meeting, I executed my escape plan. I had spent the entire day looking forward to this exciting yet petrifying adventure, and the adrenaline coursed through my veins. I was going to give Rintveld a run for their money, and they didn't even realize it. My backpack contained my pajamas, toiletries, and a water bottle. I made sure to pack only the essentials for the long walk ahead of me.

When the night nurse did her final round and said, "Lights out!" at 10:30 p.m., I promptly closed my book and jumped under the covers. The moonlight shining through the window shades illuminated the reflective patches on my North Face backpack, hidden in the corner behind the bedroom door. As I lay in bed, eyes wide open, I listened closely to the nurse's footsteps. When they trailed off into silence, my heartbeat quickened. The time for action was coming closer and closer. Was I *really* going to do this? *Hell yes, I was.*

After waiting exactly twenty minutes to ensure the coast was clear, it was time. I slipped out of bed and changed into the clothes I had set on the top shelf of my closet. Earlier that day, I had retrieved my raincoat from the coatrack in the common room, as the weather forecast showed rain all week. I slipped on my warmest socks and gently slid my feet into my waterproof sneakers. It was the middle of January, one of the coldest months in the Netherlands, so I had to be well-attired. Considering the resources at my disposal, I had done the best I could.

I placed one of my two pillows under the duvet cover, adding a few pieces of clothing near the foot of the bed. Surely, the nurse would get suspicious if I was suddenly half my size! I pulled the duvet cover high above the pillow at the top of the bed, making it appear as if my head was totally covered in the sheets. I took a moment to stare at the human-like heap in amusement, proud of my clever construction. I grabbed my backpack from the corner, cracked open the door, and cautiously peered out before stepping into the hallway. The LED lights almost blinded me, but my pupils adjusted as I tiptoed towards the nearest exit.

With every step, I glanced behind me to ensure the coast remained clear. My palms were sweaty, and I was hot in my winter clothing. *I'm almost outside*, I reminded myself. My heart pounded through the thick raincoat as I scurried down the halls like a spy, hyper-aware of the slightest possible peep. When I finally reached the exit, I gently pushed on the crash bar, glancing behind me once again. I sashayed through the opening and held my fingers on the door to ensure a silent close. Just before it locked into place, I paused: *Am I really going to do this?* As soon as the door shut, I would be locked out. I allowed it to latch and thought again, *Hell yes, I am.*

My walk home was just over one and a half hours. I was soon soaked, and my legs felt like Jell-O, but I made it. As I approached the front door, I heard my mom in a panic.

"What do you mean she's not there?" she screamed.

"Louise, calm down!" my dad said. "Livia is a smart girl. She'll turn up."

"She'll *turn up*!?" My mom's voice was angry. "Jan, they're saying she's not at the clinic. She's nowhere to be found!" Even from outside I could discern a faint voice on the other end of my mom's phone, evidently a Rintveld nurse. "I'm going for a drive. We need to find her!" My mom swung open the front door, only to be met by her exhausted and drenched daughter.

"Oh my God, Livia!" she exclaimed in relief as she rushed over to hug me. "Jan, she's here! Oh, she's here!" She squeezed me even tighter.

"I knew she was fine," my dad said in a relaxed tone that emitted a hint of pride. I smirked at him over my mom's shoulder. I knew "I told you so" is what he wanted to say.

"You're soaking wet, honey! Did you seriously walk all this way? Oh my God, I'm so glad you're safe! Come on, let's get you inside." My adrenaline rush had somehow transferred onto my mom. Now *she* was the one who was full of energy. But just as my burning energy metamorphosed into sheer exhaustion and a need for sleep, my mom's demeanor quickly switched from relief to anger. "How dare they just allow her to walk home?" my mom asked my dad. She turned to me. "How dare you just walk home like this, Livia?"

"I'm telling you, Mommy, they don't care about me," I replied. "I'm not going to get better there. Please, let me stay home."

"Well, we have to take you back," my dad said. "You know that, right?"

"Why?" I cried. By this point, my sisters stood in the doorway to the living room, rubbing their eyes and wearing matching pink pajamas.

My mom rushed over to hug them. "Oh, sweeties. Everything's okay."

"What are we supposed to do, Livia?" my dad asked.

"Allow me to come home! I'm exhausted, and I just want to sleep in my own bed."

My mom stood up and turned towards my dad. She looked at the clock on the wall. "It's 12:30 a.m. We can't drive her back at this hour." She turned to me. "Go off to bed now, but we're having a serious discussion in the morning."

I skidded to my room (my own room!) in euphoria. I didn't want to think about the discussion in the morning. Sleeping in my own bed was all that mattered right now. I fell asleep as soon as my head hit the pillow.

42

Too Complex

The next morning, my mom took me back to Rintveld for the serious discussion. I would have to go back at some point to gather the rest of my belongings, so I didn't make a fuss about getting in the car.

"Livia's ongoing defiance has proven how severe her illness really is." Those were the first words that came out of Priscilla Vilain's mouth. Her tone was different from the first time we were seated in her office. Although still direct, the underlying hope her words exuded during that first meeting was nonexistent. "It shows me that her situation is too complex to be helped."

"Too complex?" my mom asked in astonishment. "This is an eating disorder clinic! You are a specialist! How can her situation be too complex?"

Priscilla folded her hands and rested them on her desk. "Here at Rintveld, we create a therapeutic environment to support individuals recovering from their eating disorders. However, in some cases, patients do not respond to treatment. Their situation may even worsen, as we have seen with Livia. When this happens, we have to shift our focus to –"

My mom interrupted: "From what I've seen and heard, there's no therapeutic environment here! Since the day she was admitted, all we were told was that eating moments are therapy moments! In the United States, Livia engaged in all different kinds of therapy while in treatment."

"And the mealtimes aren't even therapeutic," I chimed in. "The nurses make fun of patients when they're having a hard time."

"Well, I'm not there at mealtimes and I don't know what therapy is like in the States, but I do know that we are one of the best eating disorder clinics in the country," Priscilla said with pride. "So when a patient has spent several months here without any improvement, we need to shift our focus away from recovery."

"What do you mean?" I asked.

"What I'm saying –" Priscilla pursed her lips for a moment. "You're just going to have to accept the fact that you're never going to get better."

The numbness that enveloped me overpowered any sense of devastation. *You're just going to have to accept the fact that you're never going to get better.* The words echoed in my mind, just like Natalie's original diagnosis of anorexia had; the only difference was five years and countless treatments. Not only were my parents at a loss, but *I* was at a loss. All this time, treatment had been a game for me. I had done everything I could to manipulate the system, simply wanting to prove that no one could tell me what to do. But now? There was no more manipulation to be done. I had been given up on. How was I supposed to rebel against that?

43

SINKING DEEPER

S hortly after I was kicked out of the clinic, my mom, sisters, and I migrated to a new home. My parents' relationship had completely fallen apart, making it no longer feasible for them to live together. My dad stayed behind in the rental house on the Wentlaan – the house we first moved into upon our arrival in our homeland – and my mom bought a house just a few blocks away on the Jordanlaan. Even though all hope for life seemed lost, a sliver of me was excited; a new home meant a new start, and a new start meant new hope.

My new room had a beautiful view overlooking a cherry blossom tree and a small pond. In the morning, sunlight beamed through my purple curtains while the birds whistled their daily song. I didn't have the urge to secretly exercise in my room, a tendency I later learned can be attributed to the way our brains form and maintain habits. Unfortunately, a change of home was not enough to save me from sinking deeper into my eating disorder.

Each day, the battle between my body and my mind intensified. I was exhausted but powerless in the face of my urge towards hyperactivity. I started running again, which soon became part of my daily routine. I would go to bed worrying about having to run the next day, suffocated by anxiety that subsided only once a run was complete. But that relief was only brief, as I was caught in a catch-22. Running felt like the only thing that could lessen my anxiety while it served as one of its main contributions.

At the same time, I was obsessively counting calories and macros and weighing every morsel of food that entered my mouth. I purchased a second food scale out of fear that the first one would suddenly stop working, and I kept a backup of all of my food staples just in case something was out of stock at the grocery store. Still, I would go to the store every day, as it was the only outing I enjoyed. During school, I would sit in the back of the classroom just to look up elaborate recipes and food photos without anyone seeing my laptop screen. It still floors me that I passed my exams with flying colors.

Despite my efforts to conceal my frail figure, I always felt eyes on me. I sensed people scanning my body up and down, terrified yet intrigued by my gauntness. I knew what they were thinking: *Why doesn't she just eat?* If I had known the answer, no one would have needed to ask the question in the first place.

44

INSTAGRAM

For months, I had been ghost-following a multitude of pro-files on Instagram, ranging from "healthy foodies" and "clean eaters" to "recovery accounts." At the time, I was not famil-iar with the concepts of intuitive eating or Health at Every Size, nor did I possess the knowledge I do now about how harmful diet culture is. All I knew then was that I was desperate for connection. No one in my direct environment understood what I was going through. I craved support and understanding, and based on the comments I read on others' vulnerable posts, I believed I would find it on this social media platform. So I decided to create my own Instagram account, @lilrecoveringfoodie. My username was born sheerly out of who I thought I was: a little foodie that was recovering. I didn't share my real name, my face, or anything that disclosed the person behind the profile. I chose to stay anonymous because I didn't want anyone I knew to find out about my account.

I posted on Instagram every day. I posted pictures of my meals and snacks along with elaborate captions in which I shared my deepest, darkest thoughts. I shared how anxious I was about eating a particular food or how I was struggling with the fact that one of my sisters had eaten breakfast later than me. Everything I was afraid to share with those around me felt safe to share in my online community. Reading others' victories made me long to be recovered – whatever that meant. People shared how they could have never imagined how great it felt to "be on the other side" until they decided to fully commit to recovery. They shared how scared they felt, but that facing their fears was the only way through. They shared that full recovery was possible, despite what their doctors or other "professionals" had said.

Finally, I was no longer alone. In fact, I wanted to be more than that. *I* wanted to be the one telling her story about making it to the other side. *I* wanted to be the one inspiring others in the same way these people had inspired me. *I* wanted to be the one saying they had fully recovered, despite being told that I just had to accept the fact that I was never going to get better. Cultivating an online community relit my inner fire, a fire that had been dimmed for too long. I finally knew what I had to do: rebel against those who had given up on me.

45

ASKING FOR HELP

"**M**om, I want to see a therapist," I mumbled quietly after breakfast one morning. I had just posted a photo of my protein oats with berries and nut butter, sharing in the caption how I had made the brave decision to reach out for help. In a society where asking for help is often labeled "weak," it took me a full week of rumination and sleepless nights to finally bite the bullet and say the words. I had written and rewritten my caption for that post dozens of times over, knowing that as soon as I shared my big announcement on the 'gram, I had to go through with it.

My mom smiled at me, her eyes kind. "That's wonderful, honey. Let's find you someone who understands," she said consolingly, deeply aware of how traumatic the past five years had been for me. My mom reached out to her friend Celeste, a therapist who worked with neurodivergent individuals. Celeste recommended a therapist named Monique, an experienced expert who had recovered from multiple eating disorders herself.

During my first session with Monique, I finally felt seen. Monique didn't stuff words down my throat as prior providers had. Instead, she listened to me and validated my thoughts. My first few sessions with her were promising. I opened up to her in a way I hadn't truthfully opened up before, but a large part of me was still ambivalent. I avoided the difficult questions, and when Monique suggested some challenging next steps, I no longer wanted to go.

"Why don't you give it another chance?" my mom asked when I told her I was done seeing Monique.

"She wants me to change too much at once." I was overwhelmed, spiraling into a state of paralysis.

"Maybe I can talk to her?" my mom suggested, trying to conserve this precious opportunity.

"No!" I yelled. "You've forced me through enough already." Although I was unaware of it at that moment, a deeper part of me knew that I could only be helped if I *wanted* to be helped.

A month after quitting with Monique, I was ready to try again. When I told my mom, it was clear she had been anticipating it. She exclaimed, "I'm so glad to hear that, Livia! A friend of mine knows a therapist who has a very unique therapy approach." The therapist was named Kiara, and her unique approach was Past Reality Integration (PRI). Developed by Dutch psychologist and researcher Ingeborg Bosch, PRI therapy is based on the idea that adults often continue to perceive the world through defense mechanisms developed during their childhood. According to Bosch, adults hold onto these defense mechanisms in an effort to protect themselves from the pain they endured as a child. It's this very attachment to old defense mechanisms that supposedly acts as a barrier to living in the present moment and connecting to one's true self.

My first session with Kiara was similar to my initial experience with Monique. Kiara had a kind and gentle manner, and she, too, was an experienced expert who had recovered from decades of disordered eating.

"PRI saved my life," Kiara told me during our first session. "Looking into my past made me realize that I was trying to protect myself from something I no longer needed to be protected from. My anorexia and bulimia were simply coping mechanisms for unhealed trauma. Once I healed the wounds of my past, I no longer needed the false safety of eating disorders."

Kiara's explanation sounded promising. Here I was with five years of an eating disorder under my belt, sitting across from someone who had fully recovered after *twenty years* of eating disorders. If PRI had healed her, perhaps it would do the same for me.

I don't remember every question she asked me during that first session, but it didn't take long for us to land on the subject of my birth.

"What was Livia's birth process like?" she asked my mom, who sat close by my side. One of my parents was always with me during therapy sessions, as I felt unsafe without their comforting presence.

"Well," my mom said, leaning back into the couch as if to prepare herself for what could take a while, "Livia was born two weeks late. Whereas we would have expected a bigger baby, she was tiny." My mom looked up at the high ceilings of the loft. "Oh, I remember that day like it was yesterday. You were so small and so cute, and your dad and I were so grateful you were healthy." She rocked an imaginary baby in her arms. "We were so afraid you weren't going to make it," my mom said, her tone shifting from delighted to distraught.

"The umbilical cord was wrapped around my neck," I chimed in. "*Twice*," I emphasized with a sense of pride.

"Wow." Kiara leaned forward in her seat to look me in the eyes. I averted my gaze to the floor but listened closely to her words. "It sounds like you had quite a traumatic childhood experience."

"Yeah," I mumbled.

"A lot of the time, we endure traumas we can't even remember," Kiara explained. "Our unconscious mind registers everything. I believe your eating disorder may be a coping mechanism to protect you from that pain, old pain you endured on the day you were born."

I looked up from the fluffy carpet. "But that's not possible. I don't even *remember* that day."

"Like I said," Kiara continued, "our unconscious mind contains memories we cannot consciously remember. But that doesn't mean they don't still influence our life as a whole."

I thought for a moment. "Well, I guess that makes sense. I've always hated wearing scarves. Whenever I try to wear one, I feel like I'm choking," I said. "But maybe it's because my unconscious mind is associating the scarf with being strangled by the umbilical cord!"

Kiara beamed like a proud teacher whose student had just gotten an A+ on their exam. "Yes, that's right!" she exclaimed. "And through looking at it with a PRI lens, you will learn to understand that you no longer have to protect yourself from the umbilical cord. It's old pain that you can finally let go of."

I tilted my head to the side as the edges of my lips curved upwards. I was intrigued. Was PRI the missing piece of my healing?

I engaged in weekly sessions with Kiara for several months, sharing childhood experiences as she analyzed them through a trauma lens. "It's old pain," she often said. "You no longer need to protect yourself. It's in the past now."

Although I definitely believe certain types of therapy – including PRI – have their time and place, no amount of talking about your problems is going to solve your problems. I was truthful and open during our sessions, but outside of therapy, nothing changed.

A few months later, I quit therapy with Kiara. While I felt seen and understood in the same way I had with Monique, I wasn't empowered to actually change. So I would continue to look until I did.

After letting go of Kiara, I moved on to yet another therapist: Bob van Ermengaard. An older man with a powerful presence, Bob was a master of telling philosophical stories. He had an immense passion for the Universe, often connecting seemingly inexplicable situations to a force that is light-years beyond explanation. At our first meeting, Bob immediately gave me a sense of safety and security; he was like the grandpa I never had. Even more than that, Bob had an incredible capability to understand my being. It was a mutual understanding that I felt in my soul, an understanding that led me to believe wholeheartedly his theories about our connection with the Universe. To illustrate Bob's painstakingly precise perception of me, I have chosen to translate and share his final report of our time together:

> Livia's behavior originates in the controversy between her own identity, her personal and innate drives, and the conflicting drives and values of society. She responds to this controversy from a wounded and systematically denied self-identity, which arose from her direct environment. In this, her parents

played an important role. The way in which Livia reacts indicates a powerful personality, fighting against superiority using all her resources, including disordered mechanisms she developed at the age of eleven.

This process is further enhanced by the conflict between the specific characteristics of the child brain and the adolescent brain. At sixteen, her brain should have been much more distanced from her child brain. However, she is still closely attached to the need to be cherished and protected, while at the same time wanting to apply a steering influence on her environment and herself. In doing so, she lacks the self-control that is allowed to be present during the healthy development of a sixteen-year-old.

She indicates in her reactions and use of language that she is extremely sensitive. In combination with a broad panorama of observations, a wide range of interests and experiences, great carefulness, and a lack of distinction between essences and side issues, this sensitivity leads to a strong self-perception of chaos and powerlessness.

These experiences and reactions to them have made her allergic to authorities, even if they are expressed by a voluntarily unemployed father, who burdens her with his own limitations. It is clear she is condemned to these burdens through her unconscious mind.

Her anorexia, her aggressive behavior, and her obsessive compulsion to direct and control her environment are the result of all these affordances. They are not isolated complaints that corrective orders can resolve. On the contrary, she will only resist authority more as it strives to "correct" her behavior. In doing so, her aggression and inability to eat will increase.

In the six hours that I have been able to work with Livia, she has, without noticing it herself, already given up much of her original identity. Remarkable is her powerful personality. She continuously gives congruent signals in her verbal and non-verbal communication. She is a leader, a thinker, and a feeler. She is nuanced and remarkably careful in the perception of details to which she attributes her own values. She resists authorities who impose their opinions on her, including those who will not listen to her views. She has the motives of a conqueror and of a winner, without the desire for anyone to lose as a consequence.

She does not aim to win; rather, she seeks verification of the truth through her strong sense of righteousness. Livia seems insatiably curious, but everything she encounters must "make sense" and act in harmony. In all these endeavors, Livia runs up against language barriers. She feels she lacks the words to match her expressive needs. This causes stress, uncertainty, and anger. She wants more than her age and life experience allow her. Her thinking (philosophy) demands an adult brain, while emotionally she is still too attached to her child brain. Unconsciously, she would like to skip the adolescent phase. No experiments, but certainties. She seeks power to steer and thus control her life, but experiences like these and her reactions to them have made her allergic to authorities, while at the same time feeling that her environment has tried to take away her sense of self. Her reaction is a fierceness and aggression towards not only her environment, but also herself.

Livia understands all the good intentions of her parents, her teachers, and therapists, but at the same time, senses their inability to be able to empathize with her world of experience. The only thing she wants, unspoken, is to be understood and to be helped out of her problems at her own pace and within her own capabilities and limitations.

Before she came to me for the first time, she had a lot of resistance. That resistance is gone. She experiences our time together as an adventure and a voyage of discovery, even though everything is still strange and she still finds the trip to be burdensome.

Unfortunately, the burden of the trip was the reason I stopped attending sessions with Bob. Every week, my mom and I would drive from Utrecht to Leiden, an hour-long commute. The journey to and from Bob's office, paired with the two-hour session, meant I had to sit still for over four hours at a time. Bony and frail as I was, I experienced terrible aches if I sat in one position for more than ten minutes. It wasn't even being unable to exercise that I found difficult – allowing myself to rest was a relief – it was my lack of fat and physical protection that sent shooting pains down my back while my tailbones pushed upwards into my body. I truly appreciated my sessions with Bob, but my desire to spare myself that weekly pain ended up prevailing.

46

BONI

In September 2016, I started my sophomore year of high school at my third school in Holland. After a horrible start at the Gerrit Rietveld College due to my almost immediate admission to Rintveld Clinic, I wanted to start fresh. I wanted to go to a school that didn't associate me with being "that student" who was always marked absent when the teacher took attendance.

Earlier that year, in May of 2016, I had enrolled in ISU, the International School of Utrecht. As I connected daily with my Instagram community, mostly based in the US, I grew nostalgic for my life back in Boston. I longed for the English language, the clear teaching style, and the cultural diversity I had been raised with. But going back to what I called home wasn't an option. We had just moved here. My mom had a stable new job. My sisters had new friends. There had to be a way for me to find my groove within the limitations of the country I resided in.

During the first few weeks, I loved ISU. I met people from all over the world, and the teachers were wonderful. I rode my bicycle there and back, a new movement routine that was so much more enjoyable than my compulsive runs and secret workouts. When summer vacation rolled around nearly two months later, however, I decided I wasn't going back. Attending ISU was strange; I would go to school to be surrounded by people of every nationality and culture, only to come out and be met with the harsh reality that I was living in the Netherlands. It was an inconsistency I could not get used to, a mental shift I had to make anew every day.

That summer, I sat my parents down to tell them the news. Because of the separation, any conversation with both of them had to be well-planned, which I preferred anyway.

"I want to go to another school." I looked down at their feet. I was filled with guilt for burdening them with another request, though at the same time, I knew my mom was relieved. ISU was a private school, and the two months from May to July had already cost a pretty penny. She and I both knew she would do anything to support me – even if that meant using the family savings to pay for school – but saving money was always the preferred option. Most of our belongings were secondhand, originating from yard sales, Craigslist, thrift shops, or wherever else we didn't need to pay full price. "Why would you pay extra if you can get it for less?" was my mom's motto regarding shopping.

When my parents asked which school I wanted to attend, I told them about Boni. In the same way I approached any big decision, I had spent hours researching nearby schools. St. Bonifatius College – nicknamed "Boni" – had caught my eye with its catch-phrase on the school's website: "our main focus is on the personal development and unique talents of each student." Could there be any better match for me? My parents were just as hopeful as I was. In mid-July, right before the school officially closed for the summer, my mom called the head of Boni.

"You caught us right on time!" said the man on the other end of the line. "We usually don't take new enrollments during the summer, but we should be able to assign Livia to a 4 VWO class for the upcoming year."

As was always the case when starting something new, I was equally excited and terrified. Still stuck in my ways of disordered eating and exercise, my health was in ruins. I created rules for myself about how many minutes of movement I should do each day, ensuring a minimum but also a maximum. I forced myself to eat past fullness, even if it left me physically ill. I knew that if I gave my eating disorder any additional room, it would take my life – and I wasn't going to let it. I wanted to trust that a new school – a fresh start – would be the tipping point for me not only to maintain my weight and current state of survival, but to give me the long-lost courage to *gain* weight and finally *live* again.

Unfortunately, the opposite was true. I was bullied and teased every day as children shouted, "Hey, little girl! Is your mom a teenager? Is that why you're so small?" On top of that, 4 VWO was undoubtedly more demanding than 3 VWO. Not only was I constantly overstimulated by my loud classmates and ever-increasing workload, but the fast pace and tight deadlines of assignments left me feeling incapacitated in every sense of the word. My mom helped me find tutors for the subjects I lacked confidence in, but nothing gave me the clarity and control I so desperately sought.

47

PANIC ATTACKS

J ust shy of two months after my first day at Boni, I had my first panic attack.

"I can't do this!" I screamed as I threw my economics textbook onto the floor and curled into a ball. I was hyperventilating so badly that it seemed my lungs were collapsing. "I can't breathe! I can't breathe!" I gasped for air, holding my hands around my neck to imitate a choking gesture.

My mom rushed to my side and covered my mouth with a paper bag. "Breathe into this." She rubbed my back. I pushed her away, believing a bag would further constrict my ability to get air. "Honey, you're hyperventilating. Please breathe into this. It will help," she reassured me.

"HOW?" I demanded. Even now, I needed to understand the logistics before surrendering to any new techniques.

"When you breathe into the contained space, you reuse the carbon dioxide you exhale," she explained. "It will help restore the balance of oxygen in your body." I motioned for her to place the bag on my face. "Now take deep breaths, honey. You're safe. I'm here. Everything is going to be okay."

I darted backward to free my face from the bag. "No, it won't! School is way too stressful! It's all too much, too fast, and I don't understand any of this shit! I'm so stupid!"

"You're not stupid," my mom said sternly. She despised when I put myself down, especially when it came to my scholastic capabilities. "You are one of the smartest people I know."

Although I was still trembling, my breathing started to even out. "Do you really mean that?" I asked, seeking commiseration to counteract my misery.

"You know I do." She smiled and drew me close.

"And do you love me?"

"Forever and always," she said as our hug grew tighter.

We sat on the floor, embracing, for the next twenty minutes. A wet patch formed on the shoulder of my mom's T-shirt from my tears. I played her words back in my mind. *You're safe. I'm here. Everything is going to be okay.*

The intensity and frequency of my panic attacks grew exponentially as the weeks progressed. The slightest inconsistencies or changes were enough to spark a full-blown meltdown, resulting in a looming cloud of tension throughout our home. *When is Livia going to have her next panic attack?* The fear was written all over my sisters' faces.

One night at dinner, as my mom scooped mac and cheese onto Mae's and Amélie's plates, I jumped up from my seat.

"I can't eat!" I burst out, my voice shaky. I started jumping up and down as panic blazed inside of me. *Oh no! It's happening again.* I didn't need to hear the words to understand that was exactly what they were thinking.

"You didn't put enough mac and cheese on their plates," I said. All three of them grew angry.

"We can eat however much we want!" Mae, now fourteen, exclaimed. More subtly, ten-year-old Amélie surrounded her plate with everything that stood on the table in an effort to hide its contents.

"Besides, Livia, how can you even say that?" my mom asked. "Look at your own plate." She motioned towards the small pile of plain, gluten-free pasta alongside steamed tofu and broccoli. "Our dinner is so much more calorie-dense than whatever you weighed out. You really cannot compare that to what we are eating!"

"Please," I begged.

"No. I am not going to give them more food just because you want me to."

I started hyperventilating, jumping up and down with increasing speed. "Please!" I begged once more. "I'm starting to not breathe! I'm going to die!"

My sisters' eyes transformed into chambers of terror. I knew I was the cause, but the ultimatum in my mind said otherwise. "I cannot eat until you give them more mac and cheese!" I gasped for air with every word. I started feeling faint and dropped to the floor. I would do anything to make my mom give my sisters more mac and cheese.

"Livia, no. That's my final answer. Now get up and eat dinner with us!" my mom yelled as her patience evaporated.

But I couldn't eat until they had more mac and cheese.

I jumped up, ran to the counter, grabbed the ceramic teapot my mom had spent hours painting at the Clayroom in Brookline, and smashed it into the wall. Mae's and Amélie's jaws dropped in unison as my mom gasped in pain.

"What have you done?" my mom cried, rushing to gather the scattered shards.

Tongue-tied and ashamed, I ran out the front door and into the street, my feet bare. I stopped when I was about halfway down the road, turning around to wait for my mom. I knew she was going to come after me.

"Livia! Please come home!" She stood in front of the house in her pajamas and socks. When I remained motionless, she jogged over to me. She grabbed my arm firmly, but I pulled away. "Livia, please," she whispered in desperation. "It's late, and you're not even wearing shoes."

"There's no point!" I exclaimed.

"What do you mean, there's no point?" she asked.

After what I had just done, I could barely believe she was still so loving and open. "In everything," I whimpered. "There's no point in eating, no point in school. I hate my life!"

My mom squeezed me tight. "Oh, honey. It kills me to hear you say those things."

"It kills *you*?" I scoffed as I pushed her away, even though I wanted her to stay close. "*I'm* the one that's miserable!"

"Do you think you're the only one affected by this?" She put her hands on her hips. "Do you even know how scared your sisters are of you? Or that you just destroyed a teapot that meant so much to me?"

I looked down at her fuzzy socks. "I'm sorry." Tears tumbled down my cheeks. "I can't help it! Please don't guilt-trip me!" When panic overcame me, I wasn't *me* anymore; it was as if a devil had possessed my soul and turned all the tables against me and everyone I loved. Despite all the pain I had inflicted on my family, they knew this, too. That's why, during every panic attack, they ended up surrendering...even if that meant surrendering to the devil. When I finally came home that night, instead of having fled, my sisters sat peacefully in their seats.

"We'll eat more mac and cheese," Amélie said. "We don't want to make you upset."

I smiled through my tears. "It's okay, Amie. You don't have to. I'm so sorry. It isn't me when that happens."

"We know it isn't," Amélie replied cheerfully. "We love you, Livia. I hope you always know that."

In moments like those, I didn't know what hurt more: being possessed by the devil or seeing how it affected my family.

That night at dinner was merely one of many similar occurrences. I once chased Mae around the kitchen table for not adding milk to her cereal, running after her like a wild animal would its prey. I hit my mom, bruising her when she didn't have dinner done at a specific time, and cut my dad's expensive leather shoes with scissors when he didn't eat a snack with me. I would test my mother's love by asking how many almonds I always put on my oatmeal, and when she didn't know, I threw the entire bowl on the floor and refused to eat breakfast. In May of 2017, as I lay on my bed crying and screaming in terror after yet another panic attack, I said the words that were long overdue: "I can't do this anymore."

PART 5: SAVING LIVIA

48

FUNDRAISER

Long before I hit rock bottom, I knew something had to change. I was tired, miserable, and lonely, yet unfazed by it at the same time. I knew how skeletal I looked. I knew my heart rate was too low and that daily panic attacks were not normal. Yet all the while, I was convinced it wasn't *that bad*. That evening in May, however, was different. I finally understood that my eating disorder would kill me if I didn't do something about it.

But *what* was I going to do about it? I had been kicked out of the Dutch treatment system because I was "too complex." And even though *sickcare* system would be a more appropriate name for the healthcare system in the US, a person can often find another doctor or center if the first one isn't helpful. In contrast, the Netherlands is so small (the entire country drivable from top to bottom in less than three hours) that certain treatment professionals (including Dr. Vilain) have monopolized the eating disorder space. Once you're out, you're *out*. But I wasn't going to let them kick me out just to prove their case. Instead, I was going to prove I could fully heal – and I would do whatever it took. I couldn't go at this alone though, meaning I had to find a solution not only outside of the Netherlands but entirely outside the box.

"I want to go to a treatment center in America." My parents looked at me wide-eyed. I was fully aware of how ludicrous a suggestion it was, but wasn't my situation already ludicrous? If I had any chance of getting better, I needed it to be so far away that I couldn't walk home or beg my parents to pick me up when things got tough...because things *would* get tough.

"But Livia, we don't have insurance in the US," my mom said. "There's no way we can pay for any kind of treatment outside of Holland." I knew it was true. Healthcare in the United States is insanely expensive, with residential eating disorder treatment costing upwards of $2,000 a day. Paying out of pocket would have left us broke in a matter of months, and then, ironically, we would all starve!

"There has to be another way," I said determinedly. I *had* to recover in the US.

My mom offered me a glimmer of hope. "I'm sure there is. I'll start researching tomorrow." I knew she would figure something out. I knew *we* would figure something out. After all, she was the one who always said, "Why would you pay extra if you can get it for less?"

In the days that followed, my mom and sisters barely got up from behind their laptops.

"How's this one look to you?" Mae would run over and ask, shoving her computer in my face.

"Or this one?" Amélie would butt in.

My mom's desk was covered in papers as she frantically scribbled notes and phone numbers while making international calls.

Of course, I was researching as well. After closely following one of my friends on Instagram who documented her several-month-long journey at Carolina House, I wanted to follow in her footsteps. I googled everything I could find about Carolina House. What answers I couldn't find online, I received directly from her. Among the dozens of treatment centers spread across the States, Carolina House was the clear winner for my specific situation: not only did they have a culinary program along with a no-measurement meal plan system, but Carolina House was the only treatment center we found that accepted adults from age seventeen and up. I wouldn't turn eighteen until November of that year, so any other treatment center would have only allowed me into their adolescent unit. Because most patients in adolescent eating disorder units are admitted against their will, the environment can be discouraging – or in the case of Rintveld, even dangerous. With my commitment to getting better, an equally committed community was a must-have.

With every call between my mom and the admissions office at Carolina House, the likelihood of my admission increased. Eventually the only problem that remained was cost. How on Earth would we afford tens of thousands of dollars of eating disorder treatment without health insurance? My mom's solution: we were going to raise it.

"We're starting a GoFundMe!" my mom exclaimed. "I've seen so many people start donation pages, and they really save lives."

"But it's a *lot* of money. We can't ask that of people."

"People *want* to help, Livia. For you to get better would be priceless."

"Well, I guess we can try." I realized I had nothing to lose at this point.

"I'll create an inspiring video!" Mae exclaimed as she jumped up from her laptop.

"Let's do it then, I guess," I mumbled.

"Well, what are we waiting for?" my mom asked Mae before they playfully raced each other back to their computers.

On May 31, 2017, the campaign "Saving Livia" went live on the GoFundMe website. My mom had spent days writing, deleting, rewriting, and asking me to proofread the lengthy story that would lay the foundation of our crowdfunding campaign. In the meantime, Mae created a video version of the story. She used the song "One Foot in Front of the Other," which my mom wrote for me, for the audio. The production was so moving even *I* cried while watching it. You can still view the campaign and video today at www.gofundme.com/f/SavingLivia.

After sharing the campaign on every social media platform we used, donations started trickling in. Our friends shared it with their friends, who shared it with their friends. People were calling us day and night to say, "I keep checking the crowdfunding campaign. This is so exciting!" Within two weeks of its launch, we had raised $50,000. I couldn't believe it. I was really going to Carolina House!

49

TAKING FLIGHT

On June 29, a Thursday, I flew with my mom to North Carolina. My admission to Carolina House was scheduled for the following Monday.

"Rutger!" my mom exclaimed when my uncle picked us up from Raleigh-Durham International Airport. That was yet another reason Carolina House had been our top choice: it was located in Durham, just short of a thirty-minute drive from where my aunt and uncle lived in Raleigh. With no other family in the US, what were the odds? I still believe today that it was written in the stars.

"Hi, Livia!" Rutger said in his familiar and gentle voice. I could sense his hesitancy as he hugged me, not wanting to squeeze too tight out of fear he might crush me. "How was your flight?"

"Sooo stressful," my mom said before I could open my mouth. Based on the blood tests I had gotten at the hospital the week prior, all of my markers indicated that flying – let alone internationally – was incredibly dangerous. But we made it, and I was going to spread my wings.

The weekend was filled with equal parts excitement and terror. I struggled immensely with eating at my aunt and uncle's house. The new environment, paired with the anticipation of my upcoming admission, left me in a state of paralysis.

"Hang in there." My mom rubbed my back at the dining table. I knew she was saying it to herself, too.

"What if I don't get better?" Not only was there pressure to recover for myself and my family, but now I was also doing it for the hundreds of people who donated to my crowdfunding campaign. "What if all those people wasted their money on me?"

"You will get better, honey. I just know it," my mom said. But I could hear a hint of uncertainty in her voice. This was just as much a leap of faith for her (and for the rest of my family and for the generous donors) as it was for me. Nothing was guaranteed, and everything depended on my actions.

For all these years, I had built my life around certainty. I had tried to make every aspect predictable, avoiding change at all costs. I had lied, stolen, and manipulated, all to ensure I would stay in control. But it was a false sense of control. The more I tried to control everything around me, the more those things controlled *me*. Now, it was time to let go. It was time to trust. It was time to surrender. After all, what was the alternative?

50

CAROLINA HOUSE

On the morning of July 3, my mom and I pulled into the driveway of 176 Lassiter Homestead Road. What stood before us was a large yellow house surrounded by freshly trimmed greenery. I could already imagine myself sitting in one of the big rocking chairs that lined the porch, journaling in the notebook my sister had given me on the day I left.

"Hi there! Are you Livia?" a woman asked with a bright smile.

"Yes," I replied quietly.

My mom asked, "Are you Harper? I recognize your voice from the phone!"

"Yes, I am!" Harper responded cheerfully. "We're so glad this all worked out for Livia. We've never had someone fly in all the way from Europe before!"

"It was quite the trip," my mom admitted, "but we are so grateful for this opportunity. Livia is so courageous and committed to getting better."

"That's all that matters, right? Come on over to the admissions office." She directed us towards a mini version of the main house. "Oh, and let me help you with that!" She grabbed the handle of my huge purple suitcase. I bit my tongue to prevent myself from letting out an angry *NO!* I hated it when people touched my things without asking, even if they were trying to help.

"Thanks," I said, but I didn't mean it.

Harper and my mom reviewed medical papers as I stared at the clock, tapping my feet to the beat of its ticking. When they were finally done, a blond woman came in.

"Hi, it's so nice to meet you!" Colette, the clinical director, said. "One of the most important values here at Carolina House is creating a loving and supportive environment for all patients. I want to share what you can expect while being here, but I also want to be very clear on what we expect from you." Colette spoke earnestly, but the soft edge of her voice comforted me. I nodded in understanding as Colette explained the house rules and handed me the weekly schedule. The color-blocked table was so densely packed that it made my mind tumble. I automatically pulled the page away from my face to prevent a dizzy spell. When Colette noticed, she gently took back the piece of paper and reassured me: "I know it's a lot of information. You'll have time to look over it and ask the RPAs any questions later."

"RPA?" I asked.

Colette smiled. "RPA is short for residential patient assistant. They'll explain more abbreviations on this schedule, such as DBT and CBT, and they also assist during mealtimes. If you ever need anything during your stay, just think of the RPAs as your go-to people!" she said. "Learning to communicate effectively is a vital part of treatment, which is why we expect you to be open and honest at all times." Colette continued sharing the ins and outs of residential as I nodded up and down. "And when your treatment team believes you are ready to step down, they'll share more information about PHP and IOP. But I think this is enough information for now, huh?" She grinned.

"Yes, and I'll be stepping down to PHP in four weeks," I reminded her.

Harper and Colette looked at each other, then at me, and finally at my mom.

"Did I miss something?" Colette asked.

"I'm only staying in residential for four weeks. That's the agreement." I looked at Harper, and when she appeared clueless, I looked to my mom. "Didn't you tell them?"

My mom bit her lip.

"Mom!" I said with a slight raise of my voice. "Remember what we agreed on? The only reason I came all this way is because I know I'm going to be here for four weeks!"

Colette, suddenly seeming to grasp the situation, interrupted the tension building between my mom and me. "There's no way of telling how long someone needs to be in treatment," she said. "Recovery will take as long as it needs to, and that duration is unique to each individual."

"But we're paying out of pocket. We only have enough money for four weeks anyways!" I hoped this would make them realize my ultimatum was not just a desire but a fact.

"I'm hoping to get Livia insurance," my mom stated, avoiding my gaze. She was twiddling her thumbs. "Her uncle – my brother – um, he, um, lives in Raleigh, and um, I'm going to get her covered through Obamacare as she now has an address here and can apply for insurance as a US resident."

How had she failed to tell me this? Even though I already knew the answer, I asked anyway: "Why didn't you tell me?"

"I didn't want to overwhelm you, Livia," she uttered apologetically, though I knew she wasn't the least bit sorry. "You were so stuck on the four weeks, I was afraid–"

"Afraid of what? Afraid that I wouldn't come here? Afraid that I'd disappoint everyone who donated?" I yelled. I felt betrayed and wanted to disappear from the sight of the six eyes that stared at me. Colette put her hand on my knee. The only reason I didn't pull away was because I wanted to maintain the slightest sliver of a positive first impression.

"Livia, I know this feels so scary. Recovery from your eating disorder *is* so scary. And that's what makes it all the braver that you came all this way to fight," Colette said. She was right. I hadn't come this far only to go this far. If any of this was going to work, I had to surrender – not only to treatment but to the entire journey – regardless of how long that journey would take.

51

KITCHEN RULES

The moment I stepped foot in Carolina House, I was guided into the kitchen by an RPA named Zari. Three women I gathered were other RPAs were setting out bins of food, all labeled with serving sizes and exchanges. They were all wearing baseball caps. This was one of the first rules I learned about the Carolina House kitchen: you could only enter with your hair up and covered.

"It's part of our hygiene policy," explained Regina, the culinary director, as she waltzed into the kitchen with her arms full of mixing bowls. "No one wants hair in their food!"

This rule wasn't anywhere in the pre-admission documents Harper had sent us, which made me angry. First, they deceived me about the duration of my stay, and now this? If they had forgotten something as simple as putting a hat on the packing list, what other surprises were bound to come my way?

Zari pulled out a sheet of paper: my meal plan. "For lunch, you'll be plating 2 starches, 1 dairy, 1 fruit, 2 proteins, 2 fats, and 1 vegetable," she said, as if it was the most natural way to speak about food.

"Where is everyone else?" I wondered why I was the only one making lunch.

"They're still in group," Zari replied. "You're scheduled for a medical evaluation at 12:30, so you'll eat in the nurse's office."

The large clock on the wall read 12:20. My heart started to race. "But that's in ten minutes!" I exclaimed. "I need more time to prepare my food."

"You only get ten minutes," Zari responded.

Shaking, I mentally noted kitchen rule number two: maximum of ten minutes to plate food.

After she emptied her arms, Regina instructed me on the plating process. "The serving sizes are noted on the items." She pointed to several different pieces of masking tape on which numbers had been inscribed with permanent marker. "You need two starches, so you can have potatoes, rice–" She tapped the corresponding plastic bins. "Or you can do two slices of bread and make a sandwich with the deli meats and cheeses over there," she said, gesturing to the counter lined with smaller bins.

"This asparagus looks good," I said. I couldn't remember the last time I had eaten roasted vegetables.

"That can count as your veggie! I'm sure it will go well with potatoes and this chicken piccata." She motioned towards another bin. I carefully spooned the rosemary-roasted potatoes onto my plate. "Oh, you'll need a couple more big spoonfuls of that," she said as she looked over my shoulder. Suddenly, the night of the baked potato flashed into my mind. *A couple more big spoonfuls?* I added a few more potatoes onto the plate and looked up at her for approval. "Keeeeep going." I added another potato wedge and looked up at her again. "I'll say stop," she said.

With every new spoonful, my heart skipped a beat. *Should I have gone for the rice? Would that have been less? Or perhaps the sandwich would have been more manageable?*

"Can I make a sandwich instead?" I asked, fearful that my stomach was too small to hold the pile of potatoes on my plate.

"Nope, you've already plated this," she said. "You can add sour cream to your potatoes for your fats."

I was utterly confused. "But aren't the asparagus and potatoes roasted?" I emphasized, "With oil?"

"Yep!" she replied.

"Isn't oil a fat?"

"It's not enough oil to count as an exchange," Regina said. "The asparagus counts as a vegetable, and the potatoes count as starches." She pointed to the labels on both bins to remind me. *I'm not blind.* I rolled my eyes. I should have gone for the sandwich.

As soon as I finished creating my meal of roasted potatoes and asparagus, chicken piccata, sour cream, a glass of milk, and a bowl of watermelon bigger than my head, I gulped. I couldn't remember the last time I had eaten a meal this big. Nevertheless, the plate on the counter before me was my very first victory at Carolina House: I had made a meal without measuring anything.

Sitting in the nurse's office while the nurse asked me questions, I repeated the phrase my mom had used when I was faced with that baked potato in the hospital. *One bite at a time.* That's how I was going to get through this meal, as well as every meal that followed.

To my surprise, it worked. Within twenty minutes, I had finished everything – *everything!* My second victory at Carolina House.

52

JUST IN CASE

For the remainder of the afternoon, I went in and out of different rooms at Carolina House. I met my therapist, my nutritionist, and my psychiatrist and received a tour of the house. In the meantime, two RPAs had gone through my suitcase and meticulously listed every single one of my belongings. From five sweatshirts to ten pairs of underwear, everything was listed in a table with the item name and corresponding quantity. Also on that list were my food scale and measuring cups. I knew about Carolina House's no-measurement policy. After all, I had just made my entire lunch by "eyeballing" serving sizes, just as I would make every meal and snack thereafter. I knew they wouldn't allow me to use measuring cups, let alone my own food scale. Still, I had brought it with me *just in case*.

As with everything in my life for as long as I could remember, those three words summed up my relationship with the food scale. *Just. In. Case.* It started innocently (doesn't every eating disorder behavior?) as a means to gain more control over my intake. But before I knew it, the food scale controlled *me*. I would often fiddle with the tare button for so long that I distrusted the scale's accuracy, forcing me to start the weighing process all over again. I was sure the amount I had weighed prior would still be the same, but I could never be *too* sure. So I started again – *just in case*.

I also kept spare batteries in the drawer alongside the scale at all times, *just in case* the scale suddenly turned off and I panicked.

But at one point, spare batteries were no longer enough. What if the food scale itself were to break down? What if it wasn't the batteries but the scale that had come to the end of its life? There was no way of telling when that day would be, which is why I purchased a second food scale. *Just in case.*

As I stood in my new bedroom and stared at the food scale and the measuring cups zipped away in a plastic bag, my whole body went numb. I didn't know what I would do without those objects, which had both given me control over my life and yet controlled my life at the same time. But whether or not I knew how to live without them, that choice was no longer mine to make. As one of the RPAs carefully placed my clothes and my other "allowed" belongings back into my suitcase, the second RPA grabbed the sealed bag and disappeared into a locked storage room.

53

CONTROL

S nack time was at 3:30 p.m. Instead of my usual protein bar, I ate Oreos with a big spoonful of peanut butter. Although my brain was scolding me for the lack of protein, my mouth was mesmerized by the crunchy, buttery, creamy deliciousness of this *Parent Trap*–inspired snack. Real Oreos were *so* much better than Oreo-flavored protein bars – I had just never allowed myself to admit it.

As I munched on my cookies, the women seated at my table introduced themselves. The dining room had four round dining tables in total, each named after a different flower. I was assigned a seat at the Roses table on the first day but would eventually sit in almost every chair at the Sunflowers, Daisies, and Orchids tables throughout my stay. The flower system was also how kitchen plating was organized. Each week, the entire group of Carolina House patients would be divided into smaller groups and each patient assigned to a flower and a new seat. When it was time to prepare food, an RPA would call out one of the flowers, and the clock would start counting down from ten minutes. Once a group was seated, they'd have thirty minutes to finish their meal.

Although the timing rules around food helped me relearn proper pacing, they were also one of the greatest stressors during my time in treatment. I have always felt tension under pressure, another reason I believe school was so difficult for me. Even if I knew I could hit a specific deadline or complete a task within the assigned time frame, the very fact of there *being* a deadline made me obsess about the assignment until I'd completed it. To protect myself from endless rumination, I often started projects way ahead of time – which manifested in my food preparation as well.

When I was still living at home, I would wake up super early just so I could prepare food in a kitchen that hadn't already been used by other family members. (By then, Mae and Amélie were turning into young women and would no longer allow me to pack their lunchboxes.) More specifically, I had to ensure no one had touched any of my things in the kitchen. I had my very own shelf in the fridge, along with a separate drawer with my own bowls, plates, and cutlery. And the majority of the pantry was dedicated to my collection of protein powders, nutrition bars, and any other items I believed would make me "healthy."

One Saturday afternoon, when Mae was about sixteen years old, I peeked behind the door when her friends were over. My mom was away for the weekend, and I knew they were conjuring up a plan to throw a party with alcohol. "We'll be responsible, Livia," Mae told me. But I wasn't worried about that. To communicate this to Mae without saying it aloud while her friends were there, all I needed to do was point to the fridge. "We won't touch your food – promise," she reassured me. I wanted to believe her. I *tried* to believe her. But that night, after I had already gone to bed, as she was hosting the party downstairs, her friends touched my food. The next morning, I came down to prepare my breakfast only to realize the drunken teenagers had raided all of the fresh berries and cheese I had purchased at the farmers' market the day before.

"You said they weren't going to touch anything!" I yelled as I shook Mae and her sleepy friends awake. Her bedroom reeked of beer, and I was well aware they had gone to bed mere hours before.

Mae rubbed her eyes. "What are you talking about?"

"My strawberries and blueberries are all gone! And the pack of cheese I bought for the week is open!"

"I'm so sorry, Livia. I'll buy you new berries and cheese at the grocery store later today."

"No!" I screamed. "I need it from the farmers' market, and the farmers' market is only open on Saturday! You guys totally messed up my life!"

The panic attack that followed the raiding was a wake-up call – not only for me but also for my sisters and their friends. After that morning, no one came near my items in the kitchen. But I still couldn't trust them; I had learned that lesson the hard way.

At Carolina House, I no longer had any of this control, or even the illusion of it. I couldn't start making my food before everyone else. Instead, I would sit on the couch, trembling until my flower was called. If I was lucky, my flower would be called first, as the first group to enter the kitchen always got first dibs on the food. But I couldn't always be part of the first group – which meant I had to accept eating a different fruit if the prior patients had raided the berries.

The same limitations applied to seating arrangements. Back home, I had *my* seat at the kitchen table. My seat became my seat the moment I first sat there, and whoever dared challenge me to sit somewhere else was in deep trouble. If we had people over and someone sat in my seat, I would refuse to dine unless my mom told them to move. At Carolina House, I didn't have my own consistent seat, and the unpredictability of where I would be assigned next often kept me up at night. When I voiced my concerns to my therapist, all she said was "I know change is hard, but part of recovery is learning to be flexible."

54

THE FIRST SUPPER

While I acquainted myself with what would be my home for probably more than four weeks, my mom went to Target to buy me a baseball cap, along with some new sweatshirts and pants (for all my UK readers, pants are trousers, not underwear!). Something else Carolina House had failed to mention on the pre-admission documents was the prohibition of wearing anything with hoods or pockets in the kitchen or at the table.

"I'm not going to hide food!" I exclaimed when Zari told me to take off my hoodie before snack time. At Carolina House, I had sworn to surrender and had no intentions of manipulating anyone or anything anymore.

"It's the rules," she replied. *Where had I heard that one before?* Despite my long-standing belief that "it's just the rules" is never a valid explanation, I didn't want to cause a stir. So I took off the hoodie and mentally scribbled kitchen rule number three in my brain.

Around 6:00 p.m., my anxiety began to rise. My mom and I were sitting in adjacent rocking chairs, soaking up the evening sun. I squeezed her hand tight as I treasured the moment – our last moment together for a while. As she went on about how proud she was of me, how I would be missed, and most of all, how I wasn't alone, I was distracted by the overpowering smell of meat wafting from the kitchen.

"What time is dinner?" I asked a girl reading in a nearby rocking chair.

"It's at six," Vera replied, looking at her watch. "It seems they're running a bit late."

"Thanks." I pulled my hand from my mom's. I held both sides of the chair tightly, rocking back and forth in an effort to calm myself down.

"Honey, are you okay?" my mom asked.

"The meat smell," I let out shakily. I didn't have to explain further. I hadn't eaten any meat other than chicken or turkey in years, and we both knew I wasn't about to change that. "Can we please go inside?" I needed to know what was being made and what the vegetarian alternative was.

"Of course." We stood up in unison.

I walked up to Zari and asked, "What's for dinner?"

"Pork tacos," she responded.

I froze. "What's the vegetarian option?" I remembered the section about dietary preferences in the pre-admission documents.

"There is no vegetarian option," Zari said. "Here at Carolina House, we encourage eating all foods."

"But I specified it on the form," I said. "I don't eat meat!"

"If you don't eat what is plated, there's always the option to supplement. But we do not accommodate vegetarianism because there's no way of telling if it stems from the eating disorder," Zari said.

I looked at my mom with the same desperate eyes I had looked at her with for years. But just as on the night of the baked potato, we both knew she couldn't save me. I trembled, ambivalently pondering my options like a broken record. I could eat the pork or choose to supplement – but neither was a valid option! There had to be a way out of this.

"Please, there has to be another way," I begged. "I don't eat pork. I'll eat chicken or turkey–"

Zari interrupted. "It's either the plated meal or the supplement. Sorry, but I really have to call dinner now." She stepped away to gather the patients, who were scattered across the living room and on the porch.

"What am I going to do?" I asked my mom, tears filling my eyes. "I want to eat everything, but this is so unfair! Why didn't they say they didn't allow vegetarianism? It said it on the forms! This just doesn't make any *sense*!" My words could barely keep up with my racing thoughts.

"Livia." My mom put her hand on my shoulder. My eyes darted back and forth between the number of plates Regina and the RPAs carried from the kitchen counter to the dining tables. White tortillas. Pulled pork. Sour cream. SOUR CREAM!? It couldn't be. I already had sour cream at lunch!

"I'm going to do it," I said. I took a deep breath and patted my eyes dry with the sleeve of my new sweatshirt.

"You're going to drink the Ensure?" my mom asked, knowing that everything about this meal went against every rule I had abided by for the past six years.

"No. I'm going to eat the meal. All of it," I replied determinedly. Doing so may have gone against my eating disorder's rules, but rules alone were never a valid enough reason.

As difficult as that plate of pork tacos seemed, what ended up being much harder than eating dinner was saying goodbye to my mom. Now that I didn't know how long I would be here, I couldn't say, "See you in four weeks!" The uncertainty left my stomach doing backflips.

"I love you sooo much!" my mom said as she kissed me what felt like a million times.

"I love you sooo much too!" I began to sob. In just a few days, she'd be on a plane back to Holland – over 4,000 miles away. I forced the thought into the back of my mind. I glanced at the clock. 6:12 p.m.

"It's time to say your final goodbyes," Zari said.

"I know, I know," I muttered through my tears. I hugged my mom tight, never wanting to let go.

"You're going to do great, Livia," she whispered. "Me and Mae and Amélie and Papa will be cheering you on every day. We all love you so much. Never forget that."

"I know," I whispered again as we both pulled out of the hug. I immediately jumped into my mom's arms to give her one last squeeze. The very last one.

I took my seat at the Roses table and waved out the window as she pulled the car out of the driveway. I kept waving as the moving vehicle disappeared into the distance. Then I turned to face my current mission: tackle these tacos.

One bite at a time was how the meal started, like so many had before. I couldn't believe I was actually eating pork, yet at the same time, I could. I had committed to this journey and everything it would entail, including the moments I didn't want to fathom beforehand. As I sat at the table, surrounded by women who were all smiling and eating and talking, I felt empowered. For the first time, I didn't feel alone. We were all afraid, all worried about the next challenge, and all filled with racing thoughts about the food that sat before us. But more importantly, we were all fighters. We were sick and tired of being sick and tired, and we sat here together because we had decided to do something about it.

In just twenty minutes, I had polished off my plate. When we went around the table sharing our thoughts and feelings about the meal while the RPA took notes, I was surprised by the words that came out of my mouth: "I really enjoyed this meal and am feeling really good!" It was the truth. Even though my stomach was stuffed, I was *satisfied*. I didn't dream about eating another whole plate, nor was I already thinking about my night snack. My tummy was happy – and so was I.

55

HOT AS HELL

My first two nights at Carolina House were a living hell. It was the middle of summer in North Carolina, meaning both the days and nights were *hot*. Without air-conditioning, you were almost guaranteed a lack of sleep...which is exactly what happened to me.

The second floor of the house consisted of a long hallway with four large bedrooms on each side. New patients would start their journey at the beginning of the hallway, close to the nighttime RPA's desk. When a longtime patient at the far end of the hallway was discharged, the rest of the group would "move up" to the next bed. Everyone's goal was to get to the rooms at the end of the hallway, since they had big windows and private bathrooms galore.

As a new patient, I was assigned to the room adjacent to the RPA desk. More like a storage closet than a room, it contained only a tiny ceiling window. When I noticed that the next room over – a room with windows and air-conditioning – had two free beds, I asked if I could sleep there.

"New patients start at the top of the hallway," the RPA replied.

"But there's no one in the second room, and not having windows makes me feel claustrophobic."

"Sorry, but these are the rules. Nothing I can do about it," she said coldly.

Here we go again with the rules.

"I get that it's a rule" – I chose my words wisely – "but this rule doesn't have any reasoning behind it. If there are two free beds and I can be so much more comfortable in that other room, isn't it worth considering allowing me to sleep there?"

"I don't do the room arrangements," she said. "You'll have to talk to your therapist tomorrow."

Tomorrow?

"But what about *tonight*? There are literally two free beds right there!" I exclaimed, pointing to the inside of the room.

The RPA looked at her watch. "No can do, Livia. Besides, it's time for lights-out. I'm not discussing this anymore, so please go to your room now."

I sighed in frustration and lugged myself towards the closet of a room. Five minutes after creeping into bed, however, I realized this wasn't going to work. I got up to speak to the RPA once more.

"It's way too hot in there!" I exclaimed. "I can't sleep in this heat. Please, can I sleep in the other room? I need air-conditioning!"

Due to its lack of windows, the tiny room didn't have an air conditioner like all of the rooms further down. I had always been hypersensitive to temperature, and sleeping in the heat was my ultimate nightmare.

The nurse rolled her eyes as she swiveled in her chair to face me. "Livia, I'm sorry the room isn't up to your standards. But like I said, there's nothing I can do."

Nothing you can do? "But there *is* something you can do! You can just allow me to sleep in that room!" I said loudly, gesturing to the other room once again. By this point, I was more frustrated with the RPA's lack of logic than the situation itself.

"I'm going to repeat myself one last time," she retorted. "You're not switching rooms tonight. You can talk to your therapist about this when she comes in tomorrow, but for now, you have to sleep in there." She waved towards the tiny room.

A fiery rage coursed through my visible veins, but what could I do? I was utterly powerless.

56

INDEPENDENCE DAY

When the alarm went off at 6:30 the next morning, I was already exhausted by a day that had barely begun. I had never been a morning person, especially after not sleeping. Still, I forced myself out of bed and into the shower. It was the Fourth of July, and I wasn't going to let this setback ruin my independence day.

The Fourth of July never meant much to me. Growing up in a culturally Dutch household, American Independence Day was never really taken to heart. Sure, we attended parties with patriotic-themed foods, but this made the day all the more dreadful. Besides the disruption of my usual routine, the fireworks and cheering crowds amplified my disquietude. Just like New Year's Eve, this American national holiday was always just another day to get through.

That all changed on July 4, 2017. It was my first full day at Carolina House, meaning my first full day of committing to independence from my eating disorder. I was tired, frustrated, and invalidated by my experiences there so far, but I knew this journey wasn't going to be easy. As had been done by the United States of America in 1776, I decided to declare my independence. (Isn't it ironic that Carolina House's address number is 176?) To say my first full day at Carolina House was a challenge would be an understatement. Instead of writing about my experience anew, I have decided to share my completely raw and unfiltered journal entry from July 4, 2017:

Just finished lunch and I'm feeling guilty as hell. I was shocked when I discovered what we were having: burgers + hot dogs. I thought we were going to get to choose one or the other but nope — we had to have a hamburger with a white bun AND a hot dog with a white bun! I get the whole "4th of July spirit," but these servings are seriously ridiculous. And if that wasn't enough fat and carbs, I ALSO had to have corn on the cob and watermelon on the side. The RPA said it counted as veggies but WTF, since when are corn and watermelon vegetables??? This whole system is sooo inconsistent! I wanted to do push-ups in the bathroom so badly while waiting to be called into the kitchen, but didn't do it because I don't want to get in trouble. I just sat there, anxiously waiting to get up and make that huge American plate of crap. I ate it all though. I need to rest and I need to fuel. It's the only way to get my life back.

Those early journal entries from five years ago reveal that my thoughts at the time were astoundingly food- and exercise-focused. I wrote in my journal every day at Carolina House, never missing a day since my first entry on July 3, 2017. Honestly, I don't think I would have stayed the least bit sane were it not for adopting this habit! I wrote when I was proud and wanted to document a victory, but also when I was angry and would rather have ripped out all the pages. I wrote as I peacefully sat in bed at night, but also when I was shaking with anxiety and the results looked more like scribbles than written words. Journaling allowed me to express myself without judgment, a luxury I had never permitted myself before.

My journal habits have evolved over time, and it's remarkable how massively my mindset has shifted since that day in 2017. Then, I had something to say about food daily, and some entries go on for pages about how difficult I found it to rest. At the time of writing this book, my journal habits include practicing daily gratitude. Just as I attribute my sanity to keeping a journal during my time at Carolina House, I attribute my abundance mindset to a nonnegotiable gratitude practice. In the words of Greg McKeown, one of my favorite authors and the mastermind behind the books *Essentialism* and *Effortless*:

When you focus on what you lack, you lose what you have.

When you focus on what you have, you get what you lack.

When I focused on my lack of control at Carolina House, I became frustrated and lost sight of the opportunity, which was choosing my life. When I shifted my focus to reclaiming my health, I gained just that.

57

HOMESICK

It wasn't long before I started begging my parents to pick me up. Considering the intensity of our residency at Carolina House, we had a daily block of "quiet time" from 1:30 to 3:00 in the afternoon. Most patients would either read or nap, but I received a special pass to call my family during this time. All patient phones and other electronics were locked in a box until "phone time" from 7:30 to 9:00 p.m., but due to the time difference (the Netherlands is six hours ahead of North Carolina), waiting until then, when my family was sound asleep, was obviously not an option.

Similar to how I vented in my journal each day, I poured my heart and soul into these lengthy phone calls. I had never been so distanced from my family before, let alone by an *entire ocean*.

"I miss you so much," I would cry for most of the conversation.

"We miss you too, Livia!" my family would exclaim over the phone. "What's it like there?"

I told them how I had already eaten every "unhealthy" food imaginable and how quickly the nutritionist was increasing my meal plan. I told them how much butter I put on my toast and how much sugar went into the cookies I made during culinary class. I told them how I hadn't exercised at all. Almost every time, I ended my victorious statements with the question "Are you proud of me?"

At the beginning of my recovery journey, I constantly searched for external validation. I shared all my struggles around food and exercise in an attempt to make them tangible. I believed that I was doing the right thing as long as my family was proud of me. I needed permission from others to eat and rest because it still felt wrong to grant myself that permission. And because it continued to feel wrong even with that external validation, I wanted an out.

"I've made so much progress here!" I told them after the first week. "I'm definitely in such a better place and I'm ready to come home."

Silence.

"Didn't you hear about all the foods I've eaten? And I've broken my exercise routine!" I emphasized, in support of my argument.

Silence.

"Hello?" I was tormented by the unknowingness of what was happening on the other end of the line.

"We hear you," my mom started, clearly trying to buy time as she sought her words, "and we're so beyond proud of everything you've achieved so far!"

"Yes, we are so proud of you, Livia," my dad chimed in.

"But, honey, it's not yet time to come home. You've only been there for one week," my mom said cautiously.

"But I already told you, I'm doing so well! This is *my* path and *my* recovery. This is only going to work if *I* get to make the decisions!"

"How about we talk about this in family therapy tomorrow?" my mom asked.

"Why?" I demanded. But I already knew the answer. She didn't want to say anything that had the potential to be misaligned with my treatment team's recommendations. She knew I would use any loophole to call them out on their inconsistencies.

"We just want what's best for you," my dad said.

"What's *best* for me is that *I* get to make the decisions!" I went on. "Remember what happened the last time you forced me into treatment?"

Silence.

Feeling utterly powerless in such moments, I ended many of our early phone calls by abruptly hanging up. What followed was a nagging guilt – one that could only be relieved when I would apologize twenty-four hours later and beg to "start over."

"Of course, we can start over," my family would respond in relief. "We know this is sooo hard for you, Livia!" each of them would say in their own way. "We're so proud that you keep on fighting every day."

And as long as they kept being proud of me, I could keep holding on.

58

HEALTH DRAWER

That concept of needing to be certain that my family was proud of me did not begin anew in the US. It was already an established habit by then.

When I flew to the States at the end of June, one of the hardest things to leave behind was the stockpile of protein powders and bars in my "health" drawer. I had a dozen different tubs of protein powder that I relied on religiously. I used protein powder in my morning oatmeal, in my pancakes, to make filling shakes after my light lunch, and most importantly, to make my nightly bowl of "protein fluff."

I first discovered the concept of protein fluff through one of the fitness accounts I followed on Instagram. They claimed it was the perfect recipe because it was both low-calorie and high-volume. At the time, I believed it was *indeed* the perfect recipe. If you used a specific flavor of protein powder, such as vanilla, chocolate, or – if you wanted to get extra fancy – birthday cake or salted caramel, it would taste like ice cream! Exhilarated by this inspiration, I convinced my mom to order protein powder for me.

"Why can't you just eat real food?" she asked when I first sent her the link to a supplements website.

"I already eat real food. These shakes are just to help me gain weight!" I casually omitted the fact that I didn't actually want them to help me gain weight. Of course, my mom would do anything to support weight gain, which is why she ordered with a single click.

Since incorporating protein powders into my diet, I came up with various creations and perfected my own recipe for protein fluff. Thanks to the loud whirring of the blender, my family dreaded this time of day as much as I treasured it. It took me almost forty-five minutes each evening to blend up the voluminous concoction, and another fifteen to gather my toppings and the rest of the food I'd spent the entire day looking forward to. At night, I was able to eat without guilt. At night, I was able to bask in the pleasure of eating beyond fullness and indulge in the foods that were off-limits throughout the day. Dates, nut butter, chocolate, cookies...that's how I topped my two heaping bowls of airy protein. When my fluff was ready, I would briefly place it in the freezer to make it resemble ice cream, then demand that my whole family watch while I broke the layer that had hardened on top.

"Look, look, look!" I would exclaim in childlike excitement.

"Come on, everyone. Livia's about to break the ice!" my mom would announce. My sisters recognized those keywords and gathered around me and my nighttime feast.

"Ooh," they would coo in an exaggerated tone as I struck the icy fluff with my spoon.

"Look how much this is!" I would motion towards the two bowls. "Are you guys proud of me?"

Even though they knew as well as I did that the volume was no indication of the calorie content, they would smile synthetically and say, "We are so proud of you." Only after I heard those words could I start my feast.

One evening, when my mom was intensely working on completing a work deadline, I noticed her eyes wandering during the icebreaker moment.

"You didn't look!" I cried.

"I'm sorry, honey. Can you do it again?" she asked hurriedly.

"I can't! It's already melting now. It's too late!"

"Livia, Livia, Livia, it's not too late. Just do it again with the other bowl, okay?" Mae said encouragingly.

"You don't understand! It has to be perfect! And Mama messed it all up!"

"Livia, again, I'm so sorry. Work has been crazy. I'm looking now, I promise." My mom opened her eyes wide to emphasize her attentiveness. But in my mind, it *was* too late. I truly believed my mom *had* messed it all up. I spiraled into a panic, throwing my half-melted bowl of protein fluff onto the floor and collapsing into a ball alongside it. My mom sighed and rushed over, holding me tightly in her arms. "I'm so sorry, Livia. If I had known–"

"Can you please buy me more bars now that I have to pay the price for this?" I pleaded through my tears.

"Bars?" my mom asked in confusion. "What do bars have to do with this?"

"Because you didn't look, I now have to pay the price! I had to endure another panic attack because you messed everything up!" I cried. "Buying me bars will make up for it."

Not wanting to escalate my irrationality any further, my mom nodded in agreement. "Send me the links, okay?" She winked. And just like that, my panic went from one hundred to zero.

Over time, my supplement collection accumulated to hoarder status. I had every flavor of protein powder imaginable, along with hundreds of artificially sweetened protein bars. And even while I was seriously attempting recovery at Carolina House, I knew my health drawer was waiting at home for my return.

59

FAMILY THERAPY

Although it wasn't half as bad as what my family had endured with Hedwig at Rintveld Clinic, family therapy sessions at Carolina House were always full of tension. I would sit on the couch across from Brittany, who would dial my parents' number into the phone placed on the chair next to her.

"Just pretend your parents are sitting in this chair." Brittany would tap the seat hosting the phone.

It was the stupidest thing ever. More than that though, it was strange. Engaging in family therapy without my family being physically present created a disconnect that went beyond the geographical distance, but calling them was as connected as we were going to get.

In my entire thirteen weeks Carolina House's residential, I can vividly remember only one family therapy session: the one in which we discussed my food drawer. During that call, my mom raised the question of what to do with all my supplements before I returned home.

Shit, I thought as soon as she broached the subject. But Brittany didn't seem as surprised as I was.

"When you return home, we want your environment to set you up for continued recovery success," Brittany started. I nodded, even as I mentally prepared myself for the worst. Why did everyone on my treatment team use this tactic? By starting with a positive sentence, they believed they could somehow dampen news they knew would upset me. "That's why I've been in touch with your mom and Julie about your supplement collection."

"What does Julie have to do with this?" I spoke to the phone in the chair beside Brittany. Julie was my nutritionist at Carolina House.

"I believe she can make the best assessment of which food items are appropriate for you when you come home," my mom said. "That's why I sent your team photos of the drawer."

My chest tightened. I wanted to scream at my mom for sending pictures of my things without my permission, but I withheld that emotion. I was well aware that my supplements collection at home was extensive, which is why I didn't want anyone to know about it. Yet here I was, feeling naked and exposed. *What did my treatment team think? That I was a hoarder? That I was sicker than I truly was? Would they keep me here longer now?* Fearful thoughts swirled around my head until I finally blurted out, "Please don't do anything with my food!"

"Livia" – Brittany leaned forward in her chair – "Julie and the rest of the team think it's best that you don't have triggering foods around when you return. Like I said, we all want you to succeed in recovery."

"They're not triggering!" I exclaimed. "I love my supplements. They make everything taste better!" Half of that statement was true. I did love adding protein powder to my oats and pancakes because it gave them a fluffier texture and sweeter flavor. I did love many of the bars in that drawer. But after eating real ice cream and cookies and cake, I would be lying to myself if I argued that my protein fluff and dessert-flavored protein bars could replace the real deal.

"Do *you* think they taste better, or is your eating disorder in the room with us?" Brittany asked as she tilted her head to the side. This was another remark I despised – when people acted as if my eating disorder was some sort of ghost that floated around my head and could be batted off whenever I felt like it.

"It's truly *me* who likes them! Besides, taking things away without allowing me to make the choice won't help me recover. Force doesn't work!"

Brittany said, "Well, Julie also gave her feedback on the products that *can* be kept." It became clear that the decision about what to do with my supplements had already been made before the session had even started.

"The date and nut bars are fine," my mom said, "but all those protein bars with fake sugars in them, and the powders – Julie believes they won't support a recovery mindset."

Yet again, I was placed in a position of utter powerlessness. The "coalition" had decided what was best for me. After years of finding myself in that position, I was angry and afraid that this treatment would traumatize me just as every prior treatment had. The only difference was that now I actually *wanted* to get better. I had promised to surrender and trust the process this time, so I no longer projected my anger by rebelling or manipulating. Right after family therapy that day, I grabbed my journal and allowed my thoughts to manifest into words:

> *I am so pissed off right now. Mommy sent pictures of my bar drawer to Julie, and in family therapy, Brittany told me that Mommy has to get rid of almost all my bars and powders!!! She says it's the ED that wants to keep them, but it's ME. It's one of the reasons I'm so excited to get discharged, so that I can finally eat my own food again and not the greasy and sugary crap they serve me every day!*

But at the same time, I know it's really important for me to eat all these things. The truth is, I don't know what is me or the ED sometimes. I thought I wanted to leave after 4 weeks, but it's the ED that wants to leave so I can weigh food, choose the healthy options, exercise etc. If I go home now, everything will go back to the way it was. I do need more time here and I need to trust whatever my treatment team recommends. It's going to be uncomfortable, but if it was comfortable, it wouldn't be recovery.

Over time, my ability to shift my mindset from a place of anger and resentment to a place of gratitude and trust improved. Journaling allowed me to make my thoughts tangible, which ultimately allowed my thoughts to be changeable. By consistently choosing to change rather than staying stuck in the negative thought loops, I started the neural rewiring process that is so essential to achieving full recovery.

60

WEIGHT GAIN

The mental work I did at Carolina House was merely a part of a much larger puzzle of piecing my health back together. Arguably, one of the most critical pieces was gaining weight. During my first week at Carolina House, I had no trouble being 100% meal compliant. Eating enough food made me realize how hungry I was, especially for the foods that had been off-limits for so long. It wasn't until I started receiving weekly (and sometimes more frequent) meal plan increases that my body started to fight back.

After about a month, most of my child-sized clothes no longer fit me. The idea of buying new clothes frightened me. As my body continued to change, I didn't know when it would stop or what size I'd eventually fit into. Along with what I'd eaten that day or what I'd talked about in therapy, many of my journal entries addressed the discomfort I felt about my changing body. Given that blind weigh-ins were protocol and full-length mirrors were purposely absent at Carolina House, it was difficult to quantify my body in the same ways I'd done before. But I didn't need external proof to understand that my body was changing...and it was changing *fast*.

Bloating, constipation, cramping, and nausea became the new normal. I constantly feared the next meal plan increase, yet another unpredictable factor in the equation. Oftentimes, I'd be certain there would be no increase, only to be met with "Your weight isn't trending upwards as fast as we'd like it to" in my next session with Julie.

"But how is that even possible?" I would ask in disbelief. "I feel like a whale!"

"Your body has a lot of healing to do," Julie explained. "Right now, all the energy you are consuming is going straight to the repair of bodily processes." I later learned that this is a very common phenomenon in recovery from starvation known as hypermetabolism. When malnourished, the body must economize. Because the energy consumed is inadequate to support daily life and bodily functions, the body must make energy expenditure trade-offs. Vital life processes such as heart rate, metabolism, and digestion slow, and non-essential life processes such as menstruation cease. However, when the body starts receiving enough fuel, it kicks into overdrive and demands large amounts of energy to repair all the damage caused by malnutrition. On the day of my admission, Carolina House almost didn't accept me due to my physically critical state.

"With this low of a heart rate, she should be lying in the hospital," one of the Carolina House nurses told my mom while I was meeting with my new treatment team. But because I was so committed to recovery, they allowed me to start my journey via residential. Within a few weeks of eating 100%, my heart rate doubled. When I saw the new number flash on the monitor, I was so proud. I immediately documented the victory in my journal:

I am still super bloated and nauseous from yesterday, and it SUCKS. I was hoping it would be better today, but it isn't. I guess it's just part of the process though, because this feeling is going hand in hand with my health! This morning I got my vitals done and my heart rate was 84! That's literally more than DOUBLE my admission heart rate of 41. That

IS progress. It's been very painful, but if you look at the facts, so far it's all been worth it.

Shortly after writing that journal entry, however, my feelings of triumph were dashed. Every Wednesday, we received a "progress report" with the highlights of what had been discussed during the weekly team meeting. If a patient was still on bathroom support or hadn't received other privileges such as walks and yoga, Wednesdays were especially anticipatory. Besides the privilege of chores (cleaning the kitchen and dining area after meals and snacks), I had yet to receive any other privileges. When the RPAs handed everyone their tri-folded paper of truth one Wednesday afternoon, I was certain that my new healthy heart rate would be rewarded in the form of at least one new privilege. I unfolded the paper hastily, skipping over the summary and immediately focusing on the "privileges" section.

No chores.

Surely, there must be some kind of mistake! Not only had I been granted *zero* new privileges, but my one and only privilege had been taken *away*. This didn't make any sense. I rushed to my therapist's office and demanded an explanation for this madness.

"Why can't I do chores?"

"Have a seat." Kyra motioned towards the couch and closed the door. She bent down to turn on the noise machine.

"Why don't I have any privileges?" I asked again.

"You've lost weight," she said matter-of-factly.

I was stunned. "How is that even possible? I've been eating 100% since I got here!" After a similar conversation with Julie just days before, I was positive Carolina House's scale was broken.

"And that's absolutely amazing, Livia!" Kyra gave me a big smile. "I emphasized how proud the treatment team is in your summary. Did you read it?"

I had been so focused on my lack of privileges that I had completely overlooked every positive word in the summary section of my progress report. I reopened the folded paper and skimmed Kyra's words. Instantly, the phrase "sometimes the body takes longer to catch up" stood out to me.

I read the phrase aloud. "What do you mean by that?"

"I'm sure you've discussed this with Julie, but you were in a very dangerous state when you arrived at Carolina House. Your body has a lot of healing to do, and this healing isn't always linear with the mental side of things," Kyra said. "As I wrote in your report, the whole team is so impressed with your commitment to getting better, and how you've been 100% compliant with your meal plan! Unfortunately, due to the amount of energy your body is demanding for its repairs, the meal plan hasn't been sufficient for weight gain."

I objected before Kyra could say anything more. "But I *have* gained weight! Everything feels tighter! My heart rate is double what it was on my admission day!"

She pursed her lips before continuing. "When you arrived, your weight was on the cusp of being allowed to do chores. Now, it's fallen just under that cusp. Your body has been putting so much energy into repairs, such as the doubling of your heart rate," she said, performing a mini clap in the air, "that it's not contributed to weight gain."

"But how come my clothes barely fit me anymore? The scale must be broken!" I protested.

"When the body is in such a malnourished state, everything goes out of whack. Your digestion, electrolytes–" She looked up at the ceiling as if to gather her words. "The reason your clothes feel tighter – what you are probably perceiving as weight gain – that's most likely a combination of fluid retention and gas."

"How do I make it go away?" I moaned as her words reminded me of my discomfort.

"You just keep doing what you've been doing, Livia!" she replied encouragingly. "Healing takes time and patience. I understand that it can feel hard to accept, but like I said, the body's reaction to your actions isn't always linear. Keep doing the mental work, and the body will catch up!"

Although I felt like I was being punished by having chores taken away, I kept reminding myself of Kyra's words. I was doing everything I could, and my body was simply adjusting in its own unique way. Not having control over the very thing I believed I could control was my biggest fear, but I had chosen to face this fear head-on. My initial choice to surrender and trust the process meant I had to surrender and trust my body's process, too. It meant I had to succumb to all the obstacles and unknowns in order to seize my life back, a life that would be lived on my own terms.

61

PASS

On August 27 – eight weeks after my admission to Carolina House – I was granted my first pass. By now, my longing to go home had peaked to a point that was even higher than during the initial weeks of my stay. Even though each patient's treatment trajectory varied, there was no doubt that my stay was skewing the average. Seeing patients admitted after me go on passes – and eventually on to discharge – while I still seemed to be at square one made me feel like I was running behind. Not a week went by that I didn't ask my treatment team when I could leave.

Through daily journaling, I did my best to focus on everything I had gained (besides weight!), despite not knowing when I would be set free. I celebrated when I came off bathroom support and could finally take a shit without the door being cracked open. I celebrated when I could participate in yoga after six weeks. I celebrated when I was allowed to go on my first twenty-minute walk. I even celebrated my hunger cues, which came at an increasing frequency towards the end of my stay.

When I posed the question "When can I leave?" during my weekly session with Kyra in late August, I wasn't met with a vague and unsatisfactory answer, as had consistently been the case until now. This time, she said, "Let's talk about passes!" Now *this* was a cause for celebration. Passes were the very first step on the road to discharge. They were little gems of temporary freedom, allowing you to independently test the waters of recovery.

My first pass was an on-site pass. I was allowed to go wherever I wanted, as long as I remained on the Carolina House grounds. Considering the vast acreage of these grounds, I had no doubt I would find peace and quiet for the first time in what felt like forever.

When the time finally came, I walked to the furthest possible corner of the lawn and laid out a giant white sheet behind a large willow tree. I gathered some nearby rocks to keep the sheet from blowing around with the wind and set my snack of a yogurt bowl, fruit, and granola bars in the middle. Finally, I grabbed my phone, took a selfie, and posted it on Instagram with the caption *MY FIRST PASS!* While I ate my snack, I chatted with my followers. For the remaining two hours of the pass, I called my parents.

"Tell me how it went!" Kyra exclaimed during our next session.

"It was amazing!" My tone was equally excited. "It truly felt like a brief sense of freedom. Not only from Carolina House, but freedom from my eating disorder." As I said the words, I realized it had been the first time I felt like myself again.

"What did you do?"

"I had a picnic! I ate my snack on the lawn, I engaged with my super supportive community on Instagram, and I called my parents. Time flew by so quickly!"

As soon as I shared how I had spent my three hours of freedom, Kyra frowned. "Did you take any time to just be by yourself?"

"What do you mean? I was by myself!"

Her frown turned upside down slightly as she held in a laugh. "What I mean is, did you take any time to just sit with yourself? To feel the freedom without distractions?"

"Oh," I responded with a hint of sadness. Fear of having disappointed her caused me to shudder. In many of our sessions, Kyra and I talked about how difficult I found it to sit with my thoughts. Attaching numbers to anything and everything, ensuring predictability, and withstanding change at all costs were all ways in which I distracted myself from my mental reality: a never-ending whirlwind of fear and anxiety. At the time, she attributed this compulsive distraction seeking to obsessive-compulsive disorder (OCD). If I had known about autism back then, our conversations might have been radically different.

My next few passes consisted of outings incorporating meals and snacks; I visited new restaurants, got a massage, and went on a shopping spree at the mall. With all the work I had done challenging food rules, accepting weight gain, and prioritizing self-care, my passes couldn't have gone any better! It was shopping for new clothes that caught me off guard.

62

SHOPPING

As I had documented in my journal from day one, I knew the weight gain process would be as much a mental challenge as a physical one. Throughout treatment, my hypersensitivity had been tested in every way possible – one of the most prominent being the way clothes fit on my ever-expanding body. When I asked Kyra if I could go on a pass to buy new clothes, she fully supported the idea. Before she signed off on it, however, we made a concrete plan and discussed potential challenges that might come up. Buying bigger sizes was hard for anyone in recovery, and knowing of my hyper-fixation on numbers like no one else, Kyra foresaw this outing as the ultimate challenge. And the ultimate challenge it was, alright.

As I scanned the leggings on the display table at my favorite athletic store, anxiety rose up. I automatically grabbed the smallest size as I had always done, but my hands quaked out of fear they wouldn't fit me. The only way to find out was to try them on.

When I jumped up in the air to pull on the leggings, my fear was confirmed. Alarm bells went off in my head as thoughts of wrongdoing whooshed alongside them. *I had eaten too much. I had gained too much weight. I should have never committed to recovery. There was no way I could handle this.* It wasn't even the weight gain itself that made me want to crawl out of my skin. It was the magnitude of *change* that had occurred – change that was beyond my control. I yanked the leggings off as I broke into a sweat, my heart racing and my head pounding. I looked at the label in my trembling hands, unable to fathom how it no longer matched my body.

Thankfully, Kyra and I had talked about this. There was no way to know my current size, and I had mentally prepared for it not being what it had always been. My body had changed, meaning my clothing size had changed, too. This wasn't a measurement of me or my worth. If anything, it proved how much I had grown: not just physically, but mentally as well. I no longer fit into children's clothes because *I was no longer a child*. I had done too much work, taken too much responsibility, and embarked too far on my journey to maturation to retreat to the safety and naïveté of a child now!

I took three deep breaths, put on my big-girl pants, and went back to find some *real* big-girl pants. Eventually, I walked out of the store with two pairs of the most comfortable leggings I have ever owned. Now, it was time for the next challenge: underwear.

For the first time in my life, I had breasts. My mom had been a late bloomer – I clearly remember her sharing stories about getting her first period at the age of fifteen – so when I still showed no signs of puberty at my twelve-year doctor's appointment, there wasn't much concern. But when I wasn't gaining weight or height, all eyes were on me. This "vital growth window," as the doctors liked to call it, was one of the primary reasons my falling off the growth curve was so concerning. It was the reason my doctors feared my eating disorder would become "a lifelong issue" if my parents didn't force me into treatment, and the reason my parents used at the dinner table when I refused to eat. Even though I knew – logically – they were right, none of it mattered to me. Somehow, I believed I would magically grow in height without needing to grow in weight. Of course, I was proven miserably wrong. Although I did gain a couple of inches after Carolina House, I will remain shorter than my potential height would have been had I never gotten an eating disorder.

But I *did* get an eating disorder, and the journey to recovery has taught me life lessons that could never measure up to a mark on the wall.

Nourishing myself with an abundance of food enlightened me on how innately capable the body is of healing. Some doctors told me I would never be able to have children because I had never gotten a period before, and others told me I would forever stay in the body of a child. But when I started noticing lumps in my chest after a mere two months of refeeding in treatment, I knew I was proving them wrong.

I bought my first two real bras at the mall that day. Just as leggings from the children's store no longer fit me, training bras from the kid's section would no longer cut it. After leaving the athletic store with two new pairs of women's-sized leggings, I uncomfortably stepped into a lingerie store for the first time in my life. In the past, people always looked at me like I was a child. Had I walked into the lingerie store two months earlier, an employee would likely have asked me if I'd lost my mom. But as I walked into the store with my purse in one hand and a shopping bag in the other, I was just like any other young woman in need of new bras.

63

SCALE

On September 13, I was granted my first pass home. At least, to what I called home at the time: my aunt and uncle's house. Throughout my stay at Carolina House, my aunt and uncle had come to visit me on several Sunday afternoons, reserved for visiting hours. Sundays were always the hardest day of the week for me. Seeing the moms, dads, and siblings of my fellow patients made me miss my own family all the more. The conversations I had with my aunt and uncle during those visits often revolved around how badly I wanted to go home, and the majority of the time was spent crying in their arms. Words fail me when it comes to the gratitude I have for my aunt and uncle. They were the family I relied on during one of the most difficult periods of my life, showing their love and support through it all. Rutger and M'Liss: if you're reading this, I hope you know you will forever hold a special place in my heart.

When my aunt picked me up on the day of my pass home, we stopped by the supermarket before she dropped me off at the house. She immediately had to leave to pick up my cousin at rowing practice, which meant I would have the whole place to myself. For the first time in nearly eleven weeks, I could cook my own dinner! As I unpacked the tofu, broccoli, and sweet potatoes from the shopping bag, I realized I didn't have a food scale. The last time I had made this meal – the evening before my admission – everything had been weighed out to the gram. Even though I hadn't weighed a thing since then, I was seized by an unbearable urge to know the measurements of my dinner-to-be.

As I visualized the scale and measuring cups sealed in a plastic bag collecting dust in the Carolina House attic, a wave of regret washed over me. *I should have just left them here*, I thought. I doubted my aunt and uncle owned a food scale but scoured the kitchen anyway. I opened every cabinet and every drawer. I looked on every shelf and behind every mixing bowl. *Maybe they had one but had hidden it?* I searched for almost half an hour before accepting my unlucky fate. That's when I realized I may not be so unlucky after all.

Apparently they didn't own a kitchen scale, but I knew for sure they had a personal scale. Perhaps I was going to have to eyeball my dinner portions, but I would be able to weigh myself. I double-checked the clock to ensure no one would return home soon, then tiptoed to the bathroom, where I had last weighed myself the day before my admission.

There it was. A glass-plated personal scale that stood upon metallic hinges and had a dark-gray display. *Am I really going to do it?* I knew I shouldn't, but the temptation was irresistible. I grabbed a tissue from the box next to the sink and gently wiped away the dust. I tapped the scale with my toe to awaken it. When the display lit up, I stepped on. The number that flashed back at me caused my whole body to tense up. I had gained exactly twenty-five pounds. Here is a direct quote from my journal entry that night:

> *This fact didn't make me upset or angry – it was just shocking to realize how fast it all happened...and I'm super damn proud of myself! I did this. I ate. I rested. I gained weight. I am gaining my LIFE back!*

As I cooked dinner, I couldn't get the number out of my head. It swirled alongside thoughts of what would have happened if I didn't know, questions about what my goal weight was, fears that I'd keep on gaining weight forever, and ambivalence about whether or not I should tell Kyra about weighing myself.

In our next session, I told Kyra everything. To my astonishment, she wasn't mad; quite the opposite!

"I'm so proud of you for being so open about your experience!" She smiled. And just like that, my fear that telling the truth would cause her to keep me in treatment longer was proven to be FEAR: False Evidence Appearing Real. The part of me that thought it better to keep my behavior with the scale a secret was convinced Kyra would think I wasn't ready to leave yet. But the part of me that wanted to tell the truth – the real, authentic Livia – had prevailed.

"I see the true Livia coming out more and more in each session," Kyra said. "Your honesty and willingness to be vulnerable in difficult situations show me how ready you are."

I wanted to jump up and do a happy dance. That was the first time I heard her say the word "ready" without it being preceded by the word "not."

"So when can I discharge?" I asked eagerly.

"I'll have to confirm with the team, but what do you think of next week?" I didn't have to think. I looked up at Kyra and performed the most exaggerated nod my head was capable of. "But just before we wrap up, I do want to ask you," Kyra said, "why *did* you weigh yourself?"

To answer this question truthfully, I needed a moment to think. At my aunt and uncle's house, the urge had felt so automatic – so natural – that I'd never even thought about why I'd done it in the first place.

"I wanted to confirm my progress," I replied.

"Hmm," Kyra said. "And do you think your progress can be measured by a single number?"

I knew it couldn't. Yet still, being able to attach a number to my journey made me feel that much more accomplished.

64

SCALE SMASH

A popular tradition at Carolina House was scale smashing. Before discharge, a patient would write affirmations all over a scale and then smash it to pieces with a giant hammer (while wearing safety goggles, of course). The act of physically destroying the scale symbolized letting go of the object's perceived power. Whenever I observed a scale smashing, I was proud of my friends; they were taking ownership of their recovery, and it delighted me to hear how the experience empowered them. But because I never struggled with body dysmorphia or resonated with fellow patients who would share in group therapy that "the number on the scale decided whether I'd have a good day or a bad day," I never felt inclined to participate in any scale smashing of my own. Yes, I had a complicated relationship with the scale – especially my food scale – but for me, that relationship was merely rooted in wanting to *know*. I wanted to know how much I was eating, and I wanted to know how much I weighed.

When I weighed my oatmeal, it gave me just as much anxiety to see a lower number on the scale than a higher one; the very act of weighing was so I could get the amount to be *just right*. When I weighed myself, it wasn't because I wished the number would be different than it was; I simply needed a confirmation of the facts, and seeing something as tangible as a number gave me that. It meant nothing more, nothing less.

When Kyra proposed smashing my food scale a few days before discharge, I opposed the idea. I had spent money on that scale, and if I wasn't going to keep it, I was much better off selling it on eBay!

Even after I had voiced my disagreement, Kyra said, "Before you discharge, I believe it's vital that you smash the scale."

"I really don't think that's necessary."

"Is that your opinion, or is that the eating disorder's opinion?"

Because I believed my real answer – that it was truly my opinion – would be taken for an untruth, I lied and gave Kyra the answer I knew she wanted to hear: "It's my eating disorder's opinion."

She nodded as if to say *I've taught you well*. "So, what do you say? Smash the scale on discharge day?" The poetical formulation of her sentence almost made it seem as if the entire situation had been schemed.

On September 26 – the day I would finally sleep again in a bed that wasn't on the second floor of Carolina House – I took a permanent marker and wrote nonsensical words all over my scale. Because my intuition wasn't in line with my actions, I couldn't come up with any phrases of my own.

"What should I write?" I asked my fellow patients who cheered me on during the event.

"Whatever you want!" they replied encouragingly.

But I didn't *want* to write anything because I didn't *want* to smash my scale! "Please, can you guys help me out?" I begged.

They shouted words and phrases that I thought were utterly ridiculous, but I marked them onto the small glass plate anyways. I just wanted to get this over with.

"Now, it's time for the finale!" Kyra exclaimed as she handed me a pair of goggles. She waited until I'd wrapped the scale in a plastic bag and set it on the ground before giving me the sledgehammer.

I took a deep breath.

"Put all your energy into smashing that little devil to pieces!" the crowd hollered.

I did put all my energy into the smash, but it wasn't negative energy towards the scale; it was anger towards this stupid situation.

"How did that feel?" Kyra asked, her eyes wide.

"Great!" I lied. "I really feel a sense of freedom from the scale," I added, to strengthen my statement.

The next day, I took an Uber to Target and bought myself a new food scale.

65

STEP-DOWN

S tepping down to the Partial Hospitalization Program was when I truly felt a sense of freedom. Throughout my time in residential, I had mapped out all the things I would do when I was back "home." From grocery shopping unsupervised to creating my own meals and going on my phone or watching movies outside of "screen time," I reveled in my new independence. I picked back up the daily documentation of my journey on Instagram, sharing my culinary creations with captions that served as journal entries. If my Instagram community had been a form of support and accountability before residential, it was my lifeline after it.

Sticking to my meal plan was infinitely more difficult without the constant monitoring of every meal and snack, primarily due to the shame and discomfort I felt in my new body. Because I had overshot my weight to a point where weight gain was no longer the goal, it was tempting to let things slide when I felt full or when I was out and about. *A normal person wouldn't eat right now* was often the excuse my brain came up with in such moments. But it was also in these very moments that I needed to remind myself that my situation was far from normal. My body was still healing, and if anything, most of the healing could only start now that I had put on so much weight!

For years, my body had been leaching energy from my bones, organs, and survival systems to fund the excessive amounts of exercise I engaged in. Being at a higher weight didn't mean the internal damage to my body had been mended. Just like a baby is cute and chubby and fat before sprouting into a child and eventually shooting upwards, a higher weight was necessary to ensure my body was safe enough to do the same. Still, every session with my dietitian commenced with me asking, "When can we decrease my meal plan?"

Even though I was clearly the shortest and youngest patient at Carolina House, it was no secret I had the largest meal plan of all. Because of the competitive nature of eating disorders, meal plans were never to be discussed between patients. But it was also for this very reason – not being allowed to discuss them – patients did just that.

"Livia, how many supplements did you have on your meal plan again?" my fellow patients would tease as I downed my fourth Clif Bar or Ensure shake of the day. Supplements were not a standard exchange; they were only added when one's meal plan became so high that the density of a supplement was necessary to maximize one's ability to "meet their needs." Every session, I'd go into the dietitian's little office hopeful, only to hear that my body was "still demanding high amounts of energy." *Ugh.*

Weighing and measuring food outside of treatment was how I kept myself accountable for sticking to the meal plan when no one was watching. I never told my treatment team about the purchase I made the day after I was discharged from residential, because I never allowed it to affect how I ate or plated food when I was at the program.

In PHP – and eventually IOP – I had the staff and fellow patients to hold me accountable; I didn't need the confirmation of a scale to fulfill my meal plan. When I was alone, though, an invisible force would whisper *That's too much food* or *Your meal plan is too high*, and I would be tempted to skimp on servings or cut out exchanges. Needing to hit a certain number of grams on the food scale forced me to portion more than I would have otherwise, which ultimately gave me the ability to continue hitting all my exchanges.

66

BIRTHDAY WISH

On November 7, I stepped down again, from PHP to IOP, the Intensive Outpatient Program. I wrote the following caption under a photo of my breakfast on Instagram that day:

Happy Tuesday everyone!! It's been a hot second since I've made pancakes, so here I am :) Today is my LAST day of PHP!!! Ah!! I made it through 13 weeks of residential, 6 weeks of PHP, and now I'm onto the next phase: IOP and I'm still going strong!! Recovery is the most amazing choice I have ever made. Not only have I gained my body back, I have gained my LIFE back. I have hunger cues, I can enjoy my food, I can listen to my body without feeling guilty, and I finally have interest and enjoy activities that my eating disorder stole from me for so many years. 5 months ago I didn't know what life was, and now I'm actually living it!!!

In light of my community and striving to support and encourage them in the same way they had supported and encouraged me since I created my Instagram account back in 2016, I did my best to stay positive when I shared. But in sticking to my values, I was equally open and transparent about my struggles. One of these was an ever-growing sense of "treatment burnout."

My birthday was less than two weeks away at this point, and all I wanted was to go home. I wanted to be done with the sessions and appointments and supplements. I wanted to live the life I had gained out in the real world, among my family and friends rather than other patients. Don't get me wrong – I loved the friendships I had built at Carolina House – but I was ready to have conversations that didn't revolve around food, fears, and other therapeutic topics.

"Can I please go home for my birthday?" I asked Adelyn on the first day of IOP. Adelyn had been my therapist all throughout PHP and IOP, as both programs were held in the same building. I simply couldn't imagine being away from my family on my birthday. Not only was I turning eighteen, which meant I'd officially be an adult, but there was so much more to celebrate: my health. It would be the first time in six years that I would be eating real birthday cake on my special day, which was a cause for celebration in and of itself!

"You just stepped down to IOP," Adelyn said. "I'm sorry, but it's not realistic to set a discharge date so soon."

I was heartbroken but remained hopeful. I knew this couldn't be her final answer. I was going to go home for my birthday; there was no other option! I sat across from her in silence for a few minutes, as was often the case during our sessions. This was something I loved about Adelyn – she was patient with me. She allowed me the space and time I needed to process my thoughts, something I hadn't felt with other treatment providers.

Finally, an idea hit me.

"Can I go home, just for a few days?" I asked excitedly. I didn't care if I had to come back, all I wanted – all I *needed* – was to be home. I needed to hug my mom and dad and sisters, and I needed to cuddle with Kiki and Sammy. That was my only birthday wish.

She tilted her head and looked up at the ceiling as if trying her best to conjure an answer to my out-of-the-box question. *All the way to the Netherlands? During treatment? Was that even wise?*

"I'm not even sure insurance would continue to cover IOP," she said hesitantly. When the funds from my crowdfunding campaign had run out, my mom had been able to get me insurance through the Affordable Care Act, which covered the continuation of my treatment at Carolina House. To say that my belief I would need treatment for just four weeks was wishful thinking would be a massive understatement!

"You're not sure," I said, "which means there's a possibility." I knew there was. There had to be!

"I'll talk to the team about it." Adelyn kept her tone and her gaze neutral. But it didn't matter what the team said. I had made up my mind: I was going home for my birthday.

For the next three days, I questioned Adelyn about whether she had already "talked to the team about it."

"I'll bring it up in our weekly meeting!" she confirmed, laughing at my childlike impatience. Patience had never been my strong suit, especially when paired with uncertainty. Knowing I'd have to wait a certain number of hours or days or weeks was fine – as long as I knew the specific outcome I was waiting for. But not knowing how long I'd have to wait *and* not knowing what the outcome would be? That was mental torture.

After three sleepless nights and three days of endless "what ifs," Adelyn approached me during afternoon snack.

"Come see me when you're done, okay?" she said with a smile. I devoured my meal-sized snack in five minutes flat, the realization of having eaten too fast clouded by the flutter of excitement that single smile sent through me. I may not have been a mind-reader, but I sure knew how to sense good news.

"So" – Adelyn shifted around some papers on her clipboard – "insurance approved."

I couldn't help but shriek.

"But?" I impatiently leaned forward in my seat. Judging by her lack of matching enthusiasm for this news, there was a catch.

"To keep coverage, you can't miss more than two consecutive days of the program."

I performed a mental calculation: the only way this plan could work was if I flew to Holland on Friday the 17th and back to the US the following Monday – the day after my birthday. "I won't even be home for forty-eight hours!" I cried. "That's not realistic!"

"Unfortunately, this is the only way you can go home for your birthday," Adelyn said.

I swallowed, then took a deep breath – just like I'd done on my first day of residential when deciding to surrender to eating meat for the first time in five years.

"Okay, I'll do it." The situation was far from ideal, but if flying 4,000 miles and back in three days would grant me my birthday wish, I would fly those damn miles.

67

ARRIVAL

On Friday night, I boarded the plane to Amsterdam after attending three hours of IOP that same morning. Even though I only needed clothes and toiletries for two nights, I packed my suitcase with as much of my belongings as would fit, *just in case* I decided to stay home and never return to North Carolina.

When I arrived in my homeland early Saturday morning, I was filled with every possible emotion. I was excited to see my family but equally nervous. I had changed in every way imaginable, both mentally and physically. Would my family be shocked at my new appearance? Or would they be amazed? Would they be proud? What would they say? I trembled as I waited for my purple suitcase to appear on the baggage belt, knowing that my family was waiting for me behind the doors that separated baggage claim from the rest of the world.

After thirty minutes, my suitcase still hadn't shown up. I became increasingly worried, as everyone else on my flight had already vacated the airport. Suddenly, the baggage belt stopped. My suitcase was nowhere to be seen. I conjured up every worst-case scenario I could think of. *Someone had stolen it. It was still on the plane. What if it had never even made it onto the plane back in North Carolina?* My phone buzzed in my pocket.

"You got it?" the message read. Since landing, I'd been messaging my mom, giving her updates about where I was and when I expected to come through the exit doors. Instead of responding to her message, I called her.

"Hey, honey! Any update on the suitcase?" she asked.

"The baggage belt stopped, but my suitcase still isn't here!" I cried. "Mommy, all of my things are in there! I don't know what to do!" I had just spent five months learning, growing, and challenging myself to immeasurable lengths. I had just flown across the ocean all by myself. I was officially going to be an adult in less than twenty-four hours. But in that very moment, I was filled with the fear and desperation of a child who couldn't find their mom.

"How about you meet us on the other side, and we'll help you figure out the suitcase?" my mom offered.

"Okay," I replied halfheartedly. "I'll see you guys in a sec."

I picked up my blue North Face backpack, tilted my pink carry-on suitcase towards me, and headed towards the "Nothing to Declare" exit of Schiphol Airport. As soon as the doors opened, I spotted Amélie's face. My eyes darted all around her, and before I knew it, my entire family stood before me. They held a giant sign that read *Welcome home, Livia!* surrounded by drawings of hearts in every color of the rainbow. I raced towards them, unable to reach their arms fast enough. This was real. My family was here. I was home.

After endless hugs, kisses, and positive words about how radiant I looked, I became the party pooper, whining, "I have no idea where my suitcase is."

"Yes, that's what we're going to investigate right now!" My mom sounded hopeful. "Are you sure you didn't see it next to the baggage belt?"

"No, I really looked everywhere. What if someone stole it?"

"Let's not jump to conclusions," my dad said, in his typical matter-of-fact demeanor.

"I'm sure we'll find it!" Mae yelled as she jumped on top of me in excitement. "You look AMAZING, Livia!"

"Yeah!" Amélie chimed in. "You look so healthy!"

I blushed at the compliments, grateful that I could finally share proof of my healthy self with those I loved most. Throughout my time at Carolina House, our phone conversations had evolved from food reports to more interesting topics, but nothing even came close to seeing each other in person. Not only could they now hear a healthy Livia, but they were immersed in my very presence.

"Thanks, guys," I mumbled. "I've missed you sooo much." For the first time since developing my eating disorder, I felt a soul connection that went far beyond what any combination of words could explain. A tear sprang to my eye as I recalled who I was when I last saw them. Five months prior, I was barely an older sister anymore; I was a skeleton of a body possessed by the devil, leaving terror in my wake. Oh, how much had changed since then. Happy tears rolled down my cheeks before my mom motioned for us to join her at the service desk.

"Unfortunately, the suitcase never made it onto your flight," my mom said.

"It was put on the next flight, so we can have it delivered to your house," the lady behind the desk said.

"But when will it arrive?" What would I do without all of my own things?

The lady looked at her wristwatch and then back at me. "That flight departed North Carolina a few hours ago, so I can arrange for Schiphol to have it delivered to your house by tonight."

Tonight? What was I going to wear *today*? All I wanted was to take a hot shower and change into my favorite sweatpants, T-shirt, and fuzzy socks. As soon as I started to tremble, Mae put her hand on my shoulder. "It's going to be okay, Livia! You can pick out anything you want from my closet. Finally, we can share clothes again!"

I could hear the excitement in her voice, and immediately a wave of nostalgia washed over me. I was filled with my fondest sister-hood memories: sharing clothes, baking, watching TV, playing outside, and laughing until our bellies hurt.

Everything changed when my eating disorder joined the chat. Thanks to anorexia, the baked goods were reserved for every-one besides me. The boxes of mac and cheese we used to split were only between Mae and Amélie. As my two younger sisters giggled and played, I retreated to my room to work out or do homework. We could no longer share clothes – not only because anorexia stole my generosity from me, but also because my younger sisters had simply outgrown my small size. They started shopping in the women's section while I scoured the children's departments.

"Oh my gosh, you're right!" I exclaimed in glee. "Thank you, Mae. That's so sweet of you."

"How nice, Mae!" my mom added.

Amélie chimed in. "And if you want, you can also pick something from my closet!"

It was no longer the family and anorexia. The true me was finally back, and I was part of the family.

68

A Taste of Home

The forty-five-minute drive from the airport to our home in Utrecht passed in a flash. As I soaked in the views of the Dutch farmland (and, unfortunately, the horrible stench of cow shit), I answered endless questions about the past five months.

"First of all, there are so many rules!" I exclaimed. "You have to wear a hat in the kitchen, and you only get ten minutes to make your food. You can't wear anything with hoods or pockets–"

"Ohhh, probably because they don't want you to hide food," Mae concluded.

"Yeah, and this *really* annoyed me because I wasn't going to hide food!"

"I know how committed you are to recovery." Mae gave me an awkward side hug. "I'm sooo proud of you, Livia!"

"Anyways," I continued, "we had therapy and groups ALL DAY LONG. It was super exhausting."

"I can definitely imagine how tiring that must be," my dad noted, keeping his eyes on the road. He insisted on driving after my mom offered at the airport, claiming that she was a "reckless driver who braked too abruptly." If he drove, he wouldn't be faced with "sudden accelerations or unpredictable stops."

"Each day of the week, there were different food themes for breakfast. We had Muffin Monday. Tuesday was free choice

228

breakfast, but only because lunch was plated. Usually, dinner was plated and lunch was free choice, but on Tuesdays we had culinary group, so lunch would be whatever we made, and then dinner would be free choice. Wednesdays were bagel day, and OMG! I discovered how much I looove cinnamon raisin bagels!"

My whole family burst into laughter. It seemed we were all reveling in what it was like to have the true Livia back.

"Too bad we don't have cinnamon raisin bagels in Holland," I said.

"Yeah, typical American food!" my dad said. "At least the bread here is much better."

This was true. I couldn't wait to eat a slice of fresh, whole-grain Dutch bread with a thick layer of butter and a hefty sprinkle of dark chocolate *hagelslag*. Because I needed to complete what I started, I continued sharing the weekly breakfast roundup. "Thursdays were cereal day, and Fridays were chef's choice."

"I miss American cereals!" my sisters exclaimed in unison.

Amélie wrinkled her nose and drew her eyebrows together. "But what's chef's choice?"

"Chef's choice was just whatever the culinary staff decided that morning. Sometimes, we'd be lucky, and they made oatmeal or gave us free choice, but other times, they'd come up with weird rules, like that your breakfast must contain an egg for one of your proteins."

"I know you hate rules!" Amélie said, wide-eyed. "I'm honestly so impressed how you survived all that."

As she said it, I realized how impressed I was with myself, too. "Honestly, the only reason I survived was because of how badly I wanted to live again."

My mom reached out from the front seat and laid her hand on my left knee. "You have no idea how proud I am of you."

"I'm so glad to see you guys." I placed my hand on hers. "Friday afternoons were always my favorite, because then we had Target outing! I bought lots of comfy new clothes and tried every new flavor of Clif Bar." With the amount of weight I had gained and the amount of supplements on my meal plan, a periodic restock of comfy clothes and Clif Bars were a necessity.

"What did you do on the weekend?" my mom asked.

"On Saturday, we had group outing. Sometimes we'd go bowling or go to the movies. We also got frozen yogurt once, and we went to this thrift store a bunch of times where you can buy all different books and arts and crafts for super cheap."

"That sounds fun!" Mae said.

"Yeah, it really depended," I said. "Some outings were more fun than others. The hardest day for me though, you guys, was Sunday. Everyone's family came in the afternoon, and all that did was make me miss you way too much."

"I get that it must have been super hard," Mae said, "but you're here with us now!"

I started to cry. "But only for one day! I really don't want to go back after this!"

"I know, honey," my mom said, "but you're so close to the finish line. You just have a couple more weeks of IOP and you'll be able to come home for good!"

"Do you know my discharge date?" I asked.

"I don't," she replied, "but I do know that it's not much longer. Adelyn keeps telling me how much progress you've made and that you're getting closer and closer every day."

As was the case throughout my entire treatment, I couldn't stand the thought of not knowing when this would finally be over; it felt like I was running a marathon that didn't have a clear finish line. Still, my mom's reassuring words motivated me to hold on just a bit longer.

69

KITCHEN MEMORIES

When my dad parked the car in front of the house, a pit formed in my stomach as traumatic memories zapped through my mind. Behind that front door was where everything had happened. Behind that front door was where I jumped up and down like a wild animal. Behind that front door was where I smashed my mom's teapot and threw bowls of oatmeal on the floor. Behind that front door was where my sisters quaked in terror as the demon overtook me.

As I got out of the car and stood in front of the house, I realized my parallel position. Just like I no longer had to hide my behaviors behind that door, I no longer had to hide behind the mask of an eating disorder. My body was my home, and my body was finally healthy enough to enter the family home. I took a deep breath, inhaling gratitude and love as I mentally prepared myself for the sight of what I'd been dreaming of for the past five months.

"Sammy!" I exclaimed as our cats ran towards the door. "Oh my gosh, Kiki!" I scooped up the twins, petting and kissing them as tears of joy streamed down my cheeks. Their soft fur and distinctive scent let me forget the world around me for a moment. Nothing could match up to the love and understanding I had with Sammy and Kiki.

"Livia, move over!" My mom heaved my carry-on suitcase and backpack into the house. That little suitcase was packed with all my electronics and books, the total weight probably far above what was allowed in the main cabin of the plane. Thankfully, security hadn't said anything.

I carried Sammy into the main room as Mae held Kiki, Amélie moving between us to alternately pet both cats. As I scanned the open-concept living room and kitchen, my heart warmed at the thought that my mom had cleaned up for me. The house was *never* this neat.

My mom set my things down and put her hands on her hips. "What do you think?"

"Thanks for cleaning up." I grinned. I put Sammy down and swiveled around to look at the kitchen – the origin of 99% of the panic attacks. I tensed up as soon as I noticed the counter was different.

"What did you do?" I couldn't hide the horror from my voice as I brushed my fingers over the new countertop. When I left for Carolina House, our kitchen counters were marble laminate. Now they were wood laminate.

"You don't like it?" my mom asked fretfully.

"Not really," I replied. "I liked the marble design much better than this fake wooden look." I tapped the new surface.

"I thought it would be good to change the kitchen," my mom said. "I honestly thought it would support you and welcome you into a new home."

I swallowed my upset feelings, realizing my mom had only done this out of love. Then I walked into the kitchen and stood behind the counter, where I used to stand more than six times a day, weighing and measuring every morsel of food I planned to enter my mouth. I traced my hand over the drawer handle beneath it, knowing that it no longer contained the items that were once my lifeline. Still, I opened it. As an empty white board stared back at me, I got the urge to grab my scale. It was the same urge I had when cooking dinner on my first pass at my aunt and uncle's house, only much stronger. The countertops may have been different, but standing in that spot, behind that counter, in front of that drawer – it was as if my body had developed a type of muscle memory that equated standing behind that counter with using my food scale.

Sliding the drawer shut, I wondered when my suitcase would be delivered. I had brought my food scale and measuring cups with me and was dying to know when we would be reunited. There was no way I was going to use them – at least not when my family was around – but I had brought them *just in case*. As I opened and closed all the kitchen cabinets, taking stock of items that were either used or were getting close to their expiration dates, I remembered the family session. I raced over to my supplements drawer and pulled it open with incredible speed. My sense of loss was palpable as I stared at the skimpy heap of nutritionist-approved nutrition bars. All of my sugar-free, dessert-flavored protein bars and powders were gone, leaving the drawer practically bare and, to me, incomplete. Just as I wanted to grab the scale from the drawer underneath the counter, I wanted to fill my bar drawer with everything my mom had been told to get rid of.

I turned around to face my mom. "What did you do with all of it?"

"Sold it, mostly!" she replied enthusiastically. "I can give you the money right now if you want."

"That's okay," I responded. "I'm not going to need any euros for the next month, anyways. You can keep it safe until I'm back for good." The reminder that I'd be flying back to North Carolina on Monday reminded me of the pit in my stomach. I took one last look at the small pile of remaining bars and gently closed the drawer. There was nothing I could do about the situation right now, and that was okay. All that mattered was that I was finally home.

70

CHOCOLATE CAKE AND SCRAMBLED EGGS

My eighteenth birthday was beyond anything I imagined it would be. We celebrated in the same way we'd done every birthday up until my eleventh: with cake for breakfast! When I picked out the double chocolate cake with dark chocolate ganache at the supermarket's bakery with my mom the day before, I had insisted we buy eggs as well.

"Oh my gosh, I neeeed to make scrambled eggs for breakfast tomorrow," I shrieked with excitement.

My mom looked confused but laughed. "It's your birthday, so chocolate cake and scrambled eggs for breakfast it is!"

After I placed the carton of eggs in our shopping cart, I told my mom about another one of the rules at Carolina House. "The RPAs always used the word *normative*. It was super annoying because I wasn't even allowed to put peanut butter on my bagel. They said it was *normative* to put either cream cheese or butter on a bagel, but apparently not peanut butter."

My mom frowned. "But peanut butter on a bagel is one of the most normal combinations I can think of. Not to mention, it's delicious!"

"Exactly!" My heart pounded with gratitude as I realized this was one of the first *normal* conversations we'd had about food in years. "They also didn't allow us to microwave food more than once, saying it wasn't *normative* and that it was an eating disorder behavior. I hated how they told us what was or wasn't our eating disorder." I used air quotes to emphasize "our eating disorder." "Like, how could *they* know? There was this one time when a new patient asked what they meant by the word normative, and the RPA gave the example of chocolate cake and scrambled eggs. She said it was normative to eat chocolate cake and it was normative to eat scrambled eggs, but it would not be normative to eat them together."

"I don't see anything wrong with eating them together," my mom said.

"Well, at that moment, when the RPA said it wasn't normative, I decided that for my birthday, I was going to eat chocolate cake with a side of scrambled eggs. Just because they'd say I couldn't!" I giggled.

"That sounds just like you, my little rebellious Livia," my mom replied with a wink. "How you did it" – she let out a sigh – "how you continue to do it...it's truly remarkable."

"I think so, too," I admitted.

It was at that moment in the supermarket – with chocolate cake and scrambled eggs in the shopping cart – that I finally felt normal. I was no longer afraid of the eyes that would scan me up and down, because there was no longer anything *to* scan up and down. I was no longer afraid of the judgments, because there was no longer anything *to* judge. I was no longer the skeleton of a soul that once roamed the grocery store like it was a museum. I was simply a girl at the grocery store with chocolate cake and eggs in her shopping cart.

71

CHERRY ON TOP

The last month of IOP was hands down the most difficult period of my entire treatment at Carolina House. The joy and success I experienced during my birthday weekend led me to believe the last month of IOP was unnecessary; I had proven I was capable of being home, so why did I have to go back to treatment?

"Pleeease can I just stay here?" I begged my parents on the evening of my eighteenth birthday – the evening before I would fly back to North Carolina.

"You know the answer to that," my dad said.

"Well, technically, I can stay here if I want to," I replied. "I'm eighteen now, so I can make my own decisions!"

"Oh, come on, Livia," my mom replied fearfully. "You know that wouldn't benefit anyone. You've come so far, embarked on such a beautiful journey. Don't you want to finish it with grace?"

Even though my mind and body yearned for the freedom of being home for good, I knew I hadn't come this far only to go this far. My mom was right – I had embarked on such a beautiful journey. I wasn't about to cut corners for the instant gratification I desired.

For years, I gave into the instant gratification that my eating disorder demanded – the dopamine hit that came from restricting, the runner's high after a new record, the superiority I felt when others ate more than me. They all lasted mere moments before anxiety and fear would kick in and I'd need to honor my eating disorder's wishes once more. Over time, however, the magnitude of the demands only grew. In the beginning, it was skipping a cookie or running an extra five minutes, the pleasure when I ate whole wheat pasta while the rest of my family ate white. But when you give an eating disorder an inch, it will take a mile. One cookie became all sweets, an extra five minutes became an extra five sessions, and the constant obsession with what everyone else was eating became too debilitating to bear.

The journey I had so courageously started at Carolina House came from a burning desire for something far greater than the instant gratification offered by an eating disorder behavior. It came from the unconscious knowledge that something else would give me *infinite* gratification. That "something else" turned out to be life. As I recalled the original commitment I had made in the admissions office on July 3 – to surrender to the journey, regardless of how long that journey was going to take – I grounded myself in the realization that finishing IOP was this journey's sine qua non. Just as scrambled eggs had been the finishing touch of my birthday breakfast, the last stretch of IOP would be the cherry on top of my Carolina House cake.

72

HOME FOR CHRISTMAS

On December 1, I received my discharge date for IOP. Over-joyed, I took a spontaneous selfie and posted it on Insta-gram with the following caption:

Happy Friday y'all! I used to never say "y'all," but ever since I came to North Carolina, I've become a chameleon! Anyways, I thought I'd give y'all (!!) an update! I've been at Carolina House since July 4th now, and I have truly gained my independence back. I no longer feel like a slave to my eating disorder. I often hear its voice whispering in my ear, but the difference now is that I choose not to listen. Livia chooses now. I frequently go out to restaurants and spend time with friends, I practice self-care, I eat the foods I crave and enjoy, and I am genuinely just experiencing all of the amazing things life has to offer. This past week, I got my discharge date for IOP: December 20th. This means I will be going home and it ends my time at Carolina House after almost 6 long months. On the 23rd of December, I will fly home, back to my family in the Netherlands, and I could not be more stoked. I start school at the Montessori school in January and I am SO excited to start real life again! Recovery has been (and still is) a rocky road, but it's been (and still is!) sooo worth it!!

My arrival in the Netherlands on Christmas Eve felt infinitely more special than the visit for my birthday had a month earlier. I was finally home – for good this time. Since moving back from the US, my family had celebrated "Sinterkerst" – an invented combination of Sinterklaas and Kerstmis (Christmas) around the tree. Growing up in Boston, we had always celebrated the two holidays separately, with a few small items in the shoe for Sinterklaas and a mountain of presents on Christmas morning. When we moved to Holland, however, where Sinterklaas is celebrated on December 5 with *surprises* (artistic creations in which gifts and poems are hidden, comparable to "Secret Santa" in the US) and Christmas is typically celebrated with a fancy dinner and no additional gifts, we switched up our usual traditions.

While the rest of the Dutch families (literally) wrapped up their holiday gift-giving weeks before and would simply spend their Christmas around the dinner table, our holidays were just about to begin! We made *surprises* in which poems and gifts were hidden, *and* the tree would be encircled with presents. Christmas of 2017 was a jolly time, and everyone received (almost) everything on their wish list. The greatest gift of all, however, was one that no amount of wrapping paper could cover: togetherness and health.

73

HERMAN JORDAN

I n January 2018, I attended my first day as a high school sophomore – for the third time. By now, I was onto my fourth school in the Netherlands. I had gone from Gerrit Rietveld to ISU to Boni, and now I was enrolled at the Herman Jordan Montessori Lyceum in Zeist. After my traumatic bullying and panic experiences while attending Boni, it was evident that I would not return there after treatment.

During the last months of IOP, school was a major topic of discussion in family therapy. Even though I was already eighteen, I still had three years of high school left. Upon my admission to Carolina House, I pondered several alternatives to the traditional route, knowing that my age and overall life experience would alienate me from younger classmates. I considered staying in North Carolina and living with my aunt and uncle to get my GED (High School Graduate Equivalency Degree) but swept this option from the table when I realized how badly I wanted to live with my family back in Holland. I considered enrolling in the Dutch VAVO program (education for adults) but was quickly repelled by the thought of sitting in a classroom with an unpredictable range of ages. Now that I was healthy, I craved social connection. I wanted to meet people and form relationships. Considering this, attending a "regular" Dutch high school seemed to be my best option.

Thankfully, the Herman Jordan Lyceum was not a typical Dutch school. It was a Montessori school, meaning its values revolved around creativity, personal development, and embracing the uniqueness of each student. Rather than the traditional lecture and get-to-work approach I so despised at Gerrit Rietveld and Boni, the Jordan promised to support each student on their individual learning journey. Not to mention, my very first school was a Montessori school. Perhaps attending one again, all these years later, was the path written in the stars since drawing my first rainbow in the yellow room. When I agreed to the possibility of attending the Jordan, my parents scheduled a meeting with the school dean.

Upon entering the school, I felt an immediate sense of belonging. The Jordan was a relatively small school, with around 900 total students. Fewer student mobs and a higher ratio of teachers to students was like music to my ears, because that's exactly what I needed. I needed to know I would receive support if I wanted it, and I needed to know I wouldn't get trampled over in between classes.

After a wonderful conversation in which I felt seen and understood, I would have instantly agreed to enroll if it hadn't been for one minor catch: the Jordan was right around the corner from Rintveld Clinic. When my parents and I parked our bikes in the racks in front of the school, I had flashbacks of walking down the path we looked out on – the path that led from Rintveld to home. I could almost feel the mix of fear, anger, and sadness when I had walked home in the dead of night years before, the memory metamorphosing into an experience similar to time travel.

My parents sensed my hesitancy. "I'm scared that biking here every day is going to bring back all the trauma," I said. "Rintveld ruined my life. I don't know if I can sit in a classroom every day, knowing that it's right around the corner."

My dad put his hand on my knee. "That's very understandable. But maybe enrolling here will give you a chance to create new associations?"

"That's a great way of putting it!" my mom added. I felt a flicker of happiness as my parents agreed on something.

"I guess you guys are right," I mumbled. "Rintveld will only continue to hold power over me if I allow it to."

It took me a minute to realize how much power those words possessed. This didn't apply just to Rintveld but for everything in life. Food, exercise, the scale – essentially, they were all meaningless concepts. It was only when I attached my worth and value to them that I gave these concepts the power to take over my life. Recovery taught me that I possessed my own power: the power of choice. I couldn't control many things – most of my life was in fact out of my control – but I could always control my actions. I couldn't control whether I had a flashback, an urge to exercise or restrict, or even a whisper of the eating disorder's voice in my ear. But whether or not I acted on those thoughts was always my own choice. So, at the start of 2018, I chose to enroll in 4 VWO at the Herman Jordan Montessori Lyceum in Zeist.

PART 6: REAL RECOVERY

74

NOW THE REAL WORK BEGINS

During my last therapy session at Carolina House, Adelyn and I spent a generous hour talking about the progress I had made throughout treatment. We celebrated my victories but also reflected on the lessons I learned through hardship. I had overcome my fear foods by facing them head-on. I had gained weight by surrendering. I had created new neural networks in my brain by taking terrifying actions and trusting the process.

"You have completed the Carolina House program in the way it was designed to be completed," she said during our last session. "Your persistent commitment and dedication to getting better is beyond admirable."

I blushed. "Thank you, Adelyn. That truly means so much to me."

"I am so excited for this next chapter of your life, Livia. You have grown into such a bright and capable young woman, and it has been a true honor being part of your journey."

"It's been quite a journey, indeed!"

"Well, it's definitely not over," Adelyn reminded me. "Now the real work begins."

I didn't really know what Adelyn meant by that until I started my first day of school. It turned out that Adelyn's words couldn't have been more accurate.

As I took my seat in the first row of a classroom, stares came from every direction. Although the attention made me uncomfortable, it was a new type of discomfort; and that was because it was a new type of attention. The other students weren't looking at me because of how thin I looked but simply because I was new. Little did they know I was nearly three years older than them, as my short stature and young-looking face shielded my true age.

"This is Livia, everyone," my Dutch teacher – who also happened to be the dean – announced to the class. "Livia is from the United States of America and is our newest student!"

"Woooow." The class cooed at the teacher's declaration.

After class, I was bombarded with questions about the US: Are the high schools there just like in the movies? Do you have those tall lockers? Is it true that people don't eat bread for lunch and eat elaborate meals in the cafeteria instead?

I confirmed certain truths and busted several myths with a smile. I couldn't remember the last time I felt this normal. Not only did I blend in with my new healthy body, but people wanted to be my *friend*. I was excited to have a new purpose – excelling at my schoolwork and balancing it with social interaction – completely separate from the snow globe of isolation my eating disorder had confined me to for so long.

As with any novelty, however, the excitement soon wore off. I forced myself to engage in small talk at lunchtime, but it left me exhausted. In the beginning, I said yes to parties and hangout invitations. As I became more aware of how different I felt from my peers, though, I increasingly started saying no. At the same time, I was drowning in my self-imposed pressure to get good grades and have all my schoolwork be "perfect" – I didn't even have time to socialize! Surely, my new friends had to understand this?

75

IDENTITY CRISIS

W hereas I preferred not to socialize in person at school, I willingly participated in socializing online – more specifically, with my community on Instagram. Since returning home from Carolina House, I continued to share my journey through daily food pictures paired with vulnerable captions. Closely resembling journal entries, my daily captions were a way to process my thoughts while simultaneously building the community that had supported me through thick and thin. I expressed my anxieties about school, as well as the struggles that lingered around food and eating. I explained that recovery isn't linear. I was honest about wanting to exercise yet choosing not to because my healing was still so fresh. After having a spring photo shoot with my sister, only to bawl my eyes out at the sight of my larger body, I posted one of the pictures and voiced my insecurities. All throughout my eating disorder, I hadn't struggled with body image issues. It wasn't until I overshot my weight – reaching a weight higher than my body's natural set point – that I felt a loss of identity.

All my life, I had been the little skinny girl. I was an athlete who played soccer and gymnastics and beat the class record for push-ups and pull-ups. I ran track and never scored anything other than first, second, or third place. Now I was none of that anymore. I was no longer thin, and the only movement that seemed safe to engage in was walking and bicycling. I missed aspects of my life that the eating disorder had given me. I missed the excuse that I was too sick to complete a school deadline. I missed the excuse that I was too tired to attend certain events. I missed the excuse that I would have a panic attack if others didn't listen to how I wanted things to go. I was now responsible for my actions; I was no longer the victim of an illness. This put even more pressure on me, as I didn't know who I was – let alone who I would become – without the very thing I had carried for almost half my life.

Because of this identity crisis, I continued to cling to the safety of the familiar. I couldn't let go of the meal plan or the exchanges I had used at Carolina House, and I increasingly weighed and measured my food. I never said no to a slice of birthday cake or a family dinner, but only if plans had clearly been communicated beforehand. I couldn't understand why I felt like this, and I became increasingly frustrated as I failed to pin down what was "wrong" with me. I had done all this work, and I still couldn't live a normal life! I had spent six months in treatment, and I still wanted to weigh and measure food! I endured hours upon hours of therapy, and I still struggled with anxiety! What was I missing?

In an effort to define myself in a new way – with the hope that this would somehow inspire me to act differently – I changed my Instagram username. Although I loved food, and my passion for creating and sharing recipes inspired me to nourish myself, I realized I was more than just a foodie, and spending time in the kitchen didn't define my life as a whole. I *had* done so much work, gone to treatment, and endured therapy, all because I was committed to discovering a life that was truly worth living. But at this point, freshly beginning my recovery journey outside of treatment, it sure didn't feel like it. My brain buzzed with anxious and obsessive thoughts 24/7, only ever dimming during the numbness of a depressive phase. All I wanted was for my life to be *simple*. So, in May 2018, I said goodbye to @lilrecoveringfoodie and hello to @simplybalancedliv.

Along with this username change, I started a blog. Sharing a new recipe or writing a heartfelt caption was part of my daily ritual, but the limits to how much I could share on Instagram were constricting. I wanted a platform that was my own, one where recipes didn't get lost down the feed and captions weren't limited to a certain number of characters. On my website, I wrote extensions of the stories I told on Instagram. I became even more excited to create in the kitchen now that people could land on my recipes through organic web searches. While posting, uploading, and tweaking, I discovered a new passion: graphic design.

Outside of my talent for drawing symmetrical rainbows, castles, and perfectly traced coloring pages, I was never considered "artistic." My dad had grown up with a knack for the craft, one that both my sisters inherited. I dreaded art class at school and would much rather spend hours doing algebra homework or writing persuasive essays. My sisters were completely the opposite. It was their artwork that was put on display in the school hallways, but it was my papers that got entered in the writing contests.

"Everyone has their own creative outlet," Mae reminded me every time I became frustrated with my lack of ability to sketch something.

"Easy for you to say!" I would glare at the picturesque cartoon she had generated in less than ten minutes.

I knew I had other talents, but part of me so badly wanted also to be artistic in the same way my sisters and dad were. Designing my website, photographing food, and creating graphics to go along with my posts was the format in which that ability came to life.

As with any external pursuit to unearth one's identity, however, my newfound discovery of this creativity wasn't strong enough to fully fund my healing. I woke up excited to photograph my new pancake recipe and write another inspirational blog post, but my soul still felt misaligned. Body image struggles penetrated my mind during school, as I constantly worried about what people were thinking of me. To grasp something with tangible certainty, I turned to labels.

76

LABELS

In May 2018, I announced I was going vegan. In the few months leading up to that, I had transitioned back into vegetarianism out of guilt for all the meat I had consumed at Carolina House. My relationship with animals has always been a deep one, in the sense that the connection doesn't require any of the social rules that come with humans. With animals, I can bond in silence, as our compassion is unspoken. With animals, I don't have to put on a mask, to pretend I'm someone I'm not. With animals, I can be myself without judgment. When my hamsters passed away, I truly felt like I had lost my best friends.

"They're just hamsters," a classmate said to me after I finally returned to school almost a week later.

"They're beings!" I responded angrily. "They're living souls just like you and me!" I couldn't understand how people saw animals as different, just like how I cannot understand how some people discriminate against others based on the color of their skin. Just as all humans are created equal, I believe animals are too.

I convinced myself that my going vegetarian was for ethical reasons. "I'm doing it for the animals," I said whenever someone questioned me. I sensed my family's skepticism about the return of this dietary restriction, which is why I diligently researched the animal industry: to defend my position with undeniable facts. The more I researched, however, the more I discovered that animal cruelty and inhumane practices didn't just affect meat. They affected eggs, dairy, and many other animal-containing products that line the aisles of our supermarkets today. My newfound knowledge, paired with the endless vegan Instagram accounts I was following, influenced me to finally make the switch. I was not yet aware that many of the "recovery" accounts were vegan *because* it was a socially acceptable way to restrict.

As I stretched my food choices to fit within the limitations of the vegan box, I felt as I had when I was first given a meal plan and then advised to follow the low-FODMAP diet. There were fewer options when it came to food, which naturally meant less chance of overwhelm. I only allowed myself to eat foods that were 100% plant-based, a strict rule that made eating that much easier.

For the first few weeks of adopting my new label, life was good. I had a purpose, and I was in control. Along with eating a purely plant-based diet, I focused on eating only whole foods. Not to mention, everything was still being precisely weighed and measured.

"Are you falling back into old patterns?" my mom asked me one evening.

"What are you talking about?" I said defensively.

She replied as calmly as she could. "You're weighing food again, and your diet is incredibly limited, honey." Loving worry suffused her gaze.

"My diet isn't limited! Becoming vegan has opened my world to so many new food combinations and recipes! Plus, the only reason I weigh food is to make sure I'm eating enough." All of my statements were true. Becoming vegan *had* inspired me to step out of my comfort zone when trying new foods and recipes, but only because it was within a different comfort zone – the comfort of a label. When it came to weighing and measuring my intake, it *was* because I wanted to ensure adequacy. My body still required an incredible amount of food to maintain my weight, and my hunger cues were still unreliable. Attaching numbers – labels – to food was my equivalent of a permission slip to eat.

77

PERIOD

Even though my food choices were rooted in orthorexia (an extreme obsession with health), my consistent routine around eating and resting gave my body the ability to heal. On July 11, 2018, I got my first period EVER. Despite menstruation being one of the most inner-body experiences in existence, my first period felt like the most out-of-body experience ever. I was officially a woman, a concept I had never identified with until then.

I called my mom during her work. "Mom! It finally happened!" I exclaimed.

"Oh my goodness!" she replied ecstatically. "I can't believe it!"

I didn't even need to tell her exactly *what* had happened, as impending menstruation was the most plausible explanation for what I had experienced in the days prior: cravings, cramping, digestive issues, insomnia, and more. At first, I thought nothing of it; these were all common symptoms of recovery from a restrictive eating disorder, symptoms I had come to accept and trust would pass. But the sudden spike in their intensity, not to mention the cloudy white discharge I had been seeing in my underwear for several months, indicated that my body was executing something miraculous.

That night, we celebrated my transition into womanhood with an expensive dinner and copious slices of triple chocolate cake – the latter being a pure necessity for me when it comes to celebrations of any kind! As I licked the remains of rich frosting from my plate, I felt victorious and free. But as soon as the climax of the evening had passed and I started preparing for bed, the cramps that had first been only physical started radiating through my mind as well. For exactly one year and one week, I had been working tirelessly to heal myself. I had overshot my weight, refrained from exercise, gone to therapy, and forced myself to continue doing it all...even if that meant using the food scale and following a rigid diet. Getting my first period was one of my goals from the very beginning, a milestone that proved my fulfillment of health. Now that I had reached that milestone, what came next?

Suddenly, the pressure was on. I could no longer use the excuse of "needing to become healthy first" to rest, honor my cravings, or eat past fullness. I could no longer hide behind the mask of being "in recovery" to do all the things someone in that position needs to do. The purpose that had so long been to recover – whatever that meant – had been achieved. I was healthy! Healed! Fixed! And what does one do when they are healthy? They engage in activities to maintain their health.

78

"Healthy"

Back in 2018, I didn't understand the meaning of the word "healthy" in the way I do while writing this book. My perception of health was deeply rooted in diet culture, as I held beliefs that certain foods were either "good" or "bad," that BMI was an accurate measure of overall well-being, and that forcing yourself to go to the gym – even if you dreaded it – was a health-promoting activity. However, because I had never menstruated before, I knew I lacked health, and therefore I knew diet culture statements didn't apply to me. Whole milk is "bad" and skim milk is "good"? Not if you're in recovery from an eating disorder. Going for a run is "healthy" and resting is "lazy"? Not if you're in recovery from an eating disorder. Eating a single cookie is "normal" and honoring your cravings for the whole pack is "abnormal"? Not if you're in recovery from an eating disorder. For so long, I permitted myself to be the exception to society's rules because *I was in recovery from an eating disorder*.

Now, I was no longer an exception. I believed I was just like everybody else and had to abide by society's diet-culture-infested guidelines. To do so, I adjusted my meal plan to ensure I wouldn't gain any more weight. I stopped buying the vegan versions of my fear foods, because "healthy" people don't eat "junk food." I forced myself to drink water if I was still mentally hungry because "healthy" people "stop when they're full." The most prominent persuasion of all, however, was my adherence to the plant-based lifestyle.

There wasn't a day of my being vegan that I didn't think about eating animal products. I absolutely loved (and still do!) Greek yogurt, cheese, and eggs, not to mention the benefits I got from taking collagen powder daily. But when I decided to adhere to my new label, all of that had to go. Even my Instagram bio mentioned my veganism, and I couldn't lie to my audience! Cutting corners would have made me a fraud. As I scrolled the app – pictures of thick yogurt bowls and my favorite egg-containing baked goods whizzing before my eyes – I contemplated ending my vegan voyage and returning to a way of eating that would excite me again. But after getting my period – and moreover, doing so while vegan – I was convinced that veganism was the way to health.

In the following months, I started feeling more and more like crap. What had started as a new sense of purpose and euphoria as I ate my overpriced organic produce, tofu, legumes, and whole grains transformed into persistent fatigue, nightmarish insomnia, and endless daydreams about all the foods that didn't fit within the box of my vegan label. Deep down, I knew veganism wasn't working for me...*but it had to!* It worked for so many people on social media, so why shouldn't it work for me? I read every article I could find on supplementing as a vegan, the importance of movement, and living "in line with nature." From there, I bought all the recommended pills and joined my first gym. I wasn't about to admit defeat; that would make me lazy. I needed to stay in control and would do anything I could to maintain that.

79

EXTREME HUNGER

When I got home from school one October afternoon, my body took that control from me. After oversleeping that morning and heading out in a rush, I was met with a growling stomach and commanding cravings as the clock announced the end of the school day. Fatigued, I biked home as quickly as possible and planned out exactly what I was going to eat: my usual snack plus a little more to make up for what I'd missed during the day. I raced into the kitchen and downed my daily bowl of soy yogurt with berries and a chocolate mug cake faster than I could chew, then made some peanut butter toast to finish my little feast. After gobbling up the toast, however, the feast was not over. It had only just begun.

"Okay, I'll make another slice of toast," I whispered to myself, unclipping the bread bag and popping a slice into the toaster. As the kitchen filled with bakery aromas, I grabbed the peanut butter jar and set it on the counter. "I'll just have a spoonful of this while I wait for the toast," I whispered, the urgency of my hunger increasing by the second. I slid a teaspoon of it into my mouth, mesmerized by the thick texture of the nutty paste. I placed the spoon in the sink, still waiting for the toast to pop up. I grabbed another spoon, dipped it into the jar, and repeated the process.

Finally, the toaster chimed. As I smeared peanut butter onto the crisped bread, my pulse increased at the thought of having gone over my planned nut butter amount. I covered the toast with the thinnest possible layer of peanut butter, attempting to compensate for my sinful spoon act. As I munched on the toast, unsatisfied at every bite by the measly ratio of peanut butter to bread, I reminded myself that this was simply my punishment for being impatient. But now, it was my body's turn. *Do you seriously think you're satisfied now?* I could practically hear my tummy cry out. *I'll show you what satisfaction feels like!*

Before I knew it, the contents of the peanut butter jar had vanished. Inspired by my first snack at Carolina House, I had covered ten whole Oreo cookies in it, saying, "Okay, now *this* is going to be the last one," every time I grabbed another Oreo. But when the cookies were gone and the peanut butter jar had been tossed into the recycle bin, my body screamed for more. Instead of being possessed by the devil of an eating disorder during a panic attack, I was now possessed by a black hole of hunger.

I spent the rest of the afternoon laying on my bed in discomfort as I played the event back in my mind. What had just happened? Whatever it was *couldn't* have happened. I blinked, wishing it had all been a terrible nightmare and the morning sun would glimmer through my purple curtains as it always did. But every time I opened my eyes, it had gotten slightly darker and the reality hit me harder: I had binged for the first time in my life.

Desperate, I posted a sequence of stories on Instagram, begging for advice, connection, and help. I felt so alone, so lost, so *out of control*. I had never eaten this much in one sitting – not even at Carolina House! Thankfully, the responses came pouring in.

"You've probably been under-fueling and this is your body's way of telling you it needs more!" one of the replies read.

"Whatever you do, make sure to NOT restrict after this, as that will perpetuate the binge-restrict cycle!" another read.

All of the responses confirmed something I had known all along: I had been restricting, whether I was ready to admit it or not. Even though I had been consuming enough calories, even though I had been deemed "weight restored," hell, even though I had gotten my period for the first time, I had been restricting myself. But because my restriction was neatly packaged into boxes labeled "vegan" and "healthy" – which themselves were squeezed into a larger box labeled "socially acceptable" – I'd been hiding from the truth.

On that October afternoon, I stopped turning my back on the issue. Maybe I was "healthy" to a physical extent, but clearly, I wasn't healthy enough for my body to fully trust me again. I was still thinking about food all the time, planning my meals obsessively, and attaching exercise to deserving food. I couldn't bear it any longer, so I surrendered again. Maybe I would gain more weight and everything would get worse. But what if everything got *better*? Only one thing was for sure: I had not endured this whole recovery journey only to accept an endless obsession with food and exercise.

That same day, after I changed out of my jeans and into the stretchiest pants I owned, I strode to the grocery store across from our house and bought every single item of food that had appeared in my dreams: Nutella, nut butter, sugary cereal, real ice cream, full-fat yogurt, meat, fish, cookies, granola, and everything else that didn't fit into the boxes I'd trapped myself in. I no longer cared if a vegan, whole-foods, plant-based diet worked for people on Instagram. All that mattered was that it didn't work for *me*. It was time I started living life on my own terms.

For dinner that night, I made salmon with sweet potatoes, spinach, and hard-boiled eggs, all finished off with an entire pint of real ice cream and unmeasured bowls of cereal with whole milk. For the first time in what felt like forever, I went to bed satisfied.

As I crept under the covers, I was met with the fear that I wouldn't be hungry enough for breakfast in the morning. I had eaten "too much." Surely my body would still be full the next day. Yet I couldn't have been more wrong. I woke up so ravenous, it was as if the floodgates to Hungerland had opened!

The following weeks consisted exclusively of eating, eating, and eating some more. All my body wanted at every moment was food, even when I became physically nauseous after yet another feast. I feared I was "swinging to the other side" and becoming a binge eater, a phenomenon I often read about on recovery forums or while scrolling social media. This fear increased linearly with my weight, which was rising fast.

"I'm developing binge eating disorder!" I cried after consuming an entire jar of Nutella, peanut butter, copious bowls of cereal, handfuls of cookies, and a whole pint of ice cream. I stood behind the kitchen counter, trembling as I covered my face with my hands. I didn't understand how I had let myself go like this.

"Oh, honey, I doubt that." My mom comforted me, rubbing my back as she always did when I was stressed. "You've spent years not eating enough. Your body needs all this food!"

"But I'm already weight restored!" I yelled defensively. "I can't gain more weight! I'll become so fat!"

"Livia, please don't say that," my mom said with a frown. "You are healthy now. You are finally full of life again, and I'm sure this is just a phase that's part of the recovery process."

"Exactly! I'm healthy, meaning I shouldn't be eating this much food. I'm not supposed to gain any more weight!"

"Who says? Maybe you do need to gain more weight! Maybe it's what your body needs to get even healthier!"

There wasn't a bone in my body that perceived even the slightest truth in her words. As tears poured out of my swollen eyes, I cried, "What if I never stop eating?"

80

SATISFACTION

The fear that I would never stop eating was rooted in a much deeper fear: the fear that I would never feel satisfied. On that evening after my first binge – when I finally allowed myself to eat all the foods I'd been restricting – I got a taste of what satisfaction felt like. But because it was of short duration, because I'd woken up the next morning even more ravenous, I feared my body was broken. I feared my eating disorder had started too young, that I'd restricted for too long, and that I had run myself into a bodily state beyond repair. Sure, my body had proven its healing capabilities by getting a period, but what if that was only part of a much bigger picture, one that sketched the irreparable damage my eating disorder had done to my body? What if I just had to accept that my body was different – that I was simply an anomaly?

All of the restriction – the dessert-flavored protein bars, the airy protein fluff, waiting to eat the majority of my calories until later in the day – were all ways in which I was building a "buffer" around my intake. Diet culture taught me that protein was the most satisfying of the macronutrients, which my literal mind translated into protein being the most important. Whereas I feared eating a real cookie would just leave me wanting more, a cookie-dough-flavored protein bar would guarantee physical satisfaction. Whereas I feared eating an ice cream cone would have me at the mercy of mental hunger until the entire pint was gone, two massive bowls of protein fluff would guarantee physical fullness. Whereas I feared honoring my hunger as it came – even if that meant first thing in the morning – would set me up for the black-and-white thinking trap that stated, "I've already overindulged, I might as well binge the whole day," sticking to a rigid schedule by which I would only allow myself to "indulge" in the evening protected me from "overindulging" in life.

It wasn't until I realized satisfaction is more than just a physical sensation that I started to fully heal. My extreme hunger had existed long before it turned into a physical feeling of needing to fill what seemed like an empty cavity of a stomach. It had existed in the form of mental hunger for years – I just didn't know mental hunger "counted" as hunger. I had become so obsessed with nutrition panels, ingredient lists, recipes, and everything else that had to do with food that I had conditioned my brain to lead a life that would forever revolve around food. But I hadn't truly conditioned my brain to think about food – my obsession was simply the result of my body's requirement for more of it! The reason I feared I wouldn't feel satisfied was because I never truly satisfied myself. The reason I feared I would never stop eating was because I never gave myself permission to fully start. It was only once I gave myself unconditional permission to eat – and let go of all labels – that I found freedom. This epiphany jump-started my rebrand to Liv Label Free, my recovery coaching program, and my online course Extremely Hungry to Completely Satisfied. Before I could share my new messages with the world, however, there was still lots to learn.

81

NINETEEN

On my nineteenth birthday – about six weeks after my extreme hunger started – I got my second period.

"You see?" my mom asked exuberantly, giving me the biggest hug after I broke the news.

"Yeah," I replied shyly, with the same set of mixed emotions as the first time around.

"Your body needed the extra fuel!"

I knew she was right – I knew my body was right. But just like the last time, part of my brain screamed, "Now that you're healthy again, you don't need all this extra weight!" On my nineteenth birthday, my weight was at a record high. I felt fluffy, embarrassed, and uncomfortable. Getting dressed led to distress, with only a few pairs of pants that still fit me.

"Honey, you can buy new clothes!" my mom reminded me during every frustration fit, but I never listened. I didn't *want* new clothes. I just wanted my old clothes to fit. So I kept them, saving them for the days I'd be at a lower weight again. I had read about the phenomenon of weight overshoot many times, so I was convinced that my current spike in BMI was simply part of this essential phase. But how long was this going to last? What if the weight didn't drop? What if my old clothes would forever remain my old clothes?

I wrote more blogs than I can count during the months I experienced extreme hunger. I shared how it started, I shared scientific research, and I shared what it felt like. Part of this was to inspire and support others going through the same – as I know firsthand how meaningful it is to know you're not alone – but another part of it was for me. Writing about how important it was to honor the extreme hunger and accept the weight gain acted as a reminder to myself to keep doing so.

Even though a part of me still so desperately wanted to control the situation and restrict, I knew that wasn't *really* control – and perhaps that "part of me" wasn't *really* me. Perhaps it was a lingering foot of the parasite that had been my eating disorder, trying to crawl back under my skin and spread like a virus. But I wasn't going to let it! The thoughts were going to be there – I knew they would – but my actions were always under my control. Some days were harder than others, but by challenging the ED thoughts time and time again, the parasite learned that it was wasting its time.

That next year was a year of ebbs and flows. Every day started with the same choice: to choose recovery or the parasite. Alongside the increasing demands of school, I often felt like I was walking on a tightrope, constantly teetering on the edge of burnout as I put one foot in front of the other. Through writing blogs, sharing lengthy Instagram captions, and continuing my daily gratitude practice, I motivated myself to keep choosing recovery – but this didn't come without a constant mental battle.

The year 2019 was the year in which I felt the highest of highs and the lowest of lows. There were days I would photograph multiple recipes, dancing my heart out in the kitchen with my sisters. There were days I would go for a run simply because I wanted to, floating along the pavement, my energy propelling me forward. There were days I would babble my Instagram community's ears off with how amazing life was, followed by inspirational posts regarding specific topic requests. But there were also days I was too depressed to get out of bed. Sometimes, weeks would go by during which I barely spoke. I was so exhausted that I wanted only to crawl into a hole and disappear. During this time my anxiety and OCD got much worse; I clung to cleanliness and order to replace my obsession with food and exercise.

82

GYM

Just as my community at Carolina House played a crucial role in me regaining my strength, my gym community in Utrecht did the same. I first joined the gym in September of 2018, permitting myself to explore movement after taking over a year off exercise. As I was building my mental strength, I wanted to feel physically strong, too. I wanted to start feeling confident in my body, embracing the weight gain as it paralleled increased physical strength. Not to mention, I craved a new mode of self-care. The worsening OCD, the unpredictable phases of depression, and the overall lack of lust for life were damaging me – I needed an outlet for my anxiety, something that would get me out of this lonely rut and back into the swing of social interaction.

My first few weeks at the gym were full of trial and error. I had no idea what I was doing, but I was embarrassed when a personal trainer would come over to show me how to properly use one of the machines. At the time, my main workout inspiration came from fitness accounts I followed on Instagram. I mixed and matched moves based on their videos, creating variety by learning about different training styles. Although I started this fitness journey full of excitement, the pressure to do it "perfectly" led to anxiety and comparison.

On Instagram and YouTube were girls with six-pack abs who claimed to train X days a week. There were people who said you should train for X number of hours if you wanted to get "results." There were people debating the role of cardio. There were people saying you should focus on one muscle group per session and others saying it was best to always train full body. A storm of opposing information battered me, fueling frustration and disappointment in myself and my capabilities. I had just spent the last year doing absolutely no exercise, not knowing half the names of the moves these "influencers" were referencing. So I became utterly obsessed with learning every in and out of working out. I forced myself to replicate one influencer's "training split," then another, and then decided which one I liked best. It wasn't until I came home crying one evening, exhausted after a full week of workouts, that I realized I had gotten so caught up in what other people were doing, I had completely lost sight of my own needs. In bed that night, I journaled almost as frantically as I had in Carolina House, reminding myself of where I came from and that I deserved to give myself grace.

From that moment onward, I stopped stressing about performing a certain number of reps or sets. I stopped following a strict schedule created by someone else and asked myself what *my* body needed each day. I looked around the gym and performed exercises I felt like doing, testing out machines and playing with different weights. I stopped when I felt like stopping, a stark contrast from the "no pain, no gain" mindset I swore by for years. This, too, was a series of trial and error. Sometimes I'd go to the gym only to realize five minutes later that my body wasn't feeling it. Giving myself permission to stop and leave offered me a sense of freedom I had never experienced before.

After a few months, I started to notice my confidence and strength soar – both physically and mentally. My mood stabilized, my focus increased, and my overall sense of happiness improved. As I became a "regular" at the gym, I got to know the team members, smiling and engaging in conversations here and there. Having relied solely on my Instagram community as a form of social interaction since Carolina House, I didn't realize the importance of in-person friends until I started making them at the gym.

"Have you ever tried a class?" a fitness instructor asked me after my solo session one morning. I responded that I hadn't, satisfied with my current routine of working out while blasting music in my AirPods. "You really should!" the instructor went on. "It's a super fun way to work out in a group setting."

"I don't really like doing things in groups." I had always been independent and preferred to do things at my own pace on my own time.

"What do you have to lose?" The trainer's tone was upbeat. "You can give it a try, and if you hate it, you can always fly solo!"

What *did* I have to lose? After replaying the trainer's words back in my head, I looked up and smiled. "You're right!" Then I walked to the front desk and asked, "Can you please book me for the 10:30 a.m. class on Sunday?"

After trying a mix of classes, I discovered my two favorites and became obsessed (this time in a good way!) with the group environment. It was, yet again, a testament to the value of stepping out of my comfort zone and a confirmation that trying new things wasn't always a bad thing.

Part 7: Liv Label Free

83

PANDEMIC

In March 2020, the entire world was hit by a virus that no one could have foreseen: COVID-19. I had been Liv Label Free for just over a month, feeling fully aligned with my brand name for the first time. Something had been tugging at me for almost a year before I had the epiphany about the new name and corresponding logo, one I proudly designed myself and still get excited by every time I see it. When I changed my username to Simply Balanced Liv, I thought I wanted my life to be simple and balanced. I thought that by controlling external factors through ritual and routine, I could create an equilibrium that resembled a simple math formula. If everything was always the same, simplicity was inevitable! If I always ate the same foods, moved in the same way, engaged in the same activities, and took the same approach, how could anything *not* be balanced? I knew what I had to do to avoid rocking the boat, so I kept doing that – to stay afloat.

But that's all I was doing: staying afloat. Sure, I was at a higher weight and had become drastically more flexible in my habits after Carolina House, but I still didn't feel free. The control I thought I had actually controlled me, perhaps now more than ever, as I no longer had an eating disorder to hide behind. Once I learned that life simply isn't simple and that perfect balance doesn't exist, I allowed myself to veer away from an ideal that had long held me at its mercy. Veering away was scary though, similar to the loss of identity I felt when I thought about how much my body had changed. Trying to accept that *change is the only constant* felt like jumping into deep waters without knowing if I could swim. But after everything I had been through – including having pulled myself back from the edge of death – I knew I was capable of being anything I wanted myself to be. At this point, all I wanted was to be free. I didn't know exactly what that was going to look like or how turning this new corner would unfold, but yet again, I chose to trust the process and surrender.

What started out as an inkling became a growing need to change my name. After several sleepless nights spent tossing and turning, days spent scribbling name ideas on scrap paper, and hours spent mapping out my brand vision on poster board, I finally envisioned the image of my current logo in a dream. I always knew I wanted to keep "Liv" in the name, as I could use this to signify "life" and "living." I wanted to liv(e) free, and I could only do this once I let go of labels. All the diagnoses, food judgments, and rules I had around how I was "supposed" to live were rooted in labels. Once I removed the tags, I was free to be me. Hence "Liv Label Free."

Living the label-free lifestyle made me feel like everything had fallen into place. I was healthy both physically and mentally, I had an incredible community of people that loved and supported me, and I had visions of returning to the USA after finishing school. Everything was going so well! Until quarantine happened.

When the Dutch government announced a lockdown on March 15, 2020, my first thought was about the gym closing. How was I going to work out? How was I going to stay social? The surge of stress that accompanied the announcement wasn't tied to a desire to exercise per se but rather to the change in my usual routine – a routine I had come to love and trust. When I said goodbye to my room the morning I flew to North Carolina in 2017, I had sworn to myself that I'd never exercise in there again.

The very thought of rolling out a yoga mat or doing push-ups on my bedroom floor sent shivers up my spine.

"I finally healed my relationship with exercise!" I cried as the family sat around the television. "The gym *can't* be closed!"

"You're not the only one dealing with this!" Mae exclaimed. "Schools are closed too! How am I going to see my friends?"

"I wonder what this means for my work in the lab," my mom said.

In the following days, supermarkets were raided as people hoarded toilet paper and stocked their fridges and pantries with more food than they could hold. When I saw viral videos of people joking about the situation, it reminded me distinctly of my own history with hoarding – my obsession with my bar drawer when I was restricted and malnourished.

"Huh." I chuckled to myself as the memory washed over me. The whole COVID mania shed light on the fact that my eating disorder behaviors were not anomalous; stocking up on resources during times of uncertainty was simply human. For years, my body couldn't trust my environment. *Why wasn't I eating enough? When would food be abundant again?* Even though rationally I knew that food was abundant all along, my survival brain perceived scarcity and therefore switched on a biological mechanism to ensure my survival.

This same phenomenon was now occurring in people worldwide as they gravitated towards external resources to provide them with a sense of safety. Ironically, I had no urge to stockpile resources now that I understood the biology behind it. I had taught my body that it could trust me by adopting an abundance mindset, which I believe carried me through the unpredictability and fear of the pandemic. I had survived an eating disorder. Surely I'd get through this as well! In fact, I was even more positive about getting through this pandemic because I wasn't going at it alone. My eating disorder isolated me in ways that are incomprehensible for someone who's never struggled with the illness, whereas quarantine isolated us all. Yes, everyone had to go into isolation, but everyone was going into isolation *together*.

The ways in which people and services started showing up online illustrated a creativity that could only have been harnessed when it became a necessity. From one day to the next, the world had flipped from physical to digital. Sitting in a classroom was replaced by waiting for the teacher to let you into the Zoom meeting, and dates at a coffee shop turned into FaceTime conversations with the coffee machine going in the background. Even the gyms started live-streaming their classes, which turned out to be my unforeseen gateway to fully healing my relationship with exercise.

84

WORKING OUT TRAUMA

Just as I had chosen to let go of the traumatic power Rintveld Clinic held over me when enrolling at the Herman Jordan Lyceum, I could choose to let go of the power my history of exercise addiction had over me. My oath to never work out in my room again acted as a shield from reliving the compulsions to try to squeeze in as many reps or sets as possible. But just as with any mask, it simply hid what was underneath, making the root cause all the more fragile. If I wanted to heal the traumatic experiences of my past, I had to give my brain proof that they were, indeed, experiences of the past. They no longer had to exist in the present. To regain power over movement in a way that wasn't controlled by the devilish voice in my head, I had to experiment with moving in my room.

When my gym announced the livestream of my favorite Sunday cardio class, I was equal parts excited and nervous. Sunday morning was the highlight of my week – waking up, making pancakes, posting the pictures on Instagram, and then leaving the house at precisely 10:00 a.m. had become my favorite ritual. Now, however, I would be doing the class alone – in my room. Would I be compelled to add extra reps, knowing that I could have easily slipped them in without standing out from the crowd? Maybe. Would I feel the urge to add on a YouTube workout afterward, knowing that I was already in my gym clothes and all it would take was opening a new tab? Maybe. But was it my choice whether or not to act on these compulsions? Always.

I Zoomed into the livestream and smiled at the trainer's enthusiasm on the screen. This was definitely weird, but the physical distance between us didn't seem to influence the teacher's bubbly and upbeat tone. I jumped and danced in my room, breaking a sweat on my yoga mat like I had nearly every day since the age of eleven – but this was different. I wasn't sweating as a result of self-imposed stress and pressure. I was sweating as the result of celebrating my body – not only for its physical capability to move but for my mental capacity to challenge my trauma and heal from something, releasing the power it once held over me.

After enjoying the heck out of that first online class, I grew excited to try new forms of movement that my gym didn't offer. Suddenly, the world had gone from shutting down to opening up in a completely different way! Not only could I now join the livestreams and engage in classes hosted by my local gym, but I was inspired to join my followers on Instagram in their favorite online workouts as well – workouts being done all over the world! I tried yoga, Pilates, dancing, and kickboxing. I bought weights and trained with my favorite non-diet fitness accounts. I got into running again over the summer. Experimenting with new kinds of movement in a non-social setting took the performance pressure off me and gave me much-needed time and space to learn the way I learned best: independently.

85

SCHOOL

Another massive insight resulting from the pandemic was the overarching idea of alternative paths. Even before COVID hit, in January 2019, it became clear to me that my school career was not in alignment with my health.

"You should really go home," one of my friends said right before an exam. "You don't look so good."

"I don't *feel* so good." Exhaustion emanated from my voice. I was several months into 5 VWO (equivalent to honors/advanced level junior year of high school in the US), feeling increasingly fragile as the year progressed. Besides the body image issues that spiked after my extreme hunger started in late 2018, I was beginning to comprehend what Adelyn had meant with her parting words on the day of my discharge: recovery was partially a physical battle when it came to weight gain and other bodily changes, but the "real work" had everything to do with mentality. It was a round-the-clock job to shift my mindset from a place of limitation to a place of empowerment, one that often left me drained by the end of the day. I now also understood why no time or space was made for school at Carolina House – there simply was no time or space for it in recovery.

When it came to school, I often felt I had jumped the gun. I hadn't even been home from treatment for two weeks before I was dropped into a classroom like an alien on a foreign planet. Yes, I wanted a social life and the chance to be normal, but most of me was still healing. The last thing my poor body needed was the additional strain of advanced-level classes, not to mention the social pressure of trying to "fit in" – I was still trying to fit into my new body! But I had no choice. School is mandatory in the Netherlands, and besides, "healthy" kids go to school. Too bad the brain can't be seen from the outside.

In the Netherlands, the school system is divided into elementary school and high school, except high school starts in seventh grade rather than ninth, as in the US. When leaving their elementary school, students get either a VMBO, HAVO, or VWO recommendation from their sixth-grade teacher. To quickly summarize each stream:

VMBO (Voorbereidend Middelbare Beroeps Onderwijs), meaning Preparatory Middle-Level Applied Education, is a four-year vocationally oriented stream focused on practical knowledge. It leads to vocational training (MBO) and is completed around the age of sixteen.

HAVO (Hoger Algemeen Voortgezet Onderwijs), meaning Higher General Continued Education, is a five-year middle stream that prepares students to study higher professional education at universities of applied sciences (hogescholen), where they can follow a bachelor's degree in applied sciences (HBO). HAVO students are around the age of seventeen when they graduate, equivalent to graduating after junior year in the US.

VWO (Voorbereidend Wetenschappelijk Onderwijs), meaning Preparatory Scientific Education, is the highest stream and requires six years of schooling, usually completed around the age of eighteen. It is focused on theoretical knowledge and prepares a student to pursue a bachelor's degree at a research university.

"Have you considered going to HAVO?" my mentor, Jolien, asked me on several occasions.

"I am not going to HAVO," I would respond with certainty. "I am completely capable of VWO!"

"Livia, it's not that I don't think you're capable," Jolien said during one of our weekly check-ins. "In fact, every teacher in this school believes you are one of the most capable students they've ever had!"

Ever since enrolling, I had gone all out to ensure the highest possible grades. Being a straight-A student was part of my identity, and doing it at the honors/advanced level even more so. Stepping down to HAVO would portray weakness – it would signify my failure to persevere at my highest level of intelligence.

"Isn't there a way to get more time?" I asked, willing to do anything to maintain my level of scholarship. After all, time was the reason I felt so overwhelmed. I'd been a deep learner my whole life and yearned for an abundance of space to internalize new material. When put under pressure, I froze, crushed by the fear that I wouldn't be able to complete something before the deadline. The classroom environment amplified this pressure, as it seemed impossible not to compare myself to others' locations on the timeline of assignment completion. I was three years older than them; there was no way I could feign a lower level of intelligence!

"We don't do this very often." Jolien looked up at the gray tiled ceiling. "But I could talk to the staff about spreading 5 and 6 VWO out for you. Perhaps over three years."

I took a moment to think about it, but it didn't take advanced-level mathematics to calculate my age were I to pursue this plan. "But then I'll be twenty-two when I graduate!"

"Yes," she replied. "It's obviously not ideal, but it will give you additional time and space. Of course, if you step down to HAVO, you'll be finished earlier."

Because I was already fifteen when my family moved to the Netherlands, I had not received a specific stream recommendation. However, my enrollment in VWO was a no-brainer, as I had always been a very bright student who received the highest grades at the highest level. School performance was an incredible strength of mine, but just as with my attention to detail and desire for perfection, it was also my Achilles' heel. My compulsion to prove my intelligence came at the cost of a decline in my mental health, which ultimately led to a physical breaking point.

86

HOMESCHOOL

I t was on that January afternoon in 2019, as dozens of students waited to enter the exam room, that I felt like I was going to collapse. I had already decided to pursue the path of completing 5 and 6 VWO in three years at the start of this school year, accepting the fact that I would be twenty-two at graduation. The scenario wasn't ideal, but at least I could avoid stepping down to HAVO. When my friend told me to go home because I didn't look so good – adding that I even looked pale – I knew she was right. Entering that exam room would be useless, as my brain felt like a ball of fog from which no logical thought could be transferred through pen onto paper.

"I'm going home," I told the lady in the attendance office. Whereas I feared she'd put her hands on her hips and reply with "Are you just trying to get out of taking the test?" as I'd seen her do with so many sneaky students, she immediately wrote down my name and said I was free to go. Because I was such a "special case," every staff member knew about my situation – which also meant they knew I wasn't the kind of person who would go home just to sneak out of an exam.

When I got home, I plopped onto my bed and was out like a light. I slept for five hours straight. As soon as I woke up, I knew I couldn't go back to school the next day.

In the two weeks that followed, I ate and slept. I was worn out in every way possible, utterly incapable of any activities besides those necessary for my survival. At the back of my mind, constant thoughts about school lingered. I knew I would have to go back at some point, but I also knew I couldn't go back to the way things were. Something had to change – but what?

During the meeting on my first day back, Jolien spoke on behalf of the staff. "We really think HAVO is the best choice for you, Livia." I had asked my mom to join me because I still felt fragile and needed as much support as I could get.

I nodded, unsure whether it was in agreement or mere acknowledgment. I had considered the option of HAVO during my two-week recuperation period, repeatedly reminding myself that my level of education said nothing about my worth or capabilities. I was so afraid of judgment and being deemed a "failure" for letting go of the very thing I was killing myself trying to achieve, and because of that fear, I hadn't realized the only person judging me was me. Just as I hid behind the identity of an eating disorder for so many years, I shielded myself from my true passion and purpose by studying nonstop and trying to get the highest grades. If I was the best at school and could attach numbers to my achievement, then I would be successful, right?

"I'll step down to HAVO," I stated as the meeting came to a close. At that moment, I realized that this was me achieving my highest level of success since enrolling at the Jordan. Choosing my health and happiness over external validation had always been my biggest challenge, yet there I was, making that very choice – just as I had done in so many other ways before. The streams of education were merely labels, labels that society had attached expectations to. But I wasn't born to fit the mold of society. Perhaps I wasn't going to university, but that's because I wanted to do much bigger things. To follow the VWO stream – simply to fit in the box that society labeled "success" – would only restrict me to that box. I didn't want to follow the beaten path and work a nine-to-five, let alone work for someone else. I wanted to build my business, as that was my true calling. My business was no longer going to be my "side hustle" that I made time for around school – my business was going to be my priority, and getting a school diploma was going to be a subsidiary undertaking.

Alongside my HAVO decision, I spoke up about wanting to complete school from home. The chaotic classroom environment overwhelmed me, and studying from home would allow me to complete the work at my own pace and on my own time. At first, my teachers were hesitant: "She'll miss important presentations!" and "There are several concepts in the book that need further explanation!"

"Can we just give it a try?" I asked. "If my grades drop, I'll come back to school." And with that, we had a deal. Due to the overstimulation the classroom provided, I had the utmost confidence that I would find greater clarity through doing my own research instead of listening to lectures...and I couldn't have been more right. Going through the material independently, paired with it simply being easier overall, sent my grades soaring without my having to go overboard with studying. When the pandemic hit a year later – and everyone had to do school from home – I looked back in amusement at the teachers' initial hesitancy towards my "radical" proposal.

87

WORKING TOGETHER

S pending less time on school opened up windows of opportunity to focus on my brand, which was steadily growing into so much more than a foodie Instagram account. What had started as a means of accountability and support in recovery was metamorphosing into a multidimensional resource for people from all walks of life. I received messages and emails about how my posts on extreme hunger had inspired others to go all in, and I couldn't help but smile when someone tagged me after making one of my recipes. Growing my brand also gave rise to the opportunity to collaborate with other brands – a development beyond my wildest dreams! Sure, I had seen popular Instagram accounts hashtag certain posts with #ad and #sponsored, but I never imagined that I – a relatively small account with a passion for nourishment – would be chatting with some of the brands I'd been using for years. I admit, it wasn't until someone asked me what I was charging per post that I realized I could actually be making money with partnerships. I had been doing product-for-post collaborations until that point, believing I'd totally "made it" as an influencer when I was sent free bags of granola or tubs of protein powder.

"You have that many followers and aren't asking for money?" Stéfan, a business owner whose social media I was running at the time, seemed surprised.

"Um, yeah?"

"With your quality of content and level of engagement, you could really be making good money," he said. "Anything you give for free is simply being taken advantage of!"

I was dumbfounded, but it also made total sense. I was providing free advertising! Of course I could be making money! I *should* be making money!

"What if they don't think I'm worthy of payment?" Although no one had ever told me the ins and outs of working with brands – meaning I couldn't have known how to approach paid collaborations in the first place – my underlying fear about my own worth and value manifested itself in ways that extended far beyond money. Brands were already sending me free products; how dare I ask for more? That would make me greedy and ungrateful.

"It doesn't make you either of those things," Stéfan reassured me. "You are running a business, which means you have to speak up for yourself. How do you think the biggest companies became big? Because they weren't afraid to sell."

Again, I knew he was right. For as long as I could remember, I had repressed my needs. I stayed quiet even when overstimulated, and I pretended to understand even when I was utterly confused. Life is hard enough; the last thing I wanted to do was make it harder for others. But in doing so, I was unconsciously making life harder for *myself.* Every time I had asked for help, I had been met with willingness and enthusiasm – proving that my fear of rejection really was FEAR: False Evidence Appearing Real.

From that moment onward, I started training my selling muscles. Just as with overcoming any fear, it felt uncomfortable. Doing the very thing I had conditioned myself not to do felt wrong and immoral; but that was simply because, according to my belief system, valuing my worth *was* wrong and immoral. Just as I had to take opposite actions to rid myself of my eating disorder's distorted belief system, I had to take opposite actions to rid myself of these limiting beliefs. The first step to achieving anything is believing it can be achieved; I could only achieve my entrepreneurial dream if I believed I was worthy of being an entrepreneur.

The reality of entrepreneurship is that you will face rejection, as I did many times. Several of the brands I reached out to informed me that they "didn't have the budget." This was frustrating, especially because I saw they had a budget for other creators. But staying in my own lane and sticking to my worth – regardless of whether a brand saw it or not – was what motivated me to keep reaching out and speaking up for myself. I may have gotten a hundred nos, but those nos made every yes all the more valuable. Although working with brands may seem completely separate from eating disorder recovery, I credit many of my skills as a business owner to the skills I learned on my recovery journey. Recovery is all about creating habits that support a life you want to live, and to create those habits, you must do hard things – consistently – until they become the default. The first hundred times, you'll fall down, which makes the first time you stay up all the more victorious.

Alongside an increasing number of brands requesting to work with me, I also started receiving requests from individuals in recovery wanting to work with me. They often had similar stories to mine, being labeled "too complex" and feeling lost about how to move forward. Whenever I wasn't creating content or working on school, I was answering emails or messages from people who desperately wanted to get better but didn't know where or how to start. Being their guidepost, their hand to hold, someone who truly understood what they were going through – that sparked a fire in me. It gave me a sense of purpose and meaning, one that was much deeper than the soul callings I'd felt before. This was the work I was born to do. I had survived an eating disorder because I was supposed to help others do the same.

On July 4, 2020 – my three-year recovery anniversary – I launched my first coaching offer. Within a few days of the announcement, I had several discovery calls lined up.

"Oh my goodness! People are actually interested in one-on-one coaching!" I said to my mom.

"Of course they are!" she replied. "You are doing such important work, and I'm so proud of you."

Alongside the excitement, however, was an equal amount of anxiety. "What if I suck at coaching? What if I am unable to actually help people? What if they waste their money on me?"

"Livia." My mom looked me dead in the eyes. "You are already coaching people and you are already helping them. It's about damn time you started getting paid for it!"

Her reassurance was a surefire confidence boost, but the real confidence came through the act of coaching itself. I view each individual as the unique person they are rather than just another client, establishing a relationship built on a foundation of trust and transparency. I adopted and adjusted a general roadmap for my twelve-week program but built in enough flexibility to embark on an entirely different journey with each individual. The commitment and strength of my clients continue to move me to this day, as I wholeheartedly believe recovery from an eating disorder is one of the hardest feats. Yet every day, I receive messages about overcoming a fear food or getting a period back. The gratitude my clients have expressed towards me is taken to the deepest point in my heart, but all the victories, tastes of freedom, steps closer to each individual's dream life – these are all because of the individual putting in the work. No one else can save you from an eating disorder – only you can take the necessary actions to create new habits – but being a guide along the way is one of my greatest honors.

88

AUTISM

O ne of the most beautiful aspects of being a coach is that I am constantly learning from my clients. When explaining a concept, I am often mandated to create new ways to bring it to life, resulting in insights I didn't have prior. These new insights not only allow me to better understand and help my clients, but they allow me to better understand and help myself.

Whether it was coaching, the pandemic, or a combination of both, 2020 was the year I discovered I am autistic. I had always been sensitive, in need of my own space, and desired predictability and routine – all traits that were tampered with when lockdown went into effect. Suddenly, I could no longer be in my own home without hearing sounds coming from every direction. Whether this was a blaring TV, my mom speaking loudly during a Zoom meeting (to make matters worse, her home office was adjacent to my room), or one of my sisters practicing the piano, any possibility of peace had vanished from my life. With everything in the outside world closed, there was nowhere to retreat to and recharge. Not to mention, the duration of this lockdown – along with all the other changes COVID brought with it – remained unpredictable. All of the routines I had established to support my well-being – I could kiss them goodbye.

Except I couldn't. I had to be strong, especially now that I was coaching others on their own journeys to freedom. Knowing that change is the only constant, understanding that pain is inevitable but suffering is optional, and realizing that the more I resisted the situation, the more torturous it would become, I chose to accept the unpredictability. I chose to go with the flow, trusting that this, too, shall pass. But despite my mindset work, despite closing my eyes and taking a deep breath when a loud burst of laughter from the other side of the wall broke my concentration, my brain simply would not flow. It didn't take long before this manifested physically, leaving me in a constant state of over-stimulation and anxiety. Part of me wanted to jump up and run, just as I had done for years during my eating disorder. I wanted to count calories again, to weigh my food, to attach numbers to everything and anything I could. But I didn't want to go back to my eating disorder, which made me wonder: what was really underlying these urges?

I believe I have one of my earliest clients to thank for piquing my interest in autism.

"What led you to reach out to me?" I asked her during our first session.

"I read your story on your blog, and what you shared about being labeled as "too complex" really resonated," she said. "Besides being diagnosed with anorexia, I am also autistic. No healthcare professional knew how to support me through both, saying I had to learn to cope with my autism before I could recover from my anorexia. But when I went to see a therapist to help me with the autism, all they said was that they couldn't because anorexia was hindering my ability to think clearly."

To provide the best possible support to my new client – and genuinely wanting to understand autism better – I turned to my mom's bookshelf. Over the years, she had purchased dozens of books recommended to her. She had books about the genetics behind anorexia, as well as self-help books for parents on how to support their sick child. She had books about the Maudsley Method, praising the "evidence-based" treatment approach that had only offered evidence to strengthening my eating disorder.

She had books about dealing with common comorbidities of eating disorders, including anxiety, depression, and OCD – all labels I had been diagnosed with over the years.

Out of all the books on her shelf, the most significant was *Aspergirls* by Rudy Simone. Before recommending Monique as my potential therapist, my mom's friend Celeste had suggested that my mom read the book *Aspergirls*. "I think Livia may be autistic," Celeste told my mom to support her book recommendation. Monique had said the same during one of our few sessions. Although I initially let their suggestions pass me by, Celeste and Monique's insights unfathomably shaped the way I understand myself today. But I didn't know that until I started working on myself.

While in treatment at Carolina House, I developed a love for reading novels. Before that time, I had never been the kind of person who turned to reading for pleasure or entertainment; the mandatory reading and writing assignments at school had saturated that part of my brain. But because I could no longer cook, bake, use electronics, or engage in any other of my usual pastimes when I wasn't studying, I had to find a new hobby.

One of my favorite books that I read at Carolina House was *The Rosie Project* by Graeme Simsion. It's about a man with Asperger's syndrome who is on a quest to find the "perfect" wife. As with everything in his life, he takes a systematic approach to this pursuit, learning many lessons through unforeseen obstacles and challenges. I had never heard the term Asperger's before reading Simsion's book but was enticed from the very first page. The main character's mathematical and logical thinking style, paired with his social awkwardness and tendency to take things literally, resonated with me in a way no fiction novel had before. I devoured the book with a constant smile on my face, humored by the author's witty writing style.

After finishing, I went on to read the sequels and actively sought out similar books. I became obsessed with the happiness and connection I felt when reading stories with neurodivergent characters, never thinking twice about the possibility of being neurodivergent myself. But when that autistic client of mine shared more about her experience of the world, and I noticed the title *Aspergirls* printed on the side of a book in my mom's room, I had to learn more.

After reading the first chapter of *Aspergirls*, my entire life fell into place. Everything that had never made sense about me now suddenly did. Everything that made me "weird" now made me unique. Perhaps most importantly, everything that made me feel alone now made me feel seen. I highlighted, underlined, and starred certain phrases as I whizzed through the story. Never in my life have I read a book as fast as I read *Aspergirls* by Rudy Simone.

89

A New Lens

My autism discovery gave me a new lens to look through. Everything that had appeared foggy and confusing was suddenly sharp and in focus. The symmetrical rainbow drawings, the lack of friends, the need for everything to match and make sense – autism was the piece that completed the puzzle of every trait that had been present since my youngest years. As I dove deeper into learning everything I could about autism and neurodiversity, I discovered that the puzzle piece is a very controversial symbol in the autism space. Many autistic individuals feel that the puzzle piece signifies incompleteness, a symbol that means missing a piece of oneself. Furthermore, ableist organizations (organizations that do not amplify the voices of actual autistic individuals) use the puzzle piece to imply the "puzzling" nature of the condition. After learning how this symbol is perceived in the autistic community, I hesitated to use it as a metaphor for my new diagnosis, despite my first instincts. I learned that the #actuallyautistic community prefers the following symbols:

Gold – The chemical symbol for gold is Au, the first two letters of the word "autism." The color gold is used to show the bright and shining future of people with autism, rather than the common belief that being autistic means being doomed to lifelong suffering and hardship.

Infinity – Often rainbow or gold-colored, the infinity sign represents the endless possibilities for individuals on the spectrum.

The gold color is associated with the aforementioned symbol, and the rainbow symbolizes the color spectrum that is full of wonder and light, just as autism is a spectrum full of unique traits and miraculous people.

Butterfly – A relatively newer symbol, the butterfly signifies change and diversity within the autistic community.

You can find a visual overview of these symbols at livlabelfree. com/symbols.

If a majority of the autistic community advocates for alternative symbols, why do I still use the puzzle piece to illustrate the impact of this new diagnosis? Because for me, discovering I am autistic *made me complete*. In contrast to the traditional view, I do not perceive the puzzle piece to symbolize incompleteness or puzzlement. Without the autistic label, I felt incomplete and puzzled, whereas with it – well, the rest is history!

Having just read about my relationship with labels, one may wonder *Isn't autism a label?* It very much is – but so is everything. When I advocate for a label-free lifestyle, I am advocating for a life without restrictions. I don't label food as "good" or "bad" because doing so would pressure me to restrict the "bad" foods. I don't label exercise as "productive" and sitting on the couch as "lazy" because doing so would propel me straight back into a compulsive relationship with movement. I don't label my emotions as "negative" or "positive" because all emotions are meant to be felt, and suppressing unwanted feelings would lead to a buildup of internal stress.

Just as different emotions have their time and place, so do labels. The way we communicate as a society is through labels. We make appointments based on times, go on vacations with airline tickets, and have allergen warnings printed on snacks containing peanuts. Without labels, society wouldn't be able to function! And that's the very reason for using them: they optimize functionality and serve an important purpose. Similarly, my autistic label optimizes my functionality and serves an important purpose. It allows me to understand myself better, which allows me to show up at my best.

Another nuance when it comes to autism and its place in my label-free lifestyle is that I view autism as a part of my identity rather than some sticker that's been plastered onto my forehead. When I was struggling with anorexia, never did I identify with the disease. I believe my years of denial were rooted in being labeled as "anorexic" and "disordered," because I was neither of those things. I *had* anorexia, along with the common comorbid mental health issues such as OCD and anxiety, but at my core, I was always Livia. Recognizing the eating disorder as something that I had – something separate from me – rather than viewing it as part of my identity gave me the power to let go of and ultimately recover from the illness.

When it comes to autism and neurodiversity, the semantics play out much differently. At the start of my autism journey (or should I say, at the start of my being aware I am autistic journey), I did not know there was a difference between "I am autistic" and "I have autism." Because of my history with disordered eating, I defaulted to saying, "I have autism," just as I had learned to say, "I had anorexia." It wasn't until I first opened up about being on the spectrum on my YouTube channel that a fellow autistic individual kindly pointed out that most autistic people prefer identity-first language over person-first language. I had never heard of this terminology before, so of course, I did everything I could to gain a better understanding! It is now such an honor to be able to share that knowledge with you.

Identity-First Language puts a person's condition or state before the person. In the autism community, most people prefer using terms such as "autistic," "autistic person," or "autistic individual." This is because we understand autism as an inherent part of an individual's identity, similar to how individuals in the LGBTQ+ community might prefer to be called "gay" or "queer" instead of "person with gayness" or "person with queerness." Or think about people with a specific racial/cultural background or religion. Most individuals will say, "I am African American" or "I am Jewish," as opposed to "person with African-American-ness" or "person with Jewish-ness."

Person-First Language, on the other hand, puts a person before their condition or state. In the case of autism, "person with autism" would be used. Many ableist organizations advocate for person-first language, arguing that this approach allows loved ones and caregivers to remember that the individual is a person first. But you shouldn't need specific language like this to remember that an autistic individual is a person first.

Although the official diagnostic name for autism, as stated in the DSM-5 (Diagnostic and Statistical Manual of Mental Disorders, Fifth Edition), is Autism Spectrum Disorder, this definition is completely mislabeled, as autism is not a disorder. Unlike anorexia, an illness I suffered from and thankfully recovered from, autism is not an illness or disease. I do not "suffer" from autism; I simply have a different brain! Just as biodiversity brings life to our planet, neurodiversity brings life to our thoughts. Many of the minds behind the world's greatest inventions and masterpieces are neurodivergent ones, including famous physicists, artists, and creators of the electronic devices our society has come to revolve around.

90

FULL RECOVERY

My eating disorder recovery led to my autism discovery, an interconnection that is best represented by the golden infinity symbol. For years, treatment providers attempted to heal my eating disorder by attacking my autistic traits. I was told that recovery meant eating different foods every day, being okay with unpredictability, and learning to eat without a set structure. I was told that my preference for certain temperatures and textures was rooted in the eating disorder and that I would only be fully recovered once I gave up those desires. I was told that my obsession for color-coordinating foods to "match" was "my eating disorder talking" and that my literal perception of health claims was "my disordered brain taking over." But what if all of these wants – these *needs* – had nothing to do with an eating disorder? What if all of these characteristics were simply autistic traits that had *manifested* as a problem with food and exercise? Because I was told to get rid of the very parts of myself that were intrinsically me, I felt invalidated and alone. I didn't understand why recovery seemed so impossible. I wanted it bad enough! Yet, the more I tried to fit the mold of what I believed recovery to be – an ideal inflicted upon me by the external world – the more out of control I felt. And the more out of control I felt, the more I wanted to hold onto the very thing I'd held onto since the age of eleven.

My autism discovery gave me the permission slip I needed to recover on my own terms. It allowed me to choose a life free of an eating disorder while simultaneously embracing my neurodiversity. Rather than fighting my need for predictability and routine, I used it to stick to a way of eating that kept me healthy. My newfound awareness about interoception taught me that my body always needed nourishment, even if I didn't *feel* hungry. Understanding that an overwhelming number of food choices led to analysis paralysis allowed me to protect my energy and limit my options to an amount I could oversee. Most importantly, my autism discovery taught me that freedom and boundaries are two sides of the same coin. I always believed that a life of freedom was the equivalent of living without limits. When I discovered I am autistic, I learned that freedom means knowing my limits and respecting them without judgment. I simply don't do well in situations with unforeseen changes, lots of people, or a lack of privacy. I prefer knowing what I will eat beforehand, and I prefer eating it in a certain way. This doesn't make me "disordered" or "wrong." It simply makes me the unique human I am. I believe knowledge is power and self-awareness is the key to a sustainable life of health and happiness.

Building this self-awareness is at the core of my work with clients. When someone starts coaching with me or enrolls in my course, the very first step to freedom is becoming aware of the barriers holding them back. Only when we know that we hold certain limiting beliefs can we take action to let them go. But letting go of something is hard when you don't know what will come in its place. It's this fear of emptiness that often keeps sufferers in the grasp of an eating disorder for so long. For this reason, I work with my clients to focus on cultivating the life they want – the dream life, if you will – rather than focusing solely on "recovery." Where attention goes, energy flows. When we stay hyper-focused on recovery, we will forever stay stuck in recovery, blocking us from achieving the full potential of being *recovered*. In contrast, when we focus on how we want to live and take actions that align with that desire, recovery is a natural by-product! Here's what one of my clients had to say after graduating my 12-week coaching program:

"Working with Livia changed my life. She provided the support, guidance, and encouragement to allow me to cultivate the life I want to lead. So many "recovery" programs had failed me before, but Livia's ability to change the focus to building the life I want to live instead of focusing on the eating disorder allowed me to be excited to wake-up and choose actions free from disorder. Because of Livia, I now marvel in all the small joys I'm surrounded by and feel so much more myself. Not only did I experience so much growth and change throughout the program, I also walked away with so many new skills to help me tackle all the challenges life throws my way. Words cannot express the gratitude I have for Livia."

— Paige, coaching client

After clients gain clarity on how they want to live and where they want to go, coaching entails breaking the process down into clear, actionable steps. Nothing is more discouraging than being overwhelmed. From my own journey, I know that the more pressure I felt to complete something, the less likely I was to do it. There were often so many steps that I didn't know where to start and therefore wouldn't start at all. It wasn't until I broke the process down in a way that was feasible for me (because everyone is different!) that I could take steps in the direction that led me to where I am today. I personally don't like the saying "it's a marathon, not a sprint" because of my negative history with running, but life really is about being in it for the long run. Going from a place of fear and restriction to a place of love and abundance is a journey in which every step counts. Just as with climbing a mountain, one must take small, careful steps as well as large bounds forward. The small steps are just as important as the larger bounds – it's the combination that results in reaching the mountain's summit.

91

BUILDING MY LIFE

J ust as a climber becomes more skilled with each mountain they climb, a person becomes more aware with every experience they face. When I could finally view my life through an autistic lens, I became the architect of my life as I continued to build it. Now that I had a strong foundation of self-awareness, I could adopt habits to enrich my well-being and my business, stacking them like bricks forming a wall. The overstimulation at home gave me the utmost clarity on what type of environment I function best in and provoked me to seek out my own apartment.

In October 2020, I moved to The Hague – the city where I had been born two decades earlier. Being "back home" in my own new home, it seemed like my life had come full circle. I'd moved to the USA and back, I'd survived the edge of death, and I'd discovered the true me. I was months away from (finally!) graduating high school as I poured my heart and soul into Liv Label Free. During this time, I started my podcast and created my first course, Extremely Hungry to Completely Satisfied (liv labelfree.com/extreme-hunger-course).

One of the most common topics that recurs in my work with clients (as well as via email or on social media) is extreme hunger. This is understandable, as I believe extreme hunger is one of the most terrifying parts of the recovery process. After years of having a (false) sense of control around food and a superior ability to monitor every morsel, being hit by extreme hunger can feel like being hit by a ton of bricks (although I know I'm not the only one who would have *rather* been hit by a ton of bricks!).

My extreme hunger sparked a flood of concerns. What is wrong with me? Why do I have extreme hunger while being weight restored? How do I deal with the rapid weight gain? What about all the digestive issues? Not to mention, how do I prepare for all the other changes that come with honoring extreme hunger, the changes no one really talks about? There was so much I had to say – so much I wanted to teach – that the idea of creating a course pulled at me until I finally spilled all my thoughts onto index cards. Every night and day for six months straight, I crafted my course. I wanted to create an all-in-one resource for anyone experiencing extreme hunger, guiding them step-by-step to find full satisfaction. When I finally launched my course in January 2022, I had never felt prouder of anything in my life.

"I'm even more proud of this course than I was when I left Carolina House," I told my mom on the phone one day.

"Really?" She sounded surprised. "And why is that?"

The pride that came with creating my course didn't take away from what I had achieved at Carolina House; it expanded on it. Not only had I achieved something as a result of tireless commitment and effort, but my course was a reflection of pure passion and love – for myself as well as for every single person my course would serve. I had created the world's very first resource that explained every aspect of extreme hunger, based on science combined with my own lived experience. It was the greatest gift I could give my community, and as we all know, giving is often much more gratifying than receiving.

If I'm being completely transparent, there are times when someone doesn't enroll in my course or commit to coaching because they say they don't have the money. There is no guarantee that their investment will be "worth it." And that's exactly what I thought about recovery for years, because the truth is, there is *never* a guarantee. When I finally committed to fighting for my life, there was zero proof that it would lead to anything. There was zero proof that eating and gaining weight would really free me from my obsession with food. There was zero proof that the pain, desperation, and fear would be worth it. The only proof I had – and perhaps the only proof you currently have – was that living with an eating disorder was miserable. The only way to find out if there's a better life is by making a change, by *investing* in something and giving it all you've got. Your results are a direct reflection of putting in the work, and putting in the work will inevitably initiate change!

But what if I put in the work, fully recover from my eating disorder, and still feel miserable?

Well, you can always go back! You truly have nothing to lose. It's this mindset, this idea of having a back door open, that continues to give me the courage to do hard things. Knowing that I can always go back to what's currently comfortable is comforting, because it doesn't bind me to infinite uncertainty. I know that moving forward comes with uncertainty, but to overcome my fears, I must be willing to face them.

One of these fears was moving to The Hague by myself. It was my first apartment, meaning my first time paying rent. *What if I am unable to sustain myself? What if I can't do it?* Those questions kept me awake on the nights leading up to moving day. When I became aware that they were coming from a place of fear and limitation, I was able to shift my thoughts to come from a place of love and abundance: What if I *am* able to sustain myself? What if I *can* do it? Looking at what *is* possible rather than what isn't gives us the power to take action to pursue our dreams. And if I couldn't pay my rent, I could always move back home. But I didn't want to – which is why I didn't only make it possible to sustain myself, I ensured it.

92

Next Steps

As my high school completion approached, I thought a lot about what would come next. I wanted to pursue Liv Label Free full-time and started envisioning how I wanted my life to unfold. Although I didn't know exactly what my life would look like in the coming weeks, months, or years, there was one aspect that was non-negotiable: I was going to live in the USA.

When I moved back to the Netherlands with my family in 2015, I felt like a complete foreigner. Not only because of the language barrier, cultural differences, and lack of friends, but also because I was very ill. An eating disorder has a way of isolating you beyond your perception, trapping you in an alternate reality of false allure. As time progressed, the addictive nature of the illness caused my isolation to intensify, deepening my downward spiral into the abyss. My pining to recover in the US in 2017 was rooted in a longing to go back home, back to the place where I'd been raised and where everything was familiar. I may be a purebred Dutch girl, but my heart will forever beat stronger in the States.

Initially, I didn't want to move back to my hometown of Boston. Just as I associated Zeist with Rintveld and my bedroom with exercise addiction, my thoughts of Boston were clouded by memories of hospital stays, healthcare providers, and manipulation. I feared that going back would trigger the trauma in me, trauma that was better left untouched. Desperately in need of sunshine after the pandemic spent in the dreary weather of the Netherlands, I decided to move to California. In fact, the very first episode of the Liv Label Free podcast is titled "I'm moving to San Diego!" I spent the entire month of August 2021 in SoCal, soaking up the sun and getting a long-overdue tan.

Another aspect of moving to the US that I appreciated was getting to partner with brands I had so missed overseas. This lit me up in an indescribable way, as working with brands whose values align with mine is one of my favorite parts of the job. Social media – or rather, the world – is saturated with ingenuity, and sponsored content has unfortunately received a negative rap. Many "influencers" often share or promote products purely for the compensation, making it almost impossible for their audience to gauge the transparency of the partnership. Is that brand of tea really *sooo delicious,* or is the influencer just saying that because they're getting paid a pretty penny to do so? One of the promises I made to myself when I started my business is that I would *never* sacrifice my values of trust and transparency for monetary compensation. When I work with brands, it's because I truly love and trust their product. The monetary compensation that comes with collaborating – which also goes for my own programs and courses – is simply a necessity in the world we live in today. I wish I could give out everything for free, but if I did that, I wouldn't be able to buy my own food or have a bed to sleep in!

When I returned to The Hague in early September to pack the rest of my things, I realized I didn't want to return to San Diego. I loved the city, but the vibe didn't align with my vision of home. What was I to do? My lease in The Hague would end in less than two months, and the infinite number of options immobilized me. California is huge, and the only place I was familiar with was San Diego. But if I didn't want to live there, where would I go?

In the same way I approach research for content creation, I became obsessed with learning as much as possible about California. What are the best places to live? Which cities are the most bike-friendly? Where in California is the most affordable? My mind wouldn't stop swirling with California thoughts until I had made a decision and booked my flight.

I had a moment of utter desperation as I lay on my bed in tears, my mom on the phone, when I realized it really didn't matter. Wherever I ended up going, I could always change course later on. Nothing was set in stone. With this new perspective, the answer to where I wanted to move practically fell in my lap: San Francisco. Even though it was one of the most expensive cities, it checked off all the boxes on my list of criteria. Of course, money-related fears bubbled up, but they were the same fears I'd had before moving to The Hague. I'd made it work then, so why shouldn't I be able to make it work now? I was willing to do anything to make this a reality, and where there is a will, there is a way.

93

SAN FRANCISCO

In late September of 2021, I took the twelve-hour flight from Amsterdam to San Francisco with two suitcases. I had to leave almost everything behind, which introduced me to minimalism. The concept of an object only having as much power as you attach to it was really put into practice for me during this move. At first, it was hard parting with certain items – whether it was a piece of kitchen equipment, a favorite throw pillow, or a book-shelf I'd spent hours putting together. Giving up these material items – not to mention the time I'd "wasted" building them – would surely leave me feeling deprived. But just as I clung to my eating disorder out of the uncertainty of what would replace it, I had to make space for temporary emptiness.

At the start of my recovery, I believed I'd wasted most of my life. I believed I'd wasted the stretches of time the eating disorder had stolen from me, time I would never get back. I know I wasn't alone in this; many of the people I've met on my recovery journey have expressed the same thoughts. Yet it's this very connection with like-minded individuals that I wouldn't have were it not for my eating disorder. My website, podcast, social media accounts, coaching programs, courses, this book – none of it would even exist were it not for my eating disorder! Sure, I may have missed out on many typical childhood and adolescent experiences, but what I've gained thanks to recovery is worth its weight in gold. Nothing in life is ever a waste – it's all a learning experience.

With this outlook of abundance, I flew to San Francisco with zero plan. I would arrive at an Airbnb I'd booked for a month, trusting that I'd find a more permanent place and would be able to sustain myself. During the first three weeks, I was elated. I WAS BACK IN THE USA, BABY! As my checkout date neared and there was still no sight of an apartment within my budget, however, desperation spiked.

"I feel paralyzed," I told Gwen, a sweet woman who had supported me since my arrival. Almost fifty years earlier, my grandma on my mom's side had met Gwen at an airport after their flight was canceled, taking her in and giving her a place to sleep. Ever since, she's kept in touch with our family and even visited us in Boston and the Netherlands a few times! What's even crazier: I learned from Gwen that both my grandma and my uncle had lived in Alameda, a small island to the east of San Francisco.

"I think you'd really like it there," Gwen said as we drove around San Francisco. "Do you want to go over, just to see?"

At this point, I was willing to see anything that would potentially open doors to my new home. "Let's do it."

Alameda reminded me a lot of Brookline. Kids played in front of large Victorian homes. Sturdy trees with bright green leaves lined the sidewalks. All the essential stores were close to everyone on the island.

"It looks like it's all residential," I said. "I'm sure there are no studios for rent here."

Gwen didn't say anything until we drove by a property with a "for rent" sign in front of it. "Why don't you call them?" she suggested, pointing to the sign.

"I'm sure whatever's available is way above my budget." I did not want to waste any time. But Gwen insisted, so I dialed the number on the hanging board. "Do you have any studios for rent?" I asked the woman who answered the phone.

"We don't have any studios in that building, but we do have one studio at one of our other properties. I was actually just about to list it this afternoon!"

When I inquired about the cost, my heart nearly skipped a beat. The monthly rent was my exact budget. Not only that but the building address contained both of my lucky numbers, 1 and 9. Was this even real?

Gwen and I retrieved the keys from the rental office and drove to the apartment. As soon as I unlocked the door, I knew I had found my place.

"You did it!" Gwen exclaimed on my move-in day.

"We did it," I said. "I couldn't have done this without you."

Thanks to Gwen's persistence, along with my mom's support during the contract and deposit process, I had secured a place to live for the coming year. Now, it was up to me to sustain myself there.

94

ALAMEDA

Earning enough to cover my monthly costs proved to be much harder than I had thought. I knew my budget was ambitiously lean, but considering that I was in the Bay Area, the studio I found was relatively inexpensive. I drowned myself in work, creating, posting, and coaching 24/7. When I went to bed at night, my mind couldn't shut off because I was so preoccupied with the next day's to-do list. But I didn't mind. I loved my work, so much so that it often didn't even feel like work. I loved that my brain wouldn't stop thinking about funny video ideas or insightful topics to post, as this was the polar opposite of being tortured by mental hunger!

Unfortunately, free content doesn't pay the bills, so I took part-time jobs. I babysat, dog-walked, and applied for freelance work. I had been living in my studio for over three months by now. I knew I had to build a social life, but there was simply no time. To distract myself from the loneliness, I worked even harder – the numbing justified by my belief that I was serving my audience. Parallel to the increasing stress, my body could not keep food down. I would sit behind my laptop after a meal only to be startled by a sudden urge to throw up. At first, I thought I might have just eaten something bad and this was my body's way of getting rid of it. But as the months progressed, the throwing up got worse – to the point where I had to keep a large tub next to me at all times.

Not surprisingly, I lost weight. With my history, I knew this was dangerous. My health is my biggest asset, and if I'm not healthy, my business can't be either! So I did everything I could to counteract the vomiting: I added extra nut butter to my smoothies, cooked my food in more oil, and bought nutritional shakes. It felt odd drinking Ensure again given my prior aversion to it, but at the same time, it was a testament to how far I'd come. I no longer feared weight gain, and this realization was the proof in the pudding that neural rewiring *really does work*.

A common fear I hear in my coaching work is the fear that one will recover physically but not mentally. Clients have expressed that they don't want to "risk" gaining weight because they believe that they'll "still worry about food and exercise, just at a higher weight."

"If I'm going to be obsessed with food, I might as well do it while being thin" is a common way of vocalizing this belief. The irony is rooted in the paradoxical nature of the eating disorder: the only reason you're obsessed with food is because you're not giving yourself enough. If your body is properly nourished, it simply has no reason to expend energy on thoughts about food and exercise – there are so many more important things to focus on!

"Yeah, but what if I'm an anomaly?" is a common rebuttal. "What if recovery works for everyone else, but my body is just different?" Again, this is the eating disorder doing everything it can to convince you that you need it; by thinking you're different and that recovery won't work, there's no point in even trying. But staying stuck in an eating disorder is a choice. The fact that you got one isn't your fault, but recovery is your responsibility.

Unfortunately, my efforts to gain back the weight lost with the vomiting yielded little result. As I ate more, I also threw up more – it was as if my body was trying to tell me something was wrong, something that couldn't be healed from the outside in.

"I can't stop throwing up!" I cried to my mom on one of our relatively few phone calls. The nine-hour time difference with the Netherlands made it almost impossible to keep in touch, undeniably amplifying my sense of loneliness.

"Could it be stress?" my mom asked several times, acutely aware of my hypersensitivity.

"No, it can't be!" I responded with certainty. If I admitted to the vomiting being caused by my constantly being turned "on," I would have to do something about the stress and anxiety – which I obviously didn't have time for!

95

URGENT CARE

I n the spring of 2022, I started experiencing other symptoms as a result of the weight loss: heart palpitations and insomnia, all while the vomiting kept getting worse. I completely stopped exercising, knowing my body needed to conserve all the energy it managed to keep in, and I continued eating calorie-dense foods. But nothing seemed to help.

On another phone call to my mom, I cried, "What if I've got some gastrointestinal disorder?"

"You really need to go see a doctor." Despite my mom's insistence, I never did. It wasn't that I didn't want to see a doctor – I wanted to figure out what was wrong – it was that the idea of researching all the steps necessary to find a good specialist were too overwhelming. I had spent hours on the phone with health insurance when I moved to San Francisco, an experience I felt traumatized just thinking about. No way was I going to go through that again. "Honey, I want you to go to the ER," my mom said. "You can go there straightaway to get your blood drawn and be referred to someone if they find abnormalities. I'm really worried about your electrolytes."

I was too. What if the vomiting had caused such imbalances that I could collapse at any moment? Even though I didn't think I would, I knew my body wasn't always the best at signaling my limits. On July 1, I admitted myself to the ER, reasoning that this was much more important than all the other things I could be doing with my time instead. If I wanted to serve my audience to the best of my abilities, I needed to be functioning at my best.

I spent five long hours laying in an uncomfortable hospital bed, my anxiety sky-high because I didn't know when I would be able to leave. Every time I asked for an update, I was met with "We're just waiting for your bloodwork to come back." It wasn't the waiting itself that worried me but not knowing how long I would have to wait that left me unnerved.

One of the nurses noticed my distress. "I'm autistic, so I have a really hard time with unpredictability."

I didn't expect her to understand but was pleasantly surprised when she said, "I totally get it. My brother is autistic too. What can I do to help you?" She sat by my bed as I showed her my Instagram feed, and we laughed together at reels videos I had made. Although I still struggled with the unknowns – what my blood results would be as well as when I could leave – just having someone to interact with felt like a breath of fresh air.

When my test results finally came back, nothing was wrong – at least, nothing appeared to be wrong. As much relief as this brought, it was equally frustrating. I had wanted something to be tangibly wrong so I could know what had to be fixed. But the doctor just sent me home with a pamphlet on anxiety and a prescription for an antihistamine.

Despite the lack of answers I received during my ER incident, laying in a hospital bed and being hooked up to monitors was a huge wake-up call for me.

"We're incredibly worried about your heart rate," the doctor had said when I came in. "Does your family have a history of heart issues?"

"No, the low heart rate is due to my weight loss. I was admitted to the hospital years ago due to having a heart rate of 40. It's what the body does when it's in energy deficit."

The doctor looked puzzled. "Well, what you're saying makes sense, but you look healthy! I don't think this has anything to do with your weight."

I could barely believe my ears. "But you *look* healthy?" I wouldn't have admitted myself to the ER with a heart rate of 40 if I was truly healthy! This doctor's reaction did not only emphasize how insignificant a medical degree could be for (mis)diagnosing health issues, it pained me in the deepest part of my soul. If I – someone with thin privilege – was being told certain effects of malnutrition couldn't be due to malnutrition, how on Earth were people in larger bodies being treated? Thanks to my work with clients who present with "atypical" anorexia (an eating disorder defined as matching all of the criteria for anorexia nervosa without an extremely low body weight), I know the horror stories of invalidation all too well.

My clients' experiences – along with the multitude of times I've had to explain that an eating disorder doesn't mean "just not eating" – continue to remind me of the harsh reality that professionals need educating. What they learn in their studies is based mainly on outdated, irrelevant psychoanalytical theories and often cannot be applied to real humans. Sadly, this lack of alignment is why so many patients are being written off as "too complex" and "hopeless." If the individual doesn't match the textbook protocol, the professionals don't want to be held responsible for an individual's issues worsening. I want to stress that I have nothing against professionals (if you find a good one, they're a keeper!), but from my personal experience, as I have outlined throughout this book, no amount of professionality can match lived experience when it comes to understanding and helping those struggling with eating disorders. As much as professionals are praised in our healthcare (or rather *sickcare*) system, it's important to remember that they're people too – people like you and me, people with fears, insecurities, and biases.

The internal realizations that flickered in my head in that emergency room led me to admit something long overdue: I hadn't been putting myself first. My constant search for external stimulation, which I fulfilled through overworking, had caused my body to draw the line. If I wasn't going to rest, my body would force me to. I concluded that the involuntary vomiting (and resulting weight loss) was a physical manifestation of my stress and loneliness, which could only be healed from the inside out. So, in a way, laying in that hospital bed and seeing my low heart rate on the monitor was the very thing I needed to implement change. I needed to commit to putting my health above all else, just as I had done exactly five years prior. The stress, vomiting, loneliness, weight loss – none of it was my fault, but it was my responsibility to mend myself back to health.

96

BOSTON

Admitting that my overworking was a way in which I numbed myself from negative emotions gave me permission to desire social connection again.

"Won't you be lonely, so far away from your family?" people had asked when I announced I was moving to California in 2021.

"It won't be a big deal," I responded. "I already live by myself and barely see them in person anyways." Even though The Hague is less than an hour from Utrecht by car or public transportation, most of our contact was via phone. It wouldn't make a difference if I moved to the other side of the world, I thought. If anything, I'd be closer to my audience, as the majority of my Instagram community is based in the US. Most of the brands I wanted to work with were also in the US, so moving overseas was a no-brainer when it came to expanding my business. It wasn't until the Atlantic Ocean and the entire United States of America stood between me and those I love most that I realized how much I'd underestimated the mental distance.

In April 2022, I went on an East Coast trip with my family. We both flew in from opposite ends of the world, literally meeting in the middle of the 6,000 miles that separated us. Bouncing between Airbnbs, we stayed in New York, Philadelphia, Princeton, and Boston. By then, I'd already been pondering the idea of moving to the East Coast.

"It'll be so much easier to keep in touch when it's only six hours instead of nine," my mom said.

"Oh, for sure! It'll also be easier for my international clients," I replied. "San Francisco has definitely been an experience, but it's not my home."

"So what is? Are you going to move back to Boston?"

"I want something new. Boston is too traumatic for me."

"I get that." My mom paused for a moment. "But where are you going to go?"

Good question. "I think this trip will be a great way to get a feel for different cities on the East Coast!" I replied.

As much as I dread unpredictability and change, my brain is exhilarated by the idea of new experiences. Along with giving my family endless hugs and catching up on almost a year's worth of missing each other, I was on a mission to find my next city. New York was too intense. Princeton was too boring. Philly was – an option. But it wasn't until we arrived in Boston that I knew for sure where I belonged. Driving around the familiar streets I had grown up on felt like it was just yesterday. Shopping at the Trader Joe's where I'd been given free cookies as a kid made my tummy flutter with excitement. Biking past my elementary school sent gratitude radiating through my entire being.

"I need to come back here," I said with certainty. "Boston is where my heart is."

"Didn't you say Boston is traumatic?" Mae asked.

"I did." I let out a deep breath. "But one of the most important lessons I've learned about life is that mindset is everything."

Just as I choose to view my eating disorder as a gift rather than a curse, I could choose to view Boston in a new light. I could choose to disconnect it from the doctor's appointments and the lies. I could choose to create new associations in which the city sparkled. And in that very instant, that's exactly what I did: "Boston, here I come!"

97

PERMISSION

After making my big decision, I spent my last few months in San Francisco writing this book and continuing to make ends meet. Even though the vomiting still wasn't improving (hence the ER incident that took place a mere month before my move), I had hope again. I was going back home – to friends and family and to everything I trusted.

Arriving in Boston gave me a similar feeling to that I had when reading *Aspergirls*; it was as if a part of me clicked into place. Within the first two weeks of roaming the streets of my home-town, I saw some of my best friends and smiled bigger than I had in months. The vomiting immediately ceased, and I was confident in my ability to regain much more than just my physical health.

Yet, as I type these words – just two months shy of returning to the Netherlands for an undetermined amount of time – I am reminded that I am forever learning. After bouncing between friends' houses for the first month in Boston, I was ecstatic when a dear friend found a three-month sublet within my budget. Unfortunately, shortly after I moved in, the vomiting resumed. The financial stress of needing my own space proved to be a trigger, and despite now being "only" 3,000 miles from my family as opposed to 6,000, my loneliness proved persistent.

"Why don't you come home for a little while?" my mom suggested on one of our phone calls. Luckily, these had become much more frequent with the smaller time difference.

"Omg, are you CRAZY?" I replied. "You know I can't do that. I need to be in the US for my business. I still rely on brand partnerships for a portion of my income, and you know how impossible those are to get in Holland." Despite the depth of certainty in my words, my mom's words struck a chord. What if I did go back? What if her suggestion wasn't so far-fetched after all? What if a break from the financial stress and a reunion with my family could aid in healing my anxiety? I retraced my initial answer, picking it apart in the same way I always pick the raisins out of authentic Dutch apple pie.

Everything I had said, everything I had been so certain of – these were all limiting beliefs. Was it that I couldn't move back, or was it that I wouldn't move back? Did I really rely on brand partnerships to make ends meet, or was I just afraid of trusting myself and my capabilities as a business owner? In the same way I hold up a mirror for my clients and help them become aware of their limiting beliefs, I held up a mirror for myself.

What would I tell a client if they were in my situation? I asked myself. Well, that's obvious! I'd ask them to shift the limiting belief to an empowering belief, and I would help them come up with action steps to internalize that new belief.

As I lay in bed and stared at the ceiling that night, I told myself I could build my life to be whatever I wanted it to be. I told myself what I always tell my clients: the first step to achieving is believing. I told myself that the only way to learn – the only way to make peace with what could be – was to fully immerse myself in the experience of it. And just like that, I decided I'd give Holland a chance and fell asleep at the drop of a hat.

My decision to move back home for an undetermined amount of time is an incredible testimony to how my mindset has grown. I've said it before and I'll say it again: external circumstances only have as much power as you give them the permission to have. Full recovery from my eating disorder was the result of giving myself permission to fully recover. Embracing my autistic brain was the result of giving myself permission to be autistic. Moving from Holland, to San Francisco, to Boston, and now back to where I was born will be the result of giving myself permission to trust myself and my ever-evolving story. Thank you for allowing me to share that story with you. Here's to turning every MESS into a MESSage!

WHAT DID YOU THINK?

Thank you so much for reading my book! It would mean the world to me if you could take two minutes to leave a review on Amazon and Goodreads. Your words help other people to find and read my book!

With love and gratitude,

Liv

READ MORE

Nourishing Neurodiversity: Simple Recipes to Nourish Your Body and Mind

BE THE FIRST!

Join the Liv Label Free family and be the first to receive updates on Livia's latest books and content: www.livlabelfree.com/join

ACKNOWLEDGMENTS

I would like to thank the following individuals for making this book possible:

To my mama, words cannot even begin to express what an impact you have made on me and my story. Thank you for loving me unconditionally and supporting me through it all.

To my papa, for raising me with unconditional love and giving me the nickname that became the title of this book.

To Mae, my younger sister and the most talented artist I know. The cover is stunning and I can't wait to design many more with you. Two neurodivergent brains are always better than one :)

To Amélie, my youngest sister and to me, forever a baby girl! Thank you for your empathy, understanding, and love throughout my entire journey. I know it wasn't easy watching your older sister battle an eating disorder, but with your support, she recovered from one!

To Rutger, M'Liss, and Kees: you were there for me during one of the most critical times of my life. Rutger, thank you for your sweet smiles, big hugs, and for always taking care of the tech. M'Liss, thank you for allowing me to cry on your shoulder when that's exactly what I needed. Kees, thanks for letting me sleep in your room when mine was 4,000 miles away!

To Barbie Halaby, you're the best editor I could have ever asked for! Your remarkable eye for detail is a dream for any autistic author :) I can't wait to work on many more books with you.

To my clients, for giving me the gift of infinite learning. Your hard work motivates me to keep putting one foot in front of the other myself!

To Tammy Sak, you're the best super spectrum sister! Our connection goes far beyond what any words could say. Thank you for your trust in me as a coach, but most importantly, thank you for our valuable friendship.

To Lex Lancaster, for teaching me so much about the importance of inclusive language and being one of the best friends I could have ever asked for.

To Brianna Murray, for your ongoing support and love for me and everything I stand for. I wouldn't be where I am today without you!

To Abby Sim, for spreading the Liv Label Free message in so many ways! I'm beyond grateful for our friendship.

To Mike Napier, the best helper monkey on the planet.

To Scott and Jen, for welcoming me into your home where I finished writing this book.

To Martha Huntley, for all your love and support while I finished writing this book in Boston.

To Ann Camara, for being one of my earliest teachers.

To my béta readers, for reading this book in its earliest stages and providing me with invaluable feedback.

To everyone who donated to the Saving Livia campaign: you funded my hope, my health, and my life. There are no words to express the gratitude I feel towards each and every one of you.

ABOUT THE AUTHOR

Livia Sara is an autism advocate and eating disorder survivor that now helps others overcome their own mental barriers through her courses and coaching programs. She is the author of the blog livlabelfree.com and the host of the Liv Label Free Podcast. Livia is a lifelong learner that loves listening to audiobooks, going on walks, and reading the latest science on all things neurodiversity and eating disorders!

Printed in Great Britain
by Amazon